"A window into Florida's foodways through time, from the heart to the palate."—Sandra Gutierrez, author of *The New Southern-Latino Table*

"Norman elevates flavors that are the core of Florida's cuisine. He is truly gifted in the way he makes them shine."—Nina Compton, chef-owner, Compère Lapin

"Touches on the influences—from as far as the Middle East to as close as Cuba—that have helped mold and shape the dishes and ingredients of Florida's cuisine. Delicious and compelling, it has become a regular 'go-to' cookbook in my kitchen."
—John Currence, chef-owner, City Grocery Restaurant Group

"Norman Van Aken's bright cuisine continues to shine and inspire home cooks."—Daniel Boulud, chef-owner, The Dinex Group

"Norman's new cookbook is about all of us becoming better cooks at home, with all the stories, details, methods, and know-how to make exciting and delicious recipes."—Dean Fearing, chef-partner, Fearing's Restaurant

"A lively and wonderfully usable book."—Colman Andrews, author of *My Usual Table: A Life in Restaurants*

"Inspires readers to roll up their sleeves, don their aprons, and get cooking."
—Ferdinand Metz, president emeritus, Culinary Institute of America

Norman Van Aken's Florida Kitchen

University Press of Florida

Florida A&M University, Tallahassee

Florida Atlantic University, Boca Raton

Florida Gulf Coast University, Ft. Myers

Florida International University, Miami

Florida State University, Tallahassee

New College of Florida, Sarasota

University of Central Florida, Orlando

University of Florida, Gainesville

University of North Florida, Jacksonville

University of South Florida, Tampa

University of West Florida, Pensacola

Norman Van Aken's Florida Kitchen

Norman Van Aken

Photographs by Debi Harbin

University Press of Florida

Gainesville · Tallahassee · Tampa
Boca Raton · Pensacola · Orlando · Miami
Jacksonville · Ft. Myers · Sarasota

This book is dedicated to our granddaughter, Audrey Quinn Van Aken . . . and to *all* of the children of the world. They come here from above . . . only seeking to play, grow, and share with others of *all* races, colors, creeds, and languages . . . a world that we need to make as peaceful and as delicious as possible for them.

CONTENTS

PREFACE

When I was still in my teens, a friend of mine and I took a Greyhound bus out of our native state of Illinois during the month of April, leaving the last of a brutish winter behind. As we rode south, I peered out through the bus windows, transfixed by a very green, floral place with . . . lo and behold . . . the Atlantic shimmering in its gargantuan majesty near Jacksonville. I continued gazing out the glass; and then a shadow from some trees changed the light and suddenly the glass turned to *mirror*—and I saw my own image, wide-eyed, enraptured by the spectral, unfolding scene.

The years passed, as years do. Arriving in Key West as a twenty-one-year-old, I was greeted with the Spanish welcome written on the wall of the Key West Airport: "Bienvenidos a Cayo Hueso!" My first years cooking would not be what they are without the calypso, soul, blues, and funk of the music and flavors of that storied island. As my career turned from a fledgling newcomer to an established member of the working class and a chef at that, I spent more and more time in the center of our state. The words were now dominated by the English language, with a delightful drawl at times.

From my very early days of cooking I was guided by something my grandmother Nana told me when I was younger and investigating a trove of books left behind by my Uncle Norman (who died prematurely at the age of twenty-four). She said, "Norman, you don't need to have a lot of books. You just need to have the right ones and truly read them." So the die was cast and my love of reading and learning was set by her wisdom. I decided at some point in my journey as a cook, a chef, and a writer that my goal in life would be to help shed light on the power of the cooking and foodways of Florida. Through each book I've written, the path went this way and that, but always I was guided by the hope that I was able to get it right—to translate the powerful flavors that I was finding in the kitchens I worked in or places I was fortunate enough to eat at. In some ways I still feel like that young man on the bus, looking out the windows and then catching my reflection as we go on. I hope the wonders of this state, so graced with beauty and bounty, will inspire you as they do me as we spend time sharing my Florida kitchen.

Norman Van Aken outside his restaurant in Mount Dora

1

"GOT A SPOON, GOT A SPOON, GOT A SPOONFUL..."

Soups and Stews

Ajiaco with Chicken, Potatoes, Squash, Corn, and Spinach

I first came upon this heart- and soul-warming soup years ago. Beloved by Cubans, Colombians, and now many Floridians, its name may derive from the word *aji*, which means "chile." But chiles are *not* always used. (It is no secret that many Cubans do not enjoy spicy food; our beautiful daughter-in-law, Lourdes, is a notable exception!) As with many soups and sauces, the essential ingredient is a good homemade stock.

Serves 6 to 8

1 butternut squash, halved and seeded

Kosher salt and cracked black pepper

3 tablespoons olive oil

4 bone-in, skin-on chicken thighs

3 cloves garlic, peeled and minced

1 Scotch bonnet or other chile, seeded and minced

½ sweet onion, diced

1 tomato, peeled, seeded, and roughly chopped

1 pound Yukon gold potatoes, peeled if you wish, cubed

8 ounces boniato (Cuban sweet potatoes; use regular sweet potatoes if boniato is unavailable), peeled and cubed

1 quart Chicken Stock (page 237)

3 ears of corn, kernels cut off the cob

3 cups roughly chopped spinach leaves

1 tablespoon roughly chopped fresh culantro or oregano leaves

2 tablespoons fresh cilantro leaves

3 scallions, finely chopped

2 tablespoons well-drained, rinsed, and minced capers

1 avocado

¼ cup sour cream

Preheat the oven to 350 degrees.

Season the squash with salt and pepper and place it cut side down on a rimmed nonstick baking sheet. Add some water to the pan and bake for about 40 minutes, until somewhat easily pierced with a fork. Turn the squash over and cook for about 12 more minutes. Remove from the oven. When cool enough to handle, peel the squash, cut it into large cubes, and refrigerate for the time being. You will need 2 cups cooked squash here, so save the remainder for another meal.

Increase the oven temperature to 375 degrees.

In a large soup pot set over medium-high heat, heat the oil. Season the chicken with salt and pepper and sear until golden on each side. Remove from the pan. Put the chicken in an ovenproof pan and bake for 10 to 15 minutes, until cooked through. Set aside, covered to keep warm.

Lower the stove heat to medium, add the garlic to the pot, and sauté for about 30 seconds. Add the chile and onion and cook for 5 to 7 minutes, until translucent. Add the tomato and cook for 3 minutes, seasoning with a little salt and pepper.

Add the potatoes, boniato, and stock and bring to a simmer. Cook until the potatoes are just tender, 20 to 30 minutes.

Meanwhile, in a sauté pan, cook the corn in a little butter with salt and pepper until just tender. Add to the soup along with the spinach and culantro and the 2 cups cooked squash. Season again with salt and pepper and turn the heat to low. Cook for 10 minutes.

Dice the chicken into ½-inch cubes and add it to the soup. Add the cilantro, scallions, and capers.

Peel, pit, and dice the avocado. Sprinkle with a bit of the salt. Pepper too, if you wish.

Serve in soup bowls, garnished with the avocado and sour cream as desired.

Serving suggestion: This is also nice garnished with diced hard-cooked eggs, more minced chiles, and additional herbs.

White Bean Soup

I might have fallen in love with white bean soup the same week I fell in love with Key West. Who can say that what makes us love a place cannot be something like soup? Northerners may carry the notion that Florida is always warm and sunny, but Floridians know that many Sunshine State homes have no central heating. On cold days, we dress in clothes that might have seen trendier times, put on a cockeyed grin to go with it, and have soups like this one. I might also put on an old Van Morrison or even older Fleetwood Mac album, one with Peter Green still in the lineup. They warm me up in essential ways too.

Serves 6 to 10

2 tablespoons olive oil

6 ounces smoked bacon, diced

1 Scotch bonnet or other chile, seeded and minced

3 cloves garlic, thinly sliced

1 sweet onion, diced

3 stalks celery, diced

Kosher salt and black pepper

¼ cup chipotles in adobo, finely chopped

1 (14½-ounce) can whole peeled tomatoes, pureed

2 bay leaves, broken

1 cup white wine

14 ounces dried white or Great Northern beans, rinsed and soaked in water overnight, then drained

1 smoked ham hock

2 quarts Chicken Stock (page 237)

Heat a large soup pot over medium heat. Add the oil and bacon and sauté until the bacon is almost cooked through. Stir in the Scotch bonnet chile and garlic. Cook for 1 minute. Increase the heat to medium-high, add the onion and celery, and stir to coat with the oil and fat. Stir in some salt and pepper. Cook, stirring only occasionally, until the vegetables are golden, about 6 minutes.

Add the chipotles in adobo, tomatoes, bay leaves, and wine and cook until reduced by half, 4 to 5 minutes.

Add the beans, ham hock, and stock and bring to a simmer. Skim the foam and impurities off the top as they arise and reduce the heat to medium-low. Cook until the beans are tender, 2 to 2½ hours.

Remove the hock and let it cool on a plate until you can handle it. The meat is nice to add to the soup if you harvest it. Discard the bone, hide, and cartilage.

Puree half to two thirds of the soup. It is a preference call, really. Season one last time to taste.

Spoon the soup into warm bowls and serve.

> *Serving suggestion*: Garnish with Fried Okra (page 167) or any seasonal fresh vegetable you enjoy.
>
> *Note*: We buy whole canned tomatoes and then cut, dice, or crush them as needed. The flavor is kept more intact with the whole tomato and thus preferred.

Winter in Florida Squashes Soup

We have more vegetables in this soup than most. This "nonmeat stock" does require a bit more cleaning and chopping, but the effort results in many vegetable flavors being kind of "escorted" in the soup. For years, I almost always used meat stock in such soups. But now I prefer the clarity of the vegetables shining through as they do here. The very smart "Meatless Monday" campaign has helped many see the light. Live and learn.

Serves 6 to 10

For the soup:

½ cup olive oil, divided

4 tablespoons butter, divided

2 butternut squash, peeled, seeded, and sliced into ½-inch-thick pieces

2 tablespoons sugar

Kosher salt and cracked black pepper

1 Scotch bonnet chile, seeded and minced

3 cloves garlic, minced

2 leeks, cleaned and diced, white parts only

1 sweet onion, diced

2 large carrots, peeled and diced

2 stalks celery, diced

½ large bulb fennel, cored and diced

1 teaspoon ground turmeric

½ cup fresh cilantro leaves, roughly chopped

1 cup fresh-squeezed orange juice

4 cups vegetable stock or water

2 cups heavy cream, warmed

Make the soup: Preheat the oven to 350 degrees.

Heat a large soup pot over medium-high heat and add ¼ cup of the oil and 2 tablespoons of the butter. Add the butternut squash and season with the sugar as well as some salt and pepper. Sauté for about 10 minutes, stirring occasionally. Carefully remove the squash to a baking sheet or a roasting pan; place in the oven and bake for about 30 minutes.

Meanwhile, return the soup pot to medium heat and add the remaining ¼ cup oil and 2 tablespoons butter. Add the chile, garlic, leeks, onion, carrots, celery, and fennel. Stir well. Add the turmeric and stir again.

When the vegetables are nicely cooked (about 10 minutes), add the cilantro and orange juice. Stir and cook for 2 minutes to reduce the liquid by half. Add the stock and reduce the heat to a bare simmer until the squash in the oven is ready. Add the squash to the soup pot and cook over medium heat until the soup has a nice flavor and consistency. We want the squash to be almost soft but *not* mushy at all.

Add the cream.

Remove from the heat and let the soup sit for 15 to 20 minutes to give the flavors a chance to develop even more. Blend the soup to a consistency you like. I do not strain it after this. You risk losing too much food to suit me and I like the texture a bit "rustic." And, as always, season to taste again.

For the garnish:

2 tablespoons olive oil

2 tablespoons butter

8 scallions, thinly sliced crosswise

2 cups sliced baby or mature zucchini

2 cups sliced baby or mature pattypan squash

Kosher salt and black pepper

Sour cream, if desired

Make the garnish: Heat a medium-sized nonstick skillet over medium heat. Add the oil and butter. When the butter has melted, add the scallions and cook until just barely soft. Add the zucchini and squash and cook for about 5 minutes, until just tender. Season to taste with salt and pepper. Do not stir too often so you can keep them a bit firm. Remove from the heat and keep warm until ready to serve.

To serve, ladle the soup into cups or bowls. Spoon on the cooked scallions, zucchini, and squash and dollop with sour cream, if you'd like.

> *Note:* I like to also add in some toasted squash seeds, which I make by culling from the butternut squash, cleaning, and then roasting them.
>
> *Serving suggestion:* Our Journey Bread (page 243) goes well with this soup.

Oldways Chicken, Sausage, Shrimp, and Crab Gumbo

Note: If you shell the shrimp yourself, you can use the shells to infuse your Chicken Stock (strain them out after 30 minutes), or save them for another stock or broth for the future.

Like many American chefs of my generation, I learned from Paul Prudhomme that eternal key to a great gumbo—a proper roux. In today's rush-rush world it might be a ghost method, yet there is a zen-like state you can reach as you nurse a drink of some potency, listen to an Alison Krauss ballad, and watch a roux turn from blond to a coppery hue while filling your kitchen with an ineffable nutty aroma. When I first attempted roux, I purchased an enormous black iron pan and held Chef Prudhomme's masterwork, *Louisiana Kitchen*, open with a wooden spoon. The book had color pictures to illustrate the "mother types of roux making." It would have taken a video, however, to record the sparks that erupt as you add the cut-up "holy trinity" of vegetables and spices to the finished roux! That is also the spark of genius that illuminates the comforting constancy of old foodways kept alive.

Serving suggestion: Serve the gumbo with simple white rice. Our Haitian Pikliz Slaw (page 218) is a nice tangy condiment to serve alongside too.

This is not a pretty dish. It is earthy, rustic, even peasant food. The chicken is kept on the bones. It smells heavenly and tastes deep, rooted, and resonant with the mix of land and sea that it is. Just the way I like to eat when surrounded by old friends and the growing family.

Serves 6 to 10

1 free-range chicken, cut into 8 pieces

1 teaspoon ground cayenne

1 teaspoon ground cumin

1 teaspoon kosher salt, plus more to taste

½ teaspoon black pepper

1 teaspoon fresh thyme leaves, minced

1 teaspoon fresh sage leaves, minced

¾ cup all-purpose flour, plus more for dredging

Canola or peanut oil, as needed to cook the sausage and sear the chicken

1½ pounds *uncooked* Italian (hot or mild, as desired) or andouille sausage

4 cloves garlic, minced

2 serrano chiles, seeded and minced

3 cups diced sweet onions

1½ cups diced red bell peppers

½ cup diced celery

1 cup diced fennel

1 bay leaf

2 quarts Chicken Stock (page 237)

1½ pounds large fresh shrimp, peeled, deveined, and cut into bite-size pieces

1 pound fresh crabmeat

Preheat the oven to 350 degrees.

Season the chicken with the cayenne, cumin, salt, pepper, thyme, and sage. Lightly dredge the chicken in flour. Set aside.

Heat a large Dutch oven or rondeau over medium heat. Add some oil and then the raw sausage and gently cook for about 10 minutes, turning a few times. Remove the sausage to a plate and set aside. (It will not be fully cooked yet.) Add more oil to the pot and allow it to get fairly hot. Add the chicken, skin side down, and cook, turning it until nicely colored on both sides. Leave the bits that stick to the pot, as they will make the roux much tastier.

Remove the chicken to a baking sheet and place it in the oven to roast for about 30 minutes. (It will not be fully cooked at this point.)

When ready to proceed with the roux, heat up the drippings in the pot with more oil if necessary to make ½ cup fat. When it is fairly hot, add the ¾ cup flour and cook over medium heat, whisking almost constantly, until the flour mixture turns a nutty or chocolate brown, about 25 minutes.

Add the garlic, chiles, onions, bell peppers, celery, fennel, and bay leaf, stirring well. Cook for about 5 minutes. Gradually add the stock. Whisk well and bring to just under a boil. Add salt to taste. Reduce the heat to medium-low and simmer, uncovered, for about 1 hour, stirring occasionally.

Add the partially cooked chicken and sausage, as well as the shrimp, and cook until the shrimp are pink and firm and the chicken is fully cooked. The time will vary so check it out. Remove the sausage to a board, cut it into rounds, and return them to the pot.

Add the crabmeat and simmer for about 2 minutes. Serve.

The American South

When I came up with the thesis of a "New World Cuisine," I realized very quickly that it was not only a New World that opened up for Europeans when the shores of Plymouth Rock and St. Augustine were landed upon. It was also the very idea of old and new joining as well. So the "Immigrant Songs," as I like to call them, are joined now in a choir of sorts that never existed before. *Listen to the music!* Black voices and instrumentalists created the blues and then, with the changing pace of life in the dawn of the twentieth century, wrought jazz. The foodways of the American South—bourbon, country ham, chitlins, gumbo, cornbread, collard greens—are born of an agricultural age and remain rooted to it. And we are all the more fortunate for it.

The Louisiana Purchase of 1803 was probably the greatest real estate deal in history, and it took a mere $15 million. With that acquisition, America became a nation that superseded the size of France, Britain, Italy, Spain, Portugal, and Switzerland combined. The belle of the ball of that land deal was the port city of New Orleans. The belle sure knew how to cook! The flavors of New Orleans were the very first iteration of a kind of New World Cuisine that would rival anything ever created in Europe. While leaning on traditions and techniques from the Old World, cooks of all strata created a *fusion* that still rings a mighty dinner bell (breakfast, brunch, and lunch too) in this age. And it likely will straight through to the next. Flavors don't go out of fashion—they evolve. And often they return. It is the nature of mankind to play in the surf of sensation.

As I write from my home in Florida I'm aware that many find our state somehow "less southern" than those to the north and west of us. Perhaps the notion took hold because the plantation society so prevalent in other southern states had a slightly lighter footprint in Florida. Conversely, Florida saw the arrival of a Central and South American population sooner and more steadily than other places in the South. That has certainly been true of the lower part of the state. This wonderful assimilation brings a unique hyphenation now between the South and the "Latino." Cookbook author Sandra Gutierrez wrote a book exploring that wedding with delicious reverberations. I contend that this will arc ever higher in the next decade.

Of course the well known is still rightly loved. I embrace the flavors of the Southern Foodways Alliance. Nathalie Dupree, Jessica Harris, Frank Stitt, John Besh, Emeril Lagasse, Paul Prudhomme, the Lee brothers, the insightful and witty John T. Edge, and before them Edna Lewis and Bill Neal, have books in a treasured place within my library. My early forays to Charleston and New Orleans will always be moments when I recognized the power of American-born cookery that gave me the confidence to seek it for us in Florida.

In 2007 there was a conclave of writers, chefs, and scholars who gathered in Charleston that was written about by a woman named Nancy Davidson for the *New York Sun*. Davidson wrote that there was general agreement about the nature of southern cooking. The consensus was this:

Flavors don't go out of fashion—they evolve.

The cuisine is the result of a mingling of black and white cultures—in dishes frequently prepared by black servants for wealthy, white families, as well as meals derived from African traditions passed down among slaves that stretched limited resources over long periods of time (grits or rice, for instance, with small quantities of inexpensive cuts of meat). A lack of refrigeration in the hot climate also required that foods be either very fresh or cured. The panelists also agreed that Southern cuisine is not monolithic. It is regional, and the characteristic dishes vary from place to place. "Lowcountry" is a reference to the coastline region that extends from Savannah, Ga., to just north of Charleston. It is influenced by the Gullah people, descendants of various African ethnic groups, from the coastal islands of Georgia and South Carolina, whose language and cooking derives from a creolized mix of Spanish, French, Native American, and African cultures. It was the marshy, rice-growing plantations that first marked South Carolina's place in the culinary history of the world.

"It was traditionally a rice culture with sandy soil, long growing seasons with strong influences from the coastal waters, crab, and other seafood from the estuaries," explained the chef of Charleston's Hominy Grill, Robert Stehling. "Okra and eggplant came from slave influences, brought in originally with the slave trade from rice growing areas of Africa." The Lowcountry rice casserole dish, purloo, made with chicken, sausage, and shrimp, is "similar to jambalaya and paella," Mr. Stehling said.

Immigrant Songs indeed,
then and now.

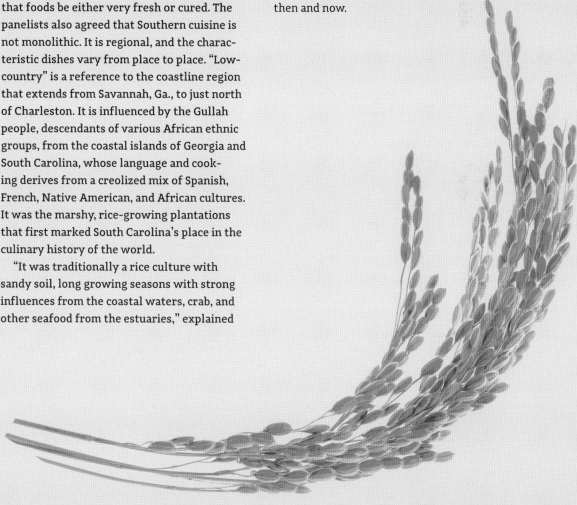

Cedar Key Creamy Clam Chowder

There is no reason to choose a red chowder over a white chowder or vice versa. There are seven days in the week, after all! And in a state like ours with *such* a bounty of seafood we have a lot of soups and stews in the repertoire. Cedar Key, a tiny island community on the Gulf of Mexico roughly 120 miles north of Tampa and 50 miles southwest of Gainesville, is a place noted for being "the real Florida." You can find this kind of soup there. (You might also find a "Shrimp Pie" at a restaurant called Frog's Landing. But let *them* make that for you.) The clams of Cedar Key make us happy as one.

Serves 6 to 8

For the soup base:

2 cups Shrimp Stock (page 238) or bottled clam juice

2 cups heavy cream

½ cup (1 stick) butter

3 cloves garlic, minced

1 jalapeño chile, seeded and minced

½ sweet onion, diced

1 stalk celery, diced

¼ cup all-purpose flour

Kosher salt and cracked black pepper

Make the soup base: Warm the stock in a saucepan and set aside for now. Warm the cream in a separate saucepan and set it aside as well.

Melt the butter in a separate large, heavy-bottomed pot over medium heat. When it is fairly hot, add the garlic, jalapeño, onion, and celery and stir. Turn up the heat to medium-high. Cook the vegetables but do not allow them to brown. When they are just barely soft (about 5 minutes), stir in the flour. Lower the heat to medium, but keep the butter bubbling some. With a whisk or a wooden spoon push the flour and vegetables around the pan until well combined.

Add the warm stock a bit at a time and whisk again. Lower the heat and simmer for 5 to 7 minutes, stirring occasionally. Season with salt and pepper to taste.

Add the warm cream and whisk or stir well again. Simmer for 7 to 8 minutes, stirring often.

Remove from the heat and carefully strain the liquid through a medium-mesh sieve while it is still nice and hot into a large bowl. (The high temperature helps promote a full yield.) Discard the vegetables in the sieve. Set the creamy base liquid aside. (This may be made a day or two in advance and refrigerated.)

For the clams:

2 tablespoons olive oil

2 shallots, sliced

60 clams, scrubbed

1 cup white wine

Kosher salt and pepper

For the soup body:

3 ounces bacon, diced

3 tablespoons olive oil

½ red or white onion, peeled and diced (red brings a bit more color but also has more punch)

1 leek, white part only, cleaned and diced

2 stalks celery, diced

½ red bell pepper, diced

½ yellow bell pepper, diced

1 jalapeño or other chile, seeded and minced

2 tablespoons butter

1 tablespoon fresh thyme leaves

1 bay leaf, broken

1 pound new potatoes, scrubbed and diced (we leave the peels on)

1½ cups fresh corn kernels

Kosher salt and cracked black pepper

1 quart half-and-half

Good bread or toasts

Make the clams: Heat a shallow saucepan that will fit the clams without too much extra room over medium heat. Add the oil and allow it to get fairly hot. Add the shallots and sauté them for a few minutes. Add the clams and then the wine. Season with a bit of salt and pepper. (Not much salt, as the clams will provide a measure of it.) Cover with a lid and steam the clams until they open. Take them out of the pan and put them into a bowl as they open. Continue to cook the liquid in the pan until it is reduced to a near syrupy consistency. Strain it through a sieve into a bowl. Discard the spent shallots. Set the liquid and the steamed clams aside.

Make the soup body: In a heavy-bottomed pan over medium heat, cook the bacon with the oil, stirring well to distribute the fat, until the bacon is almost crisp, 3 to 5 minutes.

Add the onion, leek, celery, bell peppers, and chile. Add 1 tablespoon of the butter and sauté the vegetables briskly. Cook the vegetables to a bit softer than al dente but still with nice texture.

Add the thyme and bay leaf to the vegetable mixture.

In a separate pot, cook the potatoes in plenty of boiling water and some salt until just barely tender, 2 to 3 minutes. Drain.

Add the soup base to the vegetable mixture. Add the cooked potatoes. Cook to heat through, stirring.

In a small sauté pan, quickly cook the corn in the remaining 1 tablespoon butter with some salt and pepper, until just tender, 2 to 3 minutes. Add the corn to the soup.

Add the reduced clam broth and the steamed clams to the soup and cook for 2 to 3 minutes. Stir in the half-and-half and cook to heat through. Season with more salt and pepper to taste.

Ladle the soup into warm bowls. Serve with good bread or toasts.

Note: We ask for a "heavy-bottomed pot" for the very good reason that the thickness helps prevent burning and sticking. So if you don't have one, now is a fine time to make that investment. There are good brands to choose from at various price points. A good one will last many years.

Note: Many chefs have a penchant for cutting the potatoes for chowder *too* small, I think. Knife skills are important but so is the distinguishing texture of the all-important potato "feel" in a good chowder. The rich creaminess of the chowder needs the momentary oasis of a potato's soft mitigation of that intensity.

Janet's Smoky Tomato Soup and "Those Toasts"

My "better half" is also my quieter one. But she does speak up about food! She told me many, many times in our first twenty-five years of being together that she "does not like tomatoes." When I pointed out that she loved ketchup with her fries and wouldn't dream of making her father's barbeque sauce without that condiment, she happily ignored me. But a woman can, as it has also been pointed out, change her mind. And Janet did when she announced one day that she was craving a "great simple tomato soup" to go with a grilled cheese sandwich we were having at lunch. And so I named it for her.

Serves 6 to 10

For the "smoked" tomatoes:

2½ pounds ripe, in-season tomatoes

1 tablespoon smoked pimentón

½ tablespoon toasted and cracked black pepper

½ tablespoon kosher salt

½ tablespoon sugar

Sherry vinegar, as needed

For the soup:

¼ cup extra-virgin olive oil

2 tablespoons butter

½ sweet onion, roughly chopped

4 large cloves garlic, minced

2 leeks, white parts only, cleaned and finely diced

2 cups Chicken Stock (page 237) or vegetable stock

1 tablespoon chopped fresh basil

1 tablespoon chopped fresh Italian parsley

Kosher salt and cracked black pepper, as needed

For serving:

"Those Toasts" (page 242)

Good blue cheese (optional)

Make the "smoked" tomatoes: Preheat the oven to 275 degrees. Cut the tomatoes in half crosswise so that they will remain cut side up when placed on a roasting pan. Line a rimmed baking sheet with parchment paper and place the tomatoes, cut side up, in the middle of the pan.

Stir the pimentón, pepper, salt, and sugar together in a small bowl.

Drizzle each tomato half with a few drops of vinegar. Then sprinkle with the spice mixture and roast for about 40 minutes, until their skins begin to pull away from the flesh. Remove from the oven and let them cool, then peel away and discard the skins.

Make the soup: Heat a large saucepan over medium heat. When it is pretty warm, add the oil and then the butter. Stir. Add the onion, garlic, and leeks and cook gently for 10 to 15 minutes, until tender but not browned, stirring as needed.

Add the stock. Turn up the heat and cook until the liquid is reduced by half, about 10 minutes. Add the "smoked" tomatoes, the basil, and parsley and simmer for about 15 minutes, adjusting the heat as needed to maintain a simmer. Cook until thickened and flavorful. The tomatoes will give up their water as they cook, which is good as it focuses the flavor of your soup. Season with salt and pepper if needed—the tomatoes had a good level of spices, so perhaps they won't need more. Remove from the heat and carefully puree in a blender until as smooth as desired. I just give a short spin. Do not strain it.

When ready to serve, ladle into a bowl and accompany with "Those Toasts." If you like, crumble some cheese on the toasts for a more intense dish.

Note: If you don't like the seeds of tomatoes or they don't agree with you digestively (as was my mom's experience), by all means remove them from the tomatoes.

Chowder, the Red One ... Like Sailors Make

Anywhere fishermen have set up their off-water lives you will see many food smokers in action. Fishermen have converted all kinds of items into quite serviceable smokers. Abandoned refrigerators are a favorite. We've bought locally caught and smoked fish after a quick free sample at a number of picturesque waterfront bars. A fisherman's jack-knife, a baggie, a small handful of cash, and the deal is done. Some will even have cut lemons to throw in. The smoked fish garnish we offer with this chowder makes it one like sailors make.

You will note that this makes a pretty large batch. I like to freeze the leftovers in quart-size containers and have it on hand for nights when we have less time to cook.

Makes about 5 quarts

For the fish:

Olive oil

2 pounds totally cleaned fish fillets (mahi mahi and swordfish is what we often use, but whatever is freshest is best), cut into roughly hand-sized sections

Kosher salt and freshly cracked black pepper

1 cup roughly chopped fresh Italian parsley, basil, and chervil, or a combination

Make the fish: Heat a large, flat nonstick sauté pan over medium-high heat. Add enough oil to lightly coat the bottom of the pan. Season the fish with salt and pepper. Stir 1 tablespoon oil into the herbs and coat one side of each piece of fish with the herb mixture. Working in batches, lay the fish herbed side down in the pan, dropping the fish away from you as you do. Let the fish sear for about 2 minutes on that herbed side, then flip them over and cook for 15 seconds on the second side. Remove the fish to a platter or pan. (The fish will not be cooked through, but that is the intention for now.)

For the potatoes:

1½ pounds red potatoes, scrubbed, any blemishes cut off

Note: The technique used for the potatoes does take additional time, but you might love the difference it makes from simply quartering them. At least try it once. You can always go back to the old way if you like.

Make the potatoes: Fill a large pot with cold water. Prepare the potatoes by cutting them once in half and then again by driving a knife into them and twisting the blade. (This is an old-school way of ensuring that the potatoes "break" along their natural lines and makes for a better absorption of the soup's flavors.) Add the potatoes to the cold water with some salt. Bring to a simmer and cook until just easily pierced with a knife, 15 to 20 minutes. Drain well. Set aside.

For the soup:

4 ounces bacon, diced

¼ cup olive oil

6 cloves garlic, sliced

2 jalapeño chiles, seeded and finely diced

1 large onion, diced

2 celery stalks, diced

2 carrots, peeled and diced

½ bulb fennel, cored and diced

1 red or yellow bell pepper, diced

Kosher salt and cracked black pepper

1 tablespoon (or less if you prefer) crushed red pepper

1 dried ancho or ñora chile, toasted, stem and seeds removed

2 pounds clams and mussels, scrubbed and drained well

1 (28-ounce) can peeled plum tomatoes, well crushed or pureed

1 (28-ounce) can tomato puree

2 bay leaves, broken

3 cups Shrimp Stock (page 238)

Tabasco or other hot sauce, if desired

For serving:

Mayonnaise (optional)

8 slices cross-cut baguette bread, toasted to a golden brown

2 ounces smoked fish per guest (we use local Florida fish such as wahoo, amberjack, or mullet, but smoked whitefish is a fine alternative)

Lemon wedges, if desired

Make the soup: In a very large soup pot or Dutch oven over medium-low heat, sauté the bacon with the oil. When the bacon is almost cooked, add the garlic and chiles and cook for 30 seconds. Turn up the heat to medium-high and add the onion, celery, carrots, fennel, and bell pepper. Season with some salt and pepper. Stir to coat and cook until nicely browned, 8 to 10 minutes. Add the crushed red pepper and the ancho chile.

Add the clams and mussels and cover the pot with a tight-fitting lid. Using a slotted spoon, retrieve the clams as soon as they open and set them aside in a clean bowl. Work quickly, as we don't want to over-reduce the clam liquor. You might need to replace the lid a time or two. Discard any clams and mussels that do not open.

Add the tomatoes, tomato puree, and bay leaves. Bring to a simmer, then reduce the heat. Add the cooked potatoes, along with the stock. Cut the seared fish into bite-size pieces and add them to the soup. Cook for 10 minutes more.

Season to taste. Add hot sauce if desired to taste.

Dab some mayonnaise on each piece of toast, if desired, and spoon some smoked fish on top. Serve on the side, with lemon wedges for the table, if you like.

2

SNACKS AND SMALL PLATES TO WARM THE SOUL

Hot Starters

Maduro Plantains as Taught by a Bantu Priestess

The Yoruba people were, after the Bantu, the second largest ethnic group brought on the slave ships during the abhorrent Middle Passage from Africa to Cuba. Between 1820 and 1870, close to twenty thousand of these deeply cultured people were torn from their land and their families to work the sugar plantations, since Europeans had developed an insatiable demand for sweetness in their diets. They originated from what is now called Nigeria, a country roughly twice the size of California and located on the botanically rich western shores of Africa. The Yoruba brought some native ingredients with them and adapted to the produce they found. I learned to love this dish when I first arrived in Key West, and it was cooked by a woman who was Bantu, hence the recipe's name. But it is also noteworthy to learn, as I did, that *Bantu* also means simply "human" or "people."

Serves 4

For the plantains:

Canola oil for frying

2 *very* ripe (black!) plantains, peeled and cut on a bias about ½ inch thick

For the Magic Sauce:

⅓ cup sugar

⅓ cup sherry vinegar

1 teaspoon ground cinnamon

1 teaspoon whole cloves

1 teaspoon grated lime zest

1 tablespoon butter, cut into four bits

2 teaspoons bourbon or golden rum

Note: When we say "ripe plantains" we mean nearly *alarmingly* black. This kind of shocked me when I first started cooking with them several eons ago. Now I am shocked if they are not black *enough*.

Make the plantains: Put about 1 inch of oil in a heavy pot and heat it to 300 degrees. Add the plantain slices and fry until dark golden brown on all sides. Remove the plantains to paper towels.

Make the Magic Sauce: Melt the sugar in a clean saucepan over medium-high heat and stir until it turns into a brown caramel and all lumps are gone, 3 to 4 minutes.

Carefully add the vinegar and stir until the caramel is dissolved, 1 to 2 minutes. Add the cinnamon, cloves, lime zest, and ⅓ cup water. Cook until the liquid is reduced to a caramel consistency, 3 to 5 minutes.

Add the butter, mixing it carefully into the caramel. Add the bourbon. Strain the sauce through a small fine-mesh sieve. (This yields ¼ cup.)

Put the plantains in a pan large enough to hold them all flat in a single layer. Pour the sauce over the plantains and warm them up gently when ready to serve. These can be eaten as a side dish with many dishes. I *adore* spooning them on crispy fried chicken.

Spiny Lobster Hash Cakes
WITH PICCALILLI TARTAR SAUCE

I began my restaurant work life in a classic American diner. In the specialized language of diner kitchens, the near mystical choices of what stood in for the actual names of a dish or a food-related item created a lot of fun for me. "Hash" had this one: "Gentleman will take a chance." Sounds dicey! But in fact hash is a term derived from the French term *hacher*, which simply means "to chop." Here we chop some sweet spiny lobsters to make our hash. American shrimp would be a fine substitute.

Makes 8 hash cakes

10 ounces Idaho potatoes, peeled and cut into quarters

10 ounces boniato sweet potatoes, peeled and cut into quarters

4 teaspoons butter

½ medium red onion, peeled and chopped

2 scallions, trimmed and chopped cross-wise (only some of the green included)

1 tablespoon minced garlic

1 tablespoon chopped fresh basil

½ teaspoon chopped fresh cilantro leaves

½ teaspoon chopped fresh thyme leaves

2 egg yolks, stirred

¼ teaspoon ground cayenne

Kosher salt and cracked black pepper

1 pound spiny (or other) cooked lobster meat or peeled and deveined shrimp, chopped into small- to medium-size pieces

Canola oil for sautéing

Piccalilli Tartar Sauce (page 232) or other tangy sauce

Put the potatoes and boniato in a pot of water to cover them and bring to a simmer. Simmer until just tender, 15 to 20 minutes. Drain well and put in the refrigerator to chill.

Heat a large, heavy skillet over medium-high heat and add the butter. When it foams, add the onion, scallions, and garlic, stirring to coat, and cook until softened, 3 to 5 minutes. Remove from the heat. Add the basil, cilantro, and thyme and let cool slightly, then transfer the vegetable and herb mixture to a large bowl and let cool completely.

Mix in the egg yolks, cayenne, and salt and black pepper to taste.

Shred the potatoes and boniato on the large holes of a box grater.

Combine the potatoes and boniato with the egg, vegetable, and herb mixture. Taste for seasoning and adjust if needed.

Add the lobster meat. Put ½ cup of the mash into a ring mold (or form with your hands) to shape. Slide the ring mold off and continue until you have made all the cakes, putting them on a plate. Chill the cakes very well in the refrigerator to allow them to set up.

Preheat the oven to 375 degrees.

Heat a heavy skillet over medium heat and add a little canola oil. Sauté the hash cakes until golden brown and crispy on each side. It helps to start cooking the cakes in the sauté pan *in* the ring molds (they must be heatproof of course) to keep them formed while they crisp. Take care to turn them gently. You can work in batches if you don't have eight rings.

Transfer to the oven and bake until cooked through, 5 to 8 minutes.

Serve warm with the Piccalilli Tartar Sauce.

Serving suggestion: **These would be great with poached eggs.**

Scallion-Speckled Pupusas
WITH "SALTY DOG" CHEESE

Pupusas, like many Latin Caribbean things, are making broader inroads in all of Florida. One taste and you too will be convinced, if you're not already in this camp. I mix in different things besides scallions or go classic . . . which means nothing mixed in. But you will find that all manner of both fillings and outside accoutrements can be made to dance with pupusas.

Makes 12 pupusas

For the scallions:

2 bunches scallions, sliced into
¼-inch-thick rings

2½ tablespoons peanut oil

Kosher salt and cracked black pepper

For the pupusas:

3½ cups masa harina, plus more
for dusting

½ cup all-purpose flour

2 teaspoons baking powder

1 teaspoon kosher salt

¼ cup lard, melted, or vegetable oil

2¼ cups warm water

2 cups shredded cheese: "Salty Dog"
from Cypress Point Creamery in
Florida, or queso fresco, Monterey
Jack, or mozzarella

Vegetable oil

Make the scallions: Heat a large nonstick sauté pan over medium-high heat. When the pan is hot, add the oil. Add the scallions and stir. Season with salt and pepper. Cook for 4 to 5 minutes, until the scallions are rather wilted and the water inside them is cooked out. Remove to paper towels and let cool. (This can be done a day in advance and kept in the refrigerator, covered.)

Make the pupusas: In a mixing bowl, combine the masa harina, all-purpose flour, baking powder, and salt and whisk to incorporate.

Drizzle the melted lard evenly over the dry ingredients and whisk really well until mixture is pebbly. Add the warm water. Using a wooden spoon, mix to thoroughly combine. Working with your hands now, knead the dough briefly . . . just until it comes together in a smooth ball, about 2 minutes. Work in the cooled scallions. Cover the bowl with a towel and let rest for 15 minutes before proceeding with the cheese filling.

Roll a 1½-ounce ball of the pupusa dough for the bottom of the pupusa and a 1¼-ounce ball for the top. Flatten them each in the palm of your hands. Lay 1 heaping tablespoon of the cheese on the bottom disk. Place the top disk on top of the filling and press the edges together with your fingers. If any holes appear, patch them up with more dough. If the dough sticks to your hands as you are working, rub a *little* oil on them and proceed.

Lay the filled pupusas on a lightly masa-dusted baking sheet.

Heat a lightly oiled large skillet over medium-high heat. Working in batches, add the pupusas and cook for 4 to 5 minutes on each side, until golden brown. Serve warm. They can be held in a 325 degree oven for up to 20 minutes if needed.

Serving suggestion: Serve with a sauce—Sorghum and Horseradish Sour Cream (page 232) would be good here—or slaw.

"Easter Came Early" Empanadas

Our April arrival in Key West some four decades ago brought an instant reprieve from the wintry grip that held our native state of Illinois. Janet and I quickly began to sample the local spots for food—it was all quite unique to us! Empanadas were among the treasures we encountered. We named this version for the kind of Easter spirit of transcendence we felt in the warming Florida sun as we sat on the steps of a little bodega and pulled empanadas from a bag and reveled in their simple, rustic powers.

Empanadas are the Hispanic equivalent of sandwiches to people of the United States, quiche to the French, and panini to the Italians. They come in all sizes and shapes, and with countless fillings. Their most common name is *empanada*, but they are also known as *empadas*, *empadãos*, *empadinhas*, *pasteles*, *empanaditas*, and more.

Makes 24 empanadas

For the dough:

4½ cups all-purpose flour, plus more for dusting

1 tablespoon kosher salt

2 teaspoons baking powder

1 cup vegetable shortening

1 cup icy water or enough to bind the dough

For the empanadas:

2 cups mashed roasted sweet potato (from about 1 large sweet potato)

4 ounces baked ham, finely diced

8 ounces shredded fresh mozzarella cheese

4 hard-cooked eggs, yolks pushed through a sieve, whites finely diced

2 tablespoons Creole- (or other stone-ground) prepared mustard

Kosher salt and cracked black pepper

All-purpose flour for dusting

1 egg, lightly beaten (optional)

Canola oil for deep-frying

Good-quality coarse salt such as Maldon for sprinkling

Make the dough: Combine the flour, salt, and baking powder in a large bowl. Using a pastry cutter or fork, cut the shortening into the flour until the mixture resembles coarse crumbs. Add the icy water and stir with a fork until the dough forms a ball, adding more water if needed. Wrap in plastic and refrigerate for 45 minutes to allow the dough to rest.

Make the empanadas: In a bowl, combine the sweet potato, ham, cheese, eggs, mustard, and salt and pepper to taste until well combined. Set aside.

Line a baking sheet with parchment paper and dust with flour.

On a well-floured working surface, roll out the dough as thin as possible without tearing it. Cut into rounds with a 4-inch cutter. Place ½ to 1 tablespoon of the filling on each round of dough, brush the edges with the egg (or water), and fold the dough round in half. Crimp the edges with the underside of a fork that has been dipped in flour (which helps keep it from sticking). Seal the outer edges by dabbing with the egg or some water with your fingers.

Transfer to the prepared baking sheet. Continue until all the empanadas are shaped.

In a deep-fryer or deep heavy pot, pour the canola oil to a depth of 3 inches and heat it to 350 degrees. Fry the empanadas a few at a time until golden brown, 3 to 4 minutes, turning them over as needed.

Drain on paper towels, season with a sprinkle of good salt, and serve.

Note: Our friend (and superb cookbook author and cooking instructor) Sandra Gutierrez is a guiding spirit of empanada making (and much more). For years I followed mixed trails on this topic, but when her book *Empanadas: The Hand-Held Pies of Latin America* came out, we had the go-to resource from then on.

Serving suggestion: Serve with Sorghum and Horseradish Sour Cream (page 232). If you want, add crispy prosciutto bits or bacon bits (homemade, of course) to the filling for crunch and a more intense porky flavor.

White Street Laundromat Papas Rellenas
WITH CRAB AND TUNA STUFFING

The *ventanita* or "little window" one walks up to for coffee in the Cuban form was one of my favorite aspects of island life when I arrived in my adopted state. In addition to the various types of coffee to be had (café con leche, colada, and cortadito among them), one could also get an array of "pick-me-up snacks" from the magical window emitting not only enticing aromas but all kinds of excited conversation from people standing on both sides of the glass. It remains a signature style of the many types of Florida casual eating spots. There's no question that the Versailles window is the busiest in Miami. Papas rellenas are "stuffed potato balls." While most papas are filled with meat of some kind, the fillings can be as varied as the weather, so dress accordingly. Here we go with seafood, and add salt in the form of capers and pepper in the form of a Vietnamese garlic-chile sauce.

Makes at least 50 papas

For the crab and tuna stuffing:

1 cup good-quality crabmeat, all shell removed

5 ounces drained good-quality canned tuna

3 hard-cooked eggs, chopped

½ cup mayonnaise

2 tablespoons capers, rinsed in cold water and chopped somewhat finely

1 tablespoon Vietnamese chile-garlic sauce, or other favorite hot sauce, or to taste

Kosher salt and cracked black pepper to taste

Make the crab and tuna stuffing: Mix all of the ingredients together. Chill in the refrigerator until ready to stuff the potato balls.

Note: Any leftover crab and tuna filling can be eaten on crackers, bread, or saved for another round of Papas Rellenas.

For the potatoes:

6 cups cooked and riced (in a potato ricer) or mashed Idaho potatoes, cooled

2 eggs, beaten, at room temperature

2 tablespoons milk, at room temperature

2 teaspoons kosher salt, or more to taste

1½ teaspoons black pepper

½ teaspoon ground cayenne pepper

1 tablespoon chopped fresh thyme

1 tablespoon chopped fresh Italian parsley

1 tablespoon chopped fresh basil

For breading and frying:

½ cup all-purpose flour

2 teaspoons kosher salt

1 teaspoon ground black pepper

2 eggs

1¼ cups panko breadcrumbs

Peanut or vegetable oil for frying

Make the potatoes: Put the potatoes in a large bowl and stir in the eggs, milk, salt, black pepper, cayenne, thyme, parsley, and basil. Taste for salt and adjust as needed. Cover and refrigerate the mixture for at least 30 minutes.

Form the potato mixture into 1-ounce balls. Using your forefinger, make an indentation large enough to fill with 1½ teaspoons of the crab and tuna filling. (Some folks like to mash the potato out into a small circle in their hand and then fold the filling around it.) Pinch the potato together to seal. Pat and roll gently into a smooth ball. Whichever method gets you a successful ball of stuffed potato is fine by me!

Bread and fry the potato balls: Put the flour in one bowl and season with the salt and pepper. In another bowl beat the two eggs together with 1 tablespoon water. Put the breadcrumbs in a third bowl. Dip each ball into the seasoned flour, then in the egg mixture, then roll in the breadcrumbs to coat, putting the breaded balls on a plate. Put them in the refrigerator to chill for about 30 minutes, as it helps "set" the potato better.

Pour at least 3 inches of oil into a deep heavy pot and heat it to 375 degrees. Working in batches, drop the potato balls into the oil and fry until golden brown, about 3 minutes.

Drain on paper towels and serve hot. No more sauce is really needed than, say, sour cream and lemon if you wish. Or hot sauce if your wishing goes like mine.

Apalachicola Oyster Pan Stew
WITH SHERRY CREAM AND CORN STICKS

The history of Apalachicola is one I would have loved to have seen James Michener take up. Few but he could conjure the magic of time's sweep of geology and the travails of mankind working on the boats during the past century and a half. Janet worked at an oyster and raw bar for a few years. While she pulled draft beers for tourists and locals, I chatted up the shuckers who worked that trade. I got to truly understand the joy that many who grow up in "oyster country" know. The waters that are home to oysters rely upon humans to be very conscientious or we may be one of the last generations to make a meal like the one we have here. It is a rich, creamy repast I especially like to make in the cool of winter. That time also coincides with truffle season; if you like, add that powerful delicacy to your shopping list and then thinly, *ever* so thinly, cut a few slices and drape them over your hot oyster stew.

Serves 4

For the cream sauce:

3 tablespoons butter

½ cup chopped shallots

1 clove garlic, minced

1 bay leaf

6 whole black peppercorns, lightly crushed

1 tablespoon fresh thyme leaves

½ cup white wine

About 1 cup oyster liquor (from oysters below)

2 cups heavy cream

1 cup whole milk

1 tablespoon Dijon mustard

Make the cream sauce: In a large heavy saucepan, heat the butter over medium heat until foamy. Add the shallots and garlic and cook until soft, 3 to 4 minutes.

Add the bay leaf, peppercorns, and thyme. Stir. Add the wine and cook until it is reduced almost to a glaze. Add the oyster liquor and cook until reduced by half, about 5 minutes.

Add the cream and cook over high heat (taking care not to let it boil over—this is best done by using a *large* saucepan and whisking constantly) until the sauce is thick enough to coat the back of a spoon.

Remove from the heat and let cool for a minute. Add the milk and mustard. Give it a few whisks and let the mustard infuse the sauce well. Strain the sauce through a fine-mesh sieve into a clean pan, discarding the solids. Set aside, covered to keep warm. You should have about 2 cups of this sauce.

For the pan stew:

3 tablespoons butter

1 leek, cleaned well and sliced into very thin julienne

1 zucchini, some of the peel removed if you like, sliced into very thin julienne

1 carrot, peeled and sliced into very thin julienne

1 stalk celery, sliced into very thin julienne

8 ounces cleaned farmed and/or wild mushrooms, sliced

¼ cup dry sherry

1 cup peeled and diced tomatoes, divided

24 freshly shucked fresh oysters, liquor drained but reserved (used above)

¼ cup minced fresh chives (optional)

> *Serving suggestion:* Serve with the 14 Corn Sticks (page 241) or whatever bread you prefer.

Make the pan stew: In a large heavy skillet, heat the butter over medium heat and add leek, zucchini, carrot, and celery; stir well. Add the mushrooms. Add the sherry and simmer over high heat until reduced almost to a syrup, 6 to 8 minutes. Add the cream sauce and half of the tomatoes. Bring to just under a boil. When ready to serve, add the raw oysters. Stir. Remove from the heat.

Ladle the stew into heated bowls. Garnish with the remaining tomatoes and the chives. Serve hot.

Old Winter Haven Eggplant, Bell Pepper, and Peanut Fritters

This dish celebrates the harvest of a number of Florida ingredients (though truly the ingredients can be found almost everywhere folks garden). It happens to be vegetarian and thus perfect for party entertaining in these less "meat-needy" times. Yet the basic recipe goes back at least a century. The values of things go full circle eternally. Let's just also be sure they taste like things we crave now, too.

Makes 16 to 18 fritters

4 to 5 tablespoons olive oil

2 cloves garlic, thinly sliced

½ cup diced yellow or red bell pepper

½ cup finely diced onion

Kosher salt and cracked black pepper

1 large Italian eggplant, stem and bottom cut off and discarded

2 eggs

¼ cup milk

¾ cup all-purpose flour

1 tablespoon baking powder

⅓ cup shelled unsalted peanuts, papery husks rubbed off

Vegetable or canola oil for deep-frying

Heat a medium-size nonstick skillet over medium heat. Add about 2 tablespoons of the olive oil to coat the bottom. Add the garlic, bell pepper, and onion and cook, stirring, until softened and a bit charred, 5 to 6 minutes. Season with salt and black pepper. Set aside.

Trim the eggplant peel off from about 50 percent of the vegetable. (Some skin is good. Too much is another story.) Cut the eggplant into strips.

Line a baking sheet with paper towels and lay the eggplant strips on them. Generously salt the strips, turn them over, and salt the other side. Cover them with paper towels, place another baking sheet on top, and weight it down with something heavy to extract the bitter liquid. Let sit for 30 minutes.

Put the salted strips in a colander and rinse the salt off with cold water. Drain, pat dry with a clean kitchen towel, and arrange them in a single layer on a rack to dry a bit more.

Put a large sauté pan over medium-high heat. Add 2 to 3 tablespoons olive oil and fry the eggplant until browned, turning as needed. Drain on paper towels and then chop the eggplant into a fairly large dice. (You'll need 1½ cups. Save any extra for another dish.) Combine the eggplant and the onion mixture and set aside.

In a bowl, beat the eggs together with the milk. In a separate bowl, combine the flour and baking powder. Add the egg mixture to the flour mixture. Season with about 1 teaspoon salt and 1 teaspoon pepper. Add the eggplant mixture and the peanuts. Stir to combine and distribute the ingredients evenly. (You can chill this in the refrigerator for up to overnight if it is going to be more than half an hour before you are ready to cook.)

Pour enough oil into a deep heavy pot to almost submerge the fritters and heat it to 350 degrees. Using a small scoop (like a melon baller) or two spoons, form balls of the batter and carefully add them to the hot oil. Cook in batches. Fry until the balls are cooked through: Check the center of one after about 2 minutes; larger ones could take 3 minutes. Drain on paper towels.

Serve hot. These can be kept in a low oven for 20 minutes while you freshen up your drinks and chat with your fabulous friends.

Serving suggestion: No sauce is really needed. But if you want to serve sour cream or something simple, feel as free as a bird.

3

TURN OFF
THE STOVE

Salads, Ceviches,
and Cool-Down
Dishes

Mallory Dock Hogfish Snapper Escabeche
WITH SWAMP CABBAGE SLAW

Hogfish are so named for their hog-like snout used to dig around the seafloor for food. They also have protruding canine teeth, which are perfect for crushing hard-shell prey like crabs. Many that we have served were harvested by our spearfishing friends. Some of the first hogfish we tasted were culled from the very waters over which folks now watch the Key West Sunset Celebration.

In a cross-cultural act of sharing, the Seminole Indians of Florida introduced new foods to white settlers struggling to survive. One of the things the Indians taught them was about the bounty of a kind of "vegetable" found in the sabal palm tree, also known as the cabbage palm or swamp cabbage. They noted that the palm's new growth "bud," if harvested, was both tender and delicious. Over time, however, the once-bountiful trees nearly became extinct. Now, hearts of palm are imported from Central and South America. For more than forty-five years, the small town of LaBelle, just east of Fort Myers on the Caloosahatchee River, has been celebrating swamp cabbage with a down-home festival and even a parade. A fitting way to recognize the state tree of Florida!

Serves 6 to 8

For the slaw:

3 cups peeled and very thinly sliced crosswise (on a mandoline, if possible) swamp cabbage (fresh hearts of palm)

½ cup peeled and julienned jicama

½ red bell pepper, sliced into julienne

½ yellow bell pepper, sliced into julienne

1 to 2 Scotch bonnet chiles, seeded and minced

1 small red onion, thinly sliced

6 scallions, finely chopped

Make the slaw: Mix all of the slaw ingredients together in a large bowl.

For the dressing:

1 cup olive oil

⅓ cup fresh-squeezed orange juice

6 tablespoons fresh-squeezed lime juice

2 teaspoons toasted and ground coriander

1 teaspoon sugar

1 teaspoon ground black pepper

Kosher salt to taste

Make the dressing: Mix all of the dressing ingredients together in another bowl. Pour the dressing over the slaw. Put in the refrigerator to macerate for at least 1 hour before serving.

For the escabeche:

1½ pounds boneless, skinless snapper or hogfish fillets

4 teaspoons Escabeche Spice Rub (page 220)

2 tablespoons peanut or canola oil

4 cloves garlic, thinly sliced

¾ cup thinly sliced red onion

½ cup cilantro leaves, torn

7 tablespoons gold tequila

¼ cup sherry vinegar

¼ cup fresh-squeezed lime juice

¼ cup fresh-squeezed orange juice

¼ cup olive oil

Make the escabeche: Lay the fish fillets on a flat dish. Rub the fish with the Escabeche Spice Rub on one side only.

Heat a nonstick or well-seasoned cast-iron pan over high heat with the peanut oil. When the pan is smoking hot, add the fish and sear on both sides, shaking the pan so the fish does not stick (about 40 seconds on each side). Remove to a plate and let cool.

In a nonreactive bowl, stir together the garlic, onion, cilantro, tequila, vinegar, lime and orange juices, and olive oil. Slide the seared fish into the marinade. Refrigerate, covered. The "cooking" time will vary depending on the thickness of the fish. Generally it will take 1 to 3 hours, so check it periodically. The fish is done when it can be easily chewed. Cut and taste a small piece to verify.

To serve, you can leave the hogfish in fillets atop the slaw, or break it up into bite-size pieces and toss with the slaw.

Bay Scallops and Passionfruit Ceviche
WITH TORCHED SWEET POTATO

Scallops have been harvested in the grassy flats off Cedar Key for a long, long time. Beautiful waters arrive at the gulf from the fabled Suwannee River as well as the Waccasassa, and the rivers converge in such a way that the scallops thrive there. Whether served as a ceviche or simply seared, they make a fine repast. These are the "bay scallops" noted for their sweetness. The "torched" sweet potatoes restate sweetness, while the passionfruit offers a complex, somewhat sour flavor profile that is one of the most intriguing in nature.

Serves 4

For the torched sweet potatoes:

1 pound sweet potatoes, peel left on, cut into planks

Olive oil

Kosher salt and cracked black pepper

1½ tablespoons butter

2 tablespoons sugar

Make the torched sweet potatoes: Preheat the oven to 350 degrees.

Brush the sweet potatoes with oil and season with salt and pepper. Place them on a nonreactive baking sheet and bake until fork tender, about 30 minutes. Remove from the oven. Turn up the heat on the oven to broil, or ready a mini or normal-size blowtorch.

Melt the butter in a small pan. Brush it on the sweet potato planks. Sprinkle the sugar evenly over the potatoes. Add a pinch of salt to this as well—but just a pinch, as the potatoes were salted once before they were put in the oven.

Broil or blowtorch the sweet potatoes, keeping a close eye on them, until nicely colored and caramelized, about 4 minutes under the broiler.

Let the sweet potatoes cool completely. Peel away the skins and dice the flesh. Set aside until ready to assemble and serve the ceviche.

For the passionfruit dressing:

⅓ cup passionfruit juice

½ tablespoon champagne vinegar

1 tablespoon sesame oil

½ cup canola or vegetable oil

1 tablespoon extra-virgin olive oil

Kosher salt and cracked black pepper to taste

Make the passionfruit dressing: Combine all the ingredients and put in the refrigerator to chill until you're ready to marinate the scallops. The fresher the scallops, the less marinating time they need. And just-harvested scallops are like sushi and thus need only a little dressing. This is why we give a stand-alone recipe for the dressing, so you can adjust the amount you wish to use. It also gives you a nice marinade or dressing that can be used on a variety of things.

For the ceviche:

1 pound bay scallops, cleaned

Kosher salt

¼ red onion, finely diced (we use the "hearts" of the red onion for stocks or other things and use the layers outside the heart for dicing for ceviche)

½ to 1 jalapeño chile, seeded and minced

Cracked black pepper

½ cup fresh cilantro leaves, torn

Make the ceviche: Season the scallops with a bit of salt and put them in a strainer over a bowl. After 30 minutes, discard any liquid in the bowl. (It won't be much.) Place the scallops in a clean bowl.

Dress the scallops with the passionfruit dressing. Add the onion, jalapeño, and sweet potato. Toss to combine, then season with salt and pepper if needed. Cover and chill for about 10 minutes, just until cold.

Just before serving, stir in the cilantro. Serve in small chilled bowls.

Note: Passionfruit juice is sold frozen, but when making your own fresh, you need to strain out the passionfruit seeds. It is important to not let the juices run out of the passionfruit when you cut them open. Have a strainer and a bowl set up near your cutting board. Cut about halfway through and then invert the fruit over the strainer and bowl to catch the first juice. Then, still holding the fruit over the strainer, scrape out the seeds and gather all you can. The seeds can be saved for other uses if you wish. The amount of juice in the fruit can vary. I net about ⅓ cup from 3 large passionfruit. The juice is bright and fascinatingly potent. Some recipes using the juice cause me to add a bump of honey. But for a ceviche I like it like this. Uncut.

Black Grouper Ceviche with *Leche de Tigre* and Popcorn

Peruvians' love of seafood is in perfect sync with native and longtime Floridians', and we warmly welcome their current wave of culinary influence. If you speak with ten Peruvian chefs, you will get ten versions of *leche de tigre*—it is a Peruvian custom and a constellation of recipes. The one consensus is that pristinely fresh fish and ice are key to preparing a fitting medium for a ceviche that is both flavorful and chilled to promote a firm, refreshing texture for the fish.

Serves 4

For the ceviche:

¾ cup fresh-squeezed lime juice

2 tablespoons chopped celery, preferably inner stalks

1 clove garlic, minced

1 tablespoon minced fresh ginger

½ Scotch bonnet chile, seeded and minced

2 tablespoons chopped red onion

¾ cup ice

8 ounces black grouper or other firm fish, scaled, skinned, and cubed

Kosher salt

For the garnishes:

1 sweet potato, peeled, cubed, and boiled until just tender

1 ear fresh sweet corn, kernels cut from the cob

¼ to ½ cup short thin slices red onion

½ to 1 minced chile (habanero, serrano, or other)

½ cup freshly popped popcorn or Peruvian *cancha*

A few sprigs fresh cilantro, roughly chopped

Make the ceviche: Put the lime juice, celery, garlic, ginger, chile, onion, and ice in a blender. Blend until everything is well mixed. Transfer to a bowl, add the fish and kosher salt, and stir; marinate for 30 minutes. Set aside in the refrigerator while you prepare the garnishes.

Make the garnishes: Stir the sweet potato, corn, onion, and chile into the chilled ceviche.

Spoon into serving dishes. Top with the popcorn and cilantro and serve.

Raw Diced Tuna with Backyard Mangos on Plantain Chips

We find tuna good when cooked, but much better when raw and dressed with a balanced marinade as the one here. As tartare has become incredibly popular in the past twenty years or so, the variations on raw fish are expanding—crudo and sashimi are two more. The main signal of whether a fish is fresh is often the label "sushi quality." But frankly, shouldn't all fish we eat be that fresh? Chef and ocean advocate Barton Seaver also reminds us how small a percentage of American waters are utilized for greater diversity of fish. So please consider taking this recipe as a guide and explore the many species in your town or city's fish markets. We need to support our fishermen and fisherwomen by using the entirety of their catch.

Serves 4 as an appetizer

¼ cup minced red or sweet onion

1 tablespoon finely minced fresh ginger

1 teaspoon gochujang (Korean chile paste)

½ teaspoon dark toasted sesame oil

1 tablespoon tamari

1 teaspoon grated lemon zest

8 ounces tuna, sinew, bloodline, and fat removed, finely diced

Kosher salt and toasted and ground black pepper

½ cup finely diced ripe, beautiful mango

Plantain Chips (page 244)

In a bowl, stir together the onion, ginger, gochujang, sesame oil, tamari, and lemon zest. Add the tuna and season with salt and pepper. Add the mango and stir delicately one more time. Cover and chill in the refrigerator for about 10 minutes, just until cold.

Serve with the Plantain Chips. Offer topped with the ceviche or let guests spoon it up as they like.

The Mango Gang

The Mango Gang was born after a run on Miami Beach. The "pregnancy" of course took much longer. But on a specific morning in 1992, I clocked my run from 1440 Ocean Drive to Joe's Stone Crab and returned panting to the steps of the Betsy Ross Hotel, where I had been working at a restaurant I created named "a Mano." The owner was sitting nonchalantly on the front steps, *still up* from the night before, and with him was actor-pugilist Mickey Rourke. It was like Crockett and Tubbs . . . as drawn by Ralph Steadman, the brilliant cartoonist who did many illustrations of the writings of Hunter S. Thompson. Despite the louche behavior in front of me, I turned away from the damaged men to face the water line and return to my "what if" thoughts from my run; I saw big ships floating in the distant water and realized that somehow we needed to depict the spirit of the times in a culinary form. So I reached out to the other chefs in south Florida about doing a cookbook together.

The primary members aside from myself were Douglas Rodriguez, Allen Susser, and Mark Militello. Douglas was cooking in Coral Gables at the original Yuca restaurant and was the chef in town back then that made me laugh in the way you laugh at a kind of creative brilliance. He understood the cooking of his parents and all of the Cuban émigrés that made Miami their new home, and then he did what chefs do if they have the mad chops. *He turned it on its head.* He actually regrasped it with

love and homage and showed generations past that Cuban cuisine should not be rooted and fixed but moving and flowing outward. Mark was in North Miami and was heavily Mediterranean in his take on cuisine. He had a command of technique that made his restaurant immensely popular. Allen was trained in part in France, and the touches of that Gallic classicism framed his food. But Allen was also in love with Florida's ingredients. We got an agent named John Harrisson, who found instant reception with publishing houses in New York. Suddenly it was game on. Each of us, in our own way, used Miami as our culinary laboratory. Tropical fruits and tubers became starring members on menus, and visitors who came to taste this new frontier were forced to learn a new lexicon in cuisine. The menus were a modern patois of half a dozen languages. It threw some of the old guard writers off and a few scoffed. But soon the *New York Times*, the London *Times* and even *Time* magazine were talking about "a Mano" and us—the "Mango Gang Chefs."

The fact is, however, that the hybridizations that make up regional cuisines had been happening all over the country in different ways. Charlie Trotter and I had done it in Illinois before Janet and I had returned to live in Florida. Emeril was doing it in New Orleans at Commander's Palace. Dean, Robert, Stephan, and Mark were doing it in their respective restaurants in Texas and New Mexico.

The big revelation and "fire starter" for me was how Jeremiah Tower created his Great American Regional Menus while working with Alice Waters in California during his time with the seer of Berkeley. Young American chefs *all* across the land were finding the voice and flavor of America again in distinctly regional voices and with a reawakened love for pure ingredients and the producers of them. Long before "farm to table" became a catch phrase, every important chef from Larry Forgione to Lydia Shire to Wolfgang and Jean-Georges was busy hunting down the products that would more fully illustrate the region of his or her kitchen. Those of us in Florida had to lift off the yoke of stale expectations. For too long Florida was able to swan along based primarily on her "looks." The fine weather and sandy beaches were not enough for those of us seeking to find our place within the sweeping winds and shifting tides of this New American Cuisine.

Each of us, in our own way, used Miami as our culinary laboratory.

U-Pick Strawberry Salad
WITH FLORIDA BURRATA, MARINATED KUMQUATS, AND TOASTED HAZELNUTS IN A CITRUS-VANILLA VINAIGRETTE

They're out there! Bursting through the black-dirt fields with a red-lipped lusciousness that only a woman as brazen as Mother Nature could muster. Folks, I'm talking about strawberries, if you haven't guessed yet! Skip the grocery store and pick your own at the right time of year. You will be rewarded with a brimming basket of sun-ripened strawberries and a day to revisit your childhood. I remember my earliest experiences picking berries. Our mom would drive us to a U-pick farm not very far from our Illinois home. We'd join other families in a kind of controlled foraging of the fields cared for by generations of family farmers. (I also keenly remember the mosquitoes that came after us those muggy mornings near the Wisconsin border.)

In the mid-1800s in the United States, there were only about fourteen hundred acres of cultivated strawberries. That *ain't* much—they were growing so abundantly in the wild that *no one bothered* to plant them. Strawberries are native to the New World, likely originating from Peru. Yet it was after a trip abroad and being cultivated by some of the greenest thumbs of Europe that the strawberries we know today truly came into the realm of greatness.

Serves 4

For the citrus-vanilla vinaigrette:

1 cup fresh-squeezed orange juice

1 whole vanilla bean, split in half

2 tablespoons sherry vinegar

¼ cup extra-virgin olive oil

Kosher salt and cracked black pepper

For the marinated kumquats:

2 cups thinly sliced kumquats (cut into rounds), any pips or seeds removed

½ teaspoon kosher salt

¼ cup rice vinegar

1 tablespoon sugar

Make the citrus-vanilla vinaigrette: Simmer the orange juice in a small heavy saucepan until reduced to about 6 tablespoons, 6 to 8 minutes. Remove from the heat, slip in the vanilla bean, and allow to steep for about 10 minutes.

Remove the vanilla bean and save it for another time. (It can be rinsed, patted dry, and kept in a container of sugar.) Transfer the juice to a bowl and add the vinegar, then whisk in the oil. Season with salt and pepper. Set aside.

Make the marinated kumquats: Put the kumquats in a bowl. Toss with salt and allow to sit for a few minutes. Add the vinegar and sugar. Stir and set aside. (Keep in the refrigerator if you do this in advance. The kumquats can be made a day ahead.)

For the salad:

48 hazelnuts (about ½ cup)

2 heads red leaf lettuce, cleaned, large leaves torn into smaller pieces, heavy ribbed bottoms discarded

2 cups strawberries, hulled and cut into quarters (if they are not sweet from nature, you can add a bit of sugar, honey, or agave to boost)

1 whole burrata cheese, cut into 4 sections, drained as necessary

Kosher salt and cracked black pepper

Make the salad: Preheat the oven to 325 degrees.

Spread the hazelnuts on a baking sheet. Bake for 10 to 15 minutes, until the skins split. While they are still quite warm, gather the nuts into a kitchen towel and kind of scrunch it up and massage to loosen the skins more. Discard the skins. Put the nuts on a cutting board and very coarsely chop them, or simply halve them if you prefer. Set aside.

Dress the lettuce lightly with the dressing, using just enough to coat the leaves. (Any extra can be saved.) Add 1 cup of the kumquats (save the rest for another use) and the strawberries. Add about three quarters of the hazelnuts. Toss.

Serve with a piece of burrata in the center of each plate. Top it all with the remaining toasted hazelnuts.

Squash Salad
WITH RED CABBAGE, CARROTS, MERKÉN, PEPITAS, POMELO, AND HONEY-SOY DRESSING

So often we lose the beautiful aspects of foods when we have to take the skins off. A banana is much more beautiful skin on, but we cannot eat it due to the toughness. And many of our squashes have skins we would be challenged to gnaw through. But the delicata is aptly named, as we can enjoy the skins with the interior flesh too. This salad has a strength in opposites: sesame and squash; honey and the Chilean spice merkén (which you will fall in love with if you haven't yet encountered its depth). The other new item for many will be pomelo, which, as Larry Schokman, the delightful emeritus director of the Kampong (a botanical garden in south Florida), once told me is the grandfather of the grapefruit.

Okay, so the stove has to be turned on a bit for this one. But you could slip the squash in the oven while you take a shower or sashay across the kitchen and shred the cold parts of this salad. And you will delight your vegetable-loving friends by serving a salad that could be a whole luncheon.

Serves 6 to 8

For the honey-soy dressing:

6 tablespoons soy sauce

3 tablespoons honey

2 tablespoons minced fresh ginger

¼ cup fresh-squeezed lemon juice

¼ cup rice vinegar

2 tablespoons dark toasted sesame oil

6 scallions, white part mostly, minced

2 tablespoons white sesame seeds, lightly toasted

Cracked black pepper to taste

Make the honey-soy dressing: Mix all of the ingredients together and set aside.

continued ➜

For the squash:

1 delicata or kabocha squash, or other winter squash with an edible peel

¼ cup extra-virgin olive oil

1 tablespoon honey

½ teaspoon Chilean merkén spice (or a combination of ½ teaspoon smoked pimentón and 1 teaspoon ground cumin)

1½ teaspoons kosher salt

Cracked black pepper to taste

For the salad:

7 cups cored and finely shredded (with a knife or mandoline) red cabbage

1 cup peeled and coarsely grated carrots

1 pomelo or grapefruit (to yield about 1½ cups cut up)

½ cup pepitas (if you use presalted, adjust your salt downward to taste)

1 teaspoon caraway seeds

Goat cheese (I use a soft kind and allow about 1½ ounces per guest)

Kosher salt and cracked black pepper

Make the squash: Preheat the oven to 375 degrees.

The skins of kabocha and delicata are edible. Remove any stickers that retailers too often feel compelled to add directly on the food, rinse the exteriors, and pat dry. Cut off the two ends, then cut the squash in half and scoop out the seeds. Discard or save the seeds for another use. Cut the squash again in half lengthwise and then into bite-size pieces.

Put the oil, honey, merkén, salt, and black pepper in a bowl and mix. Add the squash and toss to coat. Spread in a single layer in a roasting pan. Bake for 20 to 25 minutes, stirring once halfway through. Let cool to room temperature.

Make the salad: Soak the cabbage in cold water for about 15 minutes. Drain well, then add the carrots. Toss well and drop onto paper towels to pat dry and remove all the excess water, which will help ensure that the dressing is not diluted. Transfer to a container and refrigerate while you prepare the rest of the ingredients.

Prepare the pomelo by trimming the top and bottom off. Slice off the skin following the curves of the fruit. Cut out the sections one by one over a bowl to catch the juice, then cut them into bite-size pieces and add them to the bowl with the juice.

Put the squash, cabbage and carrots, pepitas, and caraway seeds in a salad bowl and add just enough vinaigrette to coat. Season with kosher salt and cracked black pepper to taste. Reserve any leftover dressing for another time.

Garnish with the pomelo and small spoonful-sized portions of goat cheese.

Note: If you like you can use a less creamy cheese to balance the acidity. Shaved Parmesan (add it to taste) would be nice.

"Florida Pinks" Shrimp

WITH BUTTERMILK–CREOLE MUSTARD DRESSING, LARDONS, CROUTONS, SPINACH, PECANS, AND RUBY RED GRAPEFRUIT

This salad offers a near riot of colors, textures, and flavors. Florida "pinks" refer to our legendary shrimp harvested off the waters of this long peninsular state. They are often also called "Key West Pink Shrimp" but can be harvested up and down our long coastlines. These shrimp have a mild, sweet taste with a superb texture.

Serves 4

8 cups spinach, stemmed, torn into bite-size pieces, washed, and spun dry

2 cups Buttermilk–Creole Mustard Dressing (page 225)

¾ cup pecans, toasted and cooled

12 ruby red grapefruit sections, chilled, juice saved for another use

5 or 6 hard-cooked eggs, cooled, whites diced, yolks crumbled

½ cup Lardons (page 235) or diced bacon cooked until crisp

½ cup Janet's Multigrain Croutons (page 244)

Kosher salt and cracked black pepper

12 Beer-Steamed Shrimp (page 55), cooled

Tomato wedges (optional)

> **Note:** As with so many salads, let seasonality be a guide; if the tomatoes are out, consider something else. Avocado would be a welcome guest!

Dress the spinach as desired with the Buttermilk–Creole Mustard Dressing in a large mixing bowl. Add the pecans, grapefruit, eggs, lardons, and croutons. Season with salt and pepper if needed. Toss. Divide among serving plates and surround or top with the shrimp (and tomatoes, if using). Serve immediately.

Teena's Tomatoes
WITH RADICCHIO, WATERMELON, FETA, CUCUMBERS, AND AVOCADOS

We have loved getting homegrown produce from farmer Teena Borek, of Teena's Pride, for more years than I can recall. Since I came up from the Florida Keys and began my work on the Florida mainland I've been lucky to purchase many varieties of produce from Teena. Her life is worthy of movie—a woman who rose from very humble beginnings to become a Florida icon. We wanted this salad to be colorful, bright, contrasting, and memorable. Like the woman we named it for.

Serves 4 to 6

For the white balsamic dressing:

⅓ cup Dijon or Creole mustard

2 egg yolks, at room temperature

1¾ cups extra-virgin olive oil

⅔ cup white balsamic vinegar

3 tablespoons minced shallot

¼ cup chopped Italian parsley or mint leaves

1 tablespoon dark toasted sesame oil

Kosher salt and cracked black pepper

For the macerated vegetables and watermelon:

1 cup peeled and cubed cucumber

Kosher salt

1 cup cubed tomatoes

2 cups seeded and cubed watermelon

3 tablespoons extra-virgin olive oil

1 tablespoon red wine vinegar

Cracked black pepper

For the salad:

1 avocado

½ head radicchio, cored and finely shredded

Kosher salt and cracked black pepper

3 tablespoons extra-virgin olive oil

1 tablespoon red wine vinegar

¼ cup crumbled feta cheese

Serving suggestion: **If you like, add a few slices or sections of lightly salted tomato to the plate and make the dish a celebration of tomatoes.**

Make the white balsamic dressing: In a blender, combine the mustard and egg yolks. With the machine running, pour in the oil and then the vinegar in a slow, steady stream. Transfer to a mixing bowl. Add the shallots, parsley, and sesame oil and season with salt and pepper. Set aside.

Note: **White balsamic vinegar provides a softer color to the dressing and works better than regular balsamic. The *flavor* of regular balsamic is fine if white balsamic is not on hand, though.**

Make the macerated vegetables and watermelon: Sprinkle the cucumber lightly with salt, let them stand for about 5 minutes, then rinse and blot them dry. Put the cucumber, tomatoes, and watermelon in a medium-size mixing bowl. Dress with the oil and vinegar and toss to coat. Season with salt and pepper if needed. Set aside to macerate for at least 10 minutes, then chill in the refrigerator for 10 to 15 minutes.

Make the salad: When ready to serve, peel, pit, and dice the avocado. Put the radicchio in a bowl. Season with salt and pepper, then dress with the oil and vinegar. Toss to coat. Add half of the feta and toss again.

Place a portion of the radicchio mix in the very center of each serving plate in a tight, high nest.

Drain the macerated vegetables and watermelon of the liquid that will have collected at the bottom of the bowl. (While it is not used as part of this recipe, the liquid is a nice thing to drink.)

Spoon some of the white balsamic dressing on the plate around the radicchio. Top that drizzle with the vegetable and water-melon mixture. Sprinkle the remaining feta and the avocado over the salads. Serve immediately.

Daytona Blue Crab Cocktail, "Revival Style"

The Allman Brothers were a new and immediate musical love for me the first time I landed in Key West. Though Duane and his younger brother, Gregg, were both born in Nashville, they grew up in north Florida. When their musical career morphed from high school amateurs to budding blues prodigies they played a lot in the clubs of Daytona Beach. "The social scene in Daytona Beach was simple," Duane Allman once said. "The white cats surf and the blacks play music." The Allmans changed that paradigm . . . and it was not without rancor in the Southland yet. One of the songs on the turntable when I first heard them was "Revival." The lyrics seem nearly simplistic, but the emotions deeply genuine and *hopeful*. The nature of this recipe is one that seeks revival too—through a slashing acidity or maybe a slide guitar's kind of sincere hope to grasp life.

Serves 10 to 12 as an appetizer

For the salsa puree:

1 large tomato, halved and seeded

1 jalapeño chile, halved and seeded

2 red bell peppers, halved and seeded

1 sweet onion, peeled and halved

Canola oil

6 jarred piquillo peppers, drained

¼ cup fresh-squeezed lime juice

¼ cup fresh-squeezed lemon juice

½ cup fresh-squeezed orange juice

¾ cup fresh-squeezed grapefruit juice

1 cup tomato juice

¼ cup sugar

1 teaspoon kosher salt, plus more to taste

1 teaspoon toasted and ground black pepper

Tabasco sauce to taste

Make the salsa puree: Preheat the oven to 500 degrees and line a baking sheet with parchment paper.

Place the tomato, jalapeño, bell peppers, and onion, cut sides down, on the pan. Brush with oil and roast for 15 to 30 minutes, until the skins are loose and somewhat charred. (The time frame given here is a bit broader than we usually like, but when working with high temperatures and oil on vegetables it's best to keep a watchful eye.) Set aside to cool.

Slip the skins off the tomato, jalapeño, and bell peppers and put the vegetables in a blender with the onion, piquillo peppers, citrus and tomato juices, sugar, salt, and black pepper. Blend until smooth. Add Tabasco to taste. The salsa can be made a day in advance and held, covered, in the refrigerator.

Note: This recipe is open to variances in what type of seafood is used. And if you find yourself short by a bit on seafood, you can simply use as much salsa as you need to dress the seafood you have and save the remaining puree for another day.

For the salad:

½ cup diced red onion

1 cup diced fennel

½ poblano pepper, seeded and diced (you can use bell pepper for a milder taste)

24 ounces crabmeat, cleaned of any shell and kept in nice large pieces if using lump crabmeat

Kosher salt and cracked black pepper

Lime (optional)

Fresh cilantro sprigs (optional)

Make the salad: Put the salsa puree in a large bowl and add the onion, fennel, poblano, and crabmeat. Season with salt and pepper to taste. You can also squeeze more lime at this point if you want more acidity. Cover and refrigerate until cold, about 15 minutes but no longer than 1 hour. Garnish with fresh cilantro if you like. Serve chilled.

Stone Crabs with Mustard Sauce and a Side of Sausages

Stone crabs and a side of sausages? *Yes.* A mild sausage like bratwurst or weisswurst unites beautifully with our mustard sauce at a chilled temperature. These lighter sausages, with less fat, don't require hot serving temperatures to make them easily digestible. Ask a French Canadian, or Her Majesty Alice Waters: in her ground-breaking first cookbook, she offers "Oysters on the Half Shell with Victoria's Champagne Sausages." Simply perfect!

Serves 4

For the mustard sauce:

¼ cup Creole mustard

¾ cup sour cream

2 tablespoons fresh-squeezed lime or lemon juice

A few drops of Tabasco sauce (or more or less, to taste)

For serving:

2 to 3 pounds fresh stone crabs, cooked, chilled, and cracked (they are sold cooked and chilled, so that part is easy!)

8 ounces mild sausages of your choosing, cooked, chilled, and sliced

Make the mustard sauce: Mix all of the sauce ingredients together and chill in the refrigerator.

Serve the mustard sauce with the crab and sausages, with claw crackers and cocktail forks for removing the precious sweet crab meat from the shells at the table.

Serving suggestion: You could dress this up with a simple salad or our Coleslaw (page 170) and Yuca Hash Browns (page 168).

Beer-Steamed Shrimp with Dixie Rémoulade

Yes, we sneak the stove in here, but only briefly! The simple pleasures of this dish are many and apparent. The accompanying sauces will vary in places that serve a version of these steamed shrimp, but any way you serve it, please use *American* shrimp.

Serves 6 to 8

For the Dixie rémoulade:

2 egg yolks

1 tablespoon fresh-squeezed lemon juice

1 cup olive oil

1 tablespoon Creole mustard

1 tablespoon ketchup

1 tablespoon Worcestershire sauce

2 teaspoons Dijon mustard

2 teaspoons Tabasco or other hot sauce

½ teaspoon smoked paprika

¼ cup finely diced celery (inner stalk)

¼ cup finely diced scallions

¼ cup minced fresh Italian parsley

2 tablespoons prepared or fresh grated horseradish

1 teaspoon minced garlic

Kosher salt and cracked black pepper to taste

Make the Dixie rémoulade: Put the egg yolks and lemon juice in the bowl of a heavy-duty electric mixer and beat with the wire attachment until the eggs are pale and thick. Gradually add the oil, while whisking, to achieve a thick consistency.

Stir in the remaining ingredients and set aside in the refrigerator until needed.

For the beer-steamed shrimp:

1 tablespoon allspice berries

½ tablespoon whole black peppercorns

½ tablespoon mustard seeds

1 teaspoon whole cloves

1 teaspoon fennel seeds

3 tablespoons olive oil

½ red onion, chopped

6 cloves garlic, chopped

2 bay leaves, broken

3 (12-ounce) bottles of beer

1 lemon, quartered

36 large shrimp, still in their shells

Make the beer-steamed shrimp: Heat a large saucepan over medium-high heat. Add the allspice, peppercorns, mustard seeds, cloves, and fennel seeds and toast for about 30 seconds. Add the oil and when hot add the onion, garlic, and bay leaves. Stir and cook for 2 minutes.

Add the beer and squeeze the lemon quarters into the pot and throw them in. When the beer comes to a boil, add the shrimp. When it comes back to a boil, check to see how the shrimp are doing. They may need more time. When the shrimp are fully cooked, drain in a colander and then transfer to a container and chill in the refrigerator.

Peel and devein the shrimp and serve with the rémoulade.

4

THE LUNCH AND BRUNCH BUNCH

Eggs, Sandwiches, and Daydreams

Egg Salad on Toast with Mote Marine Caviar

Two of the key women in my life are always on my mind when I make or eat this dish: my grandmother, Nana, who always seemed to peel perfectly smooth hard-boiled eggs as she peered over her pointed glasses at our kitchen sink; and my mother, who taught me countless perfect lessons—enjoying caviar among them! I particularly recommend Mote Caviar, from Florida. Mote has grown from a tiny shed where esteemed scientist Eugenie Clark began the nonprofit organization, to a ten-and-a-half-acre campus on Sarasota Bay. Mote Caviar has additional stations in Summerland Key and Charlotte Harbor, but the diamond in the group is the two-hundred-acre Mote Aquaculture Park in Sarasota County.

Serves 4 in tapas-sized portions

4 large hard-cooked eggs

½ tablespoon Dijon mustard

2 tablespoons mayonnaise

2 tablespoons minced sweet onion

1½ tablespoons minced hot and sweet pickles

Hot sauce to taste (3 dashes for us)

Kosher salt and cracked black pepper to taste

4 slices of bread (I prefer a simple white bread, but sourdough is also nice)

Butter (optional)

Caviar (as much as you like, but get the best you can)

Fresh chives, finely snipped

Peel and halve the eggs lengthwise. Without breaking the egg whites, carefully remove the yolks. Put the yolks in a small mixing bowl and mash them with a fork.

Reserve six of the best egg white halves. Mince the other two egg white halves and mix with the mashed yolk. Add the mustard, mayonnaise, onion, and pickles. Mix well and season to taste with hot sauce and salt and pepper.

Stuff the egg white halves with the egg yolk mixture. (You will have more than can fit. Enjoy the leftovers as a snack or sandwich spread!)

Cut a small hole in the center of each piece of bread with a cylinder cutter with the diameter of a nickel or quarter. When you are ready to serve, toast the bread. (Always make toast to order, please.) Butter it lightly if you like. Lay the egg halves on the hole in the toast. Top the eggs with caviar. Garnish with the chives and serve.

Serving suggestion: For a more "filled in" version we serve Pickled Roasted Gingered Beets (page 216) with this. The acidity marries well with the richness of the eggs and the delicate salinity of the caviar. But my recommendation is to eat the caviar and then the beets.

Toasted Pecan Buttermilk Pancakes
WITH FLORIDA ORANGE MARMALADE

It is customary to sweeten pancakes with maple syrup. We do it often ourselves. But we love to use the products of Florida whenever we can, and so we drizzle these with a warm mixture of half maple syrup and half Florida orange marmalade, either our homemade version or a good-quality one produced by a place like Dundee Farms in central Florida.

Serves 4

1 cup all-purpose flour

2 tablespoons sugar

½ teaspoon baking soda

½ teaspoon kosher salt

1 teaspoon ground cinnamon

1 cup pecans, toasted and chopped

2 eggs

1¼ cups buttermilk

Canola oil or clarified butter for cooking

Orange marmalade

Maple syrup

Soft butter

In a large bowl, combine the flour, sugar, baking soda, salt, cinnamon, and pecans.

In a separate bowl, beat the eggs together with the buttermilk. Stir into the flour mixture until just combined; the batter doesn't have to be perfectly smooth.

Heat a griddle or a nonstick sauté pan over medium heat and add a touch of oil per pancake. When the oil is fairly hot, add the batter and wait until bubbles form on top. Flip the pancake over and cook until the other side is nice and golden. Repeat with more oil and the remaining batter.

Meanwhile, in a small saucepan, heat about a 50/50 ratio of marmalade to syrup and set aside until ready to serve.

Serve the pancakes with butter and as much of the marmalade syrup combo spooned over as desired.

Marjorie's Corn Cakes

WITH HOUSE PORK SAUSAGE AND PINEAPPLE-LYCHEE CHUTNEY

I have an interview program called "Kitchen Conversations" on the *Daily Meal* website, which is run by my good friend and fellow music lover Colman Andrews. There are some common questions I have asked guests ranging from chef-legend Jeremiah Tower to award-winning novelist Monique Truong. One is "What three folks from history, living or otherwise, would you like to invite to a meal in your home?" This question, if asked of me, would get this response: "Marjorie Kinnan Rawlings, for one."

Serves 4 to 6

¾ cup medium-grind yellow cornmeal

¾ cup white self-rising cornmeal

¾ cups all-purpose flour

2 tablespoons baking powder

Kosher salt and cracked black pepper (pepper is nice in this breakfast/brunch cake)

4 egg yolks

2 cups whole milk, at room temperature

4 tablespoons butter, melted

5 egg whites

2 tablespoons sugar

A pinch of cream of tartar

Clarified butter, duck fat, or oil

House Pork Sausage (page 234)

Pineapple-Lychee Chutney (page 217)

Butter (optional)

Maple syrup (optional)

Combine the cornmeals, flour, baking powder, and salt and pepper to taste in a large bowl. Whisk together.

Put the egg yolks in a medium-size bowl and stir them up. Add the milk and melted butter.

In a separate bowl, whip the egg whites together with the sugar and cream of tartar to medium-stiff peaks.

Whisk the milk mixture into the cornmeal mixture. Gently fold the whipped egg white mixture into the batter.

Heat some clarified butter in a skillet or on a griddle and, working in batches, ladle in the batter to make the corn cakes and cook until small bubbles appear on the surface, 3 to 4 minutes, then turn and cook the other side for 3 to 4 minutes. Keep warm while you make all you need.

Form sausage patties and cook to the desired doneness, until the interior is at least 145 degrees. Plate warm corn cakes and sausage and serve with the chutney. Add butter and maple syrup to the table if you want to do it like we do.

Ecuadorean Potato Cake
WITH AN "EGGS BENNY" COUSIN

The potato part of this recipe I first learned when writing *New World Kitchen*. These delicious potato cakes originated during the Incan Empire, which once spread all the way from northern Chile to southern Colombia, and of course included Ecuador. When a lot of guests wanted to cut out breads, I turned the cakes into a kind of "Eggs Benedict," giving brunch a nice cross-cultural accent.

Serves 4 to 8, depending on appetites

1 pound red or Yukon gold potatoes, peels left on

1 tablespoon butter

2 tablespoons softened goat cheese or cream cheese

5 ounces cooked bacon, finely diced (optional)

2 tablespoons extra-virgin olive oil

Kosher salt and cracked black pepper

½ cup all-purpose flour

2 eggs

1 cup panko breadcrumbs, pulsed in a food processor

Canola oil

4 or 8 eggs (or more), 1 per serving

Basic and Beautiful Tomato Sauce (page 228)

Kosher salt and cracked black pepper

Pickled peppadews, finely diced

Cook the potatoes in salted water until just soft. Drain off all the water. Return the potatoes to the pot and mash them well. Add the butter, cheese, bacon (if using), and olive oil and mash again. Season to taste with salt and pepper but be sure to taste, as potatoes need a good amount of seasoning. Let cool completely.

Preheat the oven to 350 degrees.

Put the flour in a bowl and season with salt and pepper. In another bowl, beat the eggs and 3 tablespoons water together with a fork. In a third bowl, put the breadcrumbs.

Form the potato mixture into eight patties. Let them sit for a few minutes, as this step helps them stay well formed.

Dredge each patty in the flour, then dip in the egg wash, then coat with the breadcrumbs.

Heat a nonstick skillet over medium-high heat and add some canola oil. Working in batches, fry the cakes on each side until crispy. Transfer to a baking sheet, put in the oven, and bake until heated through, about 5 minutes.

Meanwhile, poach the eggs.

Spoon the tomato sauce onto serving plates. (Or put it smack dab on top of the eggs if you like. Remember—it is *your* show, I'm just a guide!) Top the sauce with one potato cake. Place a well-drained poached egg on top of each cake and sprinkle with salt and pepper. Scatter some of the pickled peppadews around the cake. Serve.

> *Serving suggestion:* If you like, cubes or slices of ripe, luscious avocado or other tropical fruits can also be served around the potato cakes.
>
> *Note:* Pickled peppadews can be found in specialty markets and online. You can use whatever you like if you can't find those particular pickled peppers. But do note that the acidity in the pickle is a key to the entire dish having the punch we like.

Crabmeat "Imperial" in Ginger Scallion Pancakes

We have been making a version of these pancakes for eons. They are capable of wrapping many kinds of food and even eaten as is for a snack. But dining at a Lauderhill Korean restaurant inspired me to stuff them with crabmeat. Crabs are fascinating, and the Latin word for them translates as "beautiful swimmer." And about that term *Imperial*? I am told it is a holdover from the 1950s or '60s when the dish dressed up some very swank dinner parties. Perhaps the term comes from the really huge wine bottles of the same name. I would be happy to drink from one soon while eating these with friends. Our Imperial is served as a chilled salad within the cylinder of the rolled-up pancakes.

Serves 8 as a snack or more if cut into pieces

For the pancakes:

4 tablespoons unsalted whole butter

½ cup thinly sliced scallions, white and light green parts only

1½ tablespoons minced fresh ginger

½ to 1 Scotch bonnet chile, seeded and minced

1 whole egg

1 egg yolk

1 cup milk

½ teaspoon kosher salt

½ teaspoon cracked black pepper

¾ cup all-purpose flour

Clarified butter or canola oil for brushing the pan

Make the pancakes: Put the whole butter in a small- to medium-size heavy saucepan and place it over medium heat to melt. Add the scallions, ginger, and chile. Cook until soft and very fragrant, 3 to 5 minutes. Remove from the heat and let cool some.

In a medium bowl, beat the whole egg and egg yolk together. Whisk in the milk, salt, and pepper. Set aside.

Sift the flour into a large bowl. Make a well in it and whisk in the egg-milk mixture. Set aside to let the flavors marry for a few minutes. Add the cooked ginger, scallion, and butter mix.

Heat an 8-inch nonstick sauté pan over medium-high heat. Brush a (very) little clarified butter into the pan. (Due to the butter in the batter, you will not need much additional fat as you work.) Tilt the pan around a bit as you spoon or ladle about ¼ cup of the batter into the pan, rotating the pan until the batter covers the bottom of the pan and is evenly distributed. (This is not a classic crêpe so we don't need to make this "see-through thin" or have the batter hug the sides of the pan.)

Cook until golden and "lacy" on the bottom. (The heat of your pan can make a difference in the cooking time, but about 45 seconds is good.) Turn the pancake over and cook for about 10 seconds on the other side. (We use a rubber spatula so as to not risk gouging our pans with metal.) Slide the cake a bit and then flip it over again, pretty side up, onto a clean plate. Set aside while you make the rest. The pancakes can be made in advance and reheated in a 350-degree oven.

For the crab filling:

1 pound lump crabmeat, any shells picked out

½ cup mayonnaise

¼ cup small capers, well rinsed

½ cup extra-virgin olive oil

½ to 1 Scotch bonnet chile or other chile (optional), seeded and minced

1 tablespoon minced fresh Italian parsley

1 tablespoon plus 1 teaspoon fresh-squeezed lemon juice

1 cup diced ripe mango

Kosher salt and cracked black pepper to taste

Make the crab filling: Stir all the ingredients together in a bowl.

To fill the pancakes, lay each one flat on a cutting board and spoon in about 2 tablespoons of the crab filling. Roll it up. They may be cut into bite-sized "tasters" if you like. Serve immediately.

Serving suggestion: You can garnish the pancakes with all manner of salad greens in a vinaigrette; our Plantain Chips (page 244) would be great here too.

Route 27 Turkey Neck Tamales

During our first stay in Key West, Janet and I got homesick for Illinois, so in the spring of 1974, we hitchhiked up out of the Florida Keys. That first full day on the highway, somewhere on Route 27, we got a ride from a trucker just as a rainstorm was baptizing the world. His windshield wipers squeaked the windshield clear, and we looked out at the muddy, verdant fields many don't associate with Florida. Our trucker was seriously concerned about us being out on the road and so young. We were too naïve to share his paternal concerns. When hunger pangs hit us, it was our good luck to find a lady selling tamales out of small roadside stand. We have loved tamales since. For people who have not made tamales before, the process may seem a bit daunting, but we will show you how. And once you make the basic tamale you will find many ways to put your own spin on it, as the recipe is infinitely variable. You will be transported, just like we were on Route 27.

The yield will depend on how thick you make your tamales. We like them pretty full, which will make a baker's dozen.

continued →

For the tamale dough:

½ cup lard

2¾ cups tamale flour (instant corn masa mix)

2 cups water heated to 115 degrees when ready to incorporate

1½ teaspoons kosher salt

4 tablespoons butter, softened

1 (4-ounce) can green chiles, stems removed if there are any, all liquid drained and discarded, chiles pureed

For the filling:

¼ cup olive oil

8 ounces button or other mushrooms, cleaned and sliced

Kosher salt and cracked black pepper

¼ cup sherry vinegar

1 pound meat from Braised Turkey Necks (page 236), all bones removed (save any leftovers for other uses)

2 tablespoons duck fat or olive oil

2 cloves garlic, minced

1 jalapeño chile, seeded and minced

½ onion, diced

½ cup port wine

1 cup Chicken Stock (page 237) or vegetable stock

For stuffing and serving the tamales:

16 to 20 large corn husks, soaked, rinsed, well drained, and patted dry

Tomatillo Salsa (page 223)

Make the tamale dough: Using the whisk attachment in a stand mixer, beat the lard on medium-high speed until it's fluffy, 3 to 5 minutes. (This can be done with a beater attachment or hand-held beater but will take longer.)

In another large bowl, combine the tamale flour, warm water, and salt until you have a well-mixed batter.

Add half of this batter to the lard and beat to combine. Add the butter and the remaining batter to the lard mixture and beat on medium-high speed for a few minutes. Add the green chiles and beat again until the dough has a nice whipped butter consistency. Here is one of the ways of testing for the perfect tamale texture: Fill a small bowl with water. Roll a small ball of the dough and drop it in the water. If it drops to the bottom, it needs to be mixed more; if it floats, it's ready.

Make the filling: Heat a sauté pan over medium-high heat. Add the oil. When hot, add the mushrooms, season with salt and pepper, and toss. Cook, tossing occasionally, until the mushrooms are cooked through, 4 to 5 minutes. Add the vinegar and cook until the liquid is almost all evaporated. Put the mushrooms in a large mixing bowl and add the cooked turkey neck meat. Season to taste. Set aside.

Heat a medium-size heavy saucepan over medium heat. Add the duck fat and then, when it is hot, add the garlic, jalapeño, and onion. Stir to coat. Let the vegetables get soft with some caramelized color on their edges. Add the wine and cook until reduced by half. Add the stock and cook until it is reduced and fairly thick (about 1 cup in volume), 5 to 8 minutes. Add this to the turkey neck and mushroom mixture. Stir it in to mix well. (You can make the filling a day or more in advance and keep it in the refrigerator until ready to use.)

Stuff the tamales: Pull apart a few of the smaller corn husks, so that you have "strings" for tying up the ends. (Or just use butcher's twine, as we do most of the time.)

Take a larger, well-formed corn husk and lay it flat on a work surface, curved side of the husk curling up toward you. Spread about ⅓ cup of the tamale dough into the center of the husk. Then spoon 3 tablespoons of the filling on top of the dough. Wrap the husk and dough around the filling, enrobing it and leaving the top end of the tamales open. Fold the husk from the narrow end over the tamale, then wrap the two sides over. Fold up the narrower pointier bottom of the husk and tie it with a piece of string (or corn husk). Tie another string around the tamale's midsection. Take care not to create a "waist." You just want to keep it snug, not cinch it. Repeat to make the remaining tamales.

Fill a tamale steamer pot or a heavy pasta pot with water up to the bottom of the steamer insert. Place the tamales in the steamer insert with the open end up. Cover the tops of the open tamales with a sheet of aluminum foil to trap steam. Then top with a cloth towel and finally the lid. If you don't have a tight-fitting lid, you can use a double layer of heavy-duty foil.

Steam over medium-high heat for about 90 minutes. Steaming is a less precise form of cooking than others; to check for doneness, open a tamale wrapper: You want to see the masa pulling away from the husk a bit. Steam can burn you, so use caution when you open a tamale to test it. When done, let the tamales sit in the steamer but with the heat source off for about 15 minutes. This lets the tamales "set" better.

Open and enjoy topped with Tomatillo Salsa.

"Spanglish" Tortilla

WITH HASH BROWNS, CREAMED SPINACH, AND SERRANO HAM

In Spain this dish is known as a *tortilla*. Unlike the Mexican tortilla, the Spanish tortilla derives its name from *torte* due to its cake-like shape. The wizard of Spanish cuisine in our century, Ferran Adrià, blew many minds when he presented a Spanish tortilla using potato chips *from a bag*. We loved it when he made one for our small group when visiting with him in Spain. Continuing with the license taking, we riff off the American passion for potato hash, and the term *Spanglish* pushes open the door widely, *deliciously*, too. Oh, and one more element to push with is the classic often found in our American steak houses—creamed spinach.

Serves 8

For the tortilla:

2 tablespoons pure olive oil

½ jalapeño or serrano chile, seeded, if you wish, and minced

½ sweet onion, thinly sliced

Kosher salt and cracked black pepper

8 eggs

2 tablespoons Chicken Stock (page 237)

3 cloves garlic, very thinly sliced

¼ cup fresh basil or 2 tablespoons fresh oregano (your preference), stemmed and chopped

3 ounces firm, aged, dry Monterey Jack or other similar cheese, shredded

Make the tortilla: Preheat the broiler and have a rack about 4 inches from the heat source.

Heat a 10-inch nonstick broiler-proof sauté pan over medium heat. Add the oil, then add the jalapeño and onion and stir. Add a little salt and pepper. Cook until the onion is soft, 8 to 10 minutes.

Meanwhile, whisk the eggs and stock in a large mixing bowl. Whisk in the garlic, basil, and about 1 teaspoon salt and 1 teaspoon pepper or to taste. Pour the mixture into the pan and evenly distribute it across the bottom.

Allow the mixture to cook over medium heat for 8 to 10 minutes. Shake the skillet from time to time. Tip the pan and slide a spatula under the egg mixture to allow some of it to run underneath and meet the pan's surface. Do this a few times to cook the egg mixture more.

Carefully place the pan under the broiler (if the handle is plastic, keep it outside the oven so it doesn't melt) and allow to cook and brown for 2 to 3 minutes.

Remove the pan from the broiler. Turn off the broiler. Scatter the cheese over the tortilla. Let the oven cool to about 350 degrees and if the eggs are still not "set," put the pan in the oven again; the residual heat will allow the mixture in the pan to set completely—5 minutes should do it. A knife, when inserted to the middle, should come out clean.

Put a large round plate over the pan and invert the tortilla onto it. Serve, or let it cool, cover, and set aside for later. That last sentence might bear re-reading. If you are not familiar with the original, the Spanish do serve their tortillas hot *or* cool. But ours will be served very warm (excepting the serrano ham). The tortilla can be made ahead to this point and even chilled. You will need to gently warm it up again in the oven before serving if you take that step.

continued ➜

For the hash browns:

2 Idaho potatoes, scrubbed well, peeled if desired

¼ cup rendered bacon fat, olive oil, or clarified butter (or any combination)

Kosher salt and cracked black pepper

½ teaspoon ground cayenne

½ teaspoon smoked pimentón

½ tablespoon butter

For the creamed spinach:

1 tablespoon olive oil

1 tablespoon butter

1 shallot, thinly sliced

10 ounces spinach, trimmed of any thick stems

Kosher salt and cracked black pepper

¼ cup heavy cream

¼ cup finely grated Parmesan cheese

For serving:

Thinly sliced serrano ham

Make the hash browns: Shred the potatoes into a large bowl filled with cold water. Stir until the water is cloudy. Drain and cover the potatoes again with fresh cold water. Stir again to remove excess starch. Drain the potatoes well and dry with paper towels, squeezing out any excess moisture. (It is best to squeeze them out in a clean towel using a lot of hand pressure to make the potatoes as dry as can be.)

Heat the fat in a large nonstick or well-seasoned cast-iron sauté pan or skillet over medium heat. Lay the shredded potatoes into the hot fat and season with salt, black pepper, cayenne, and pimentón. Form the potatoes into a circle in the pan. Sort of pack the potatoes around the edges to help form a compact cake.

Cook the potatoes until a nice crust forms on the bottom, 12 to 15 minutes. Midway through this process, add the butter and let it slide under the cooking "cake." This creates both the amazing flavor and golden hue that only butter gives. Using two spatulas (or mad short-order cook skills), flip the hash "cake" over. Continue to cook until the potatoes are browned on the bottom, 5 to 8 more minutes. Set aside, covered to keep warm.

Make the creamed spinach: Heat a large nonstick skillet over medium-high heat. Add the oil and butter and allow the butter to foam. Add the shallot and stir. Cook until almost soft. Add the spinach and season with salt and pepper. Let the spinach wilt completely. Add the cream and cook until it is reduced and thick, 3 to 4 minutes. Add the cheese and stir. Set aside.

Have the tortilla nicely warmed up if needed. Top with the hash browns. Top that with an even coating of the hot creamed spinach. Feel free to leave excess cream in the pan; it can be saved to make an omelet later if you like. Crown with the slices of ham. You can roll them up or offer them in a somewhat artistic fashion if you like. Serve immediately.

Serving suggestion: Basic and Beautiful Tomato Sauce (page 228) would be excellent here. For something a bit more exotic you might try the Charred Scallion–Toasted Almond Romesco (page 230).

Quesadillas from a Gardener and Cured Meats from a Charcutier

The modern brunch offerings are now a dazzling cornucopia of international dishes. So in that vein we work with Mexican and European roots in this dish, being sure we hit our Florida farmers' markets to get the inspiration for possible fillings in the "From a Gardener" part. Here, we use a succotash recipe for our quesadillas. Don't feel confined to the recipe here—use it as a guide, but let your local market shopping be the lead.

Serves 2

4 (6-inch) flour tortillas

1 cup Succotash (page 169)

Canola oil (not much)

1 cup shredded Monterey Jack or other melting cheese

3 ounces mixed cured meats such as serrano ham, prosciutto, mortadella, soppresatta, chorizo, or lomo

For serving:

Tomatillo Salsa (page 223) or another sauce or salsa

Preheat the oven to 400 degrees.

Place two flour tortillas on a cutting board. Spread some Succotash on each, stopping about an inch from the edge. Place shredded cheese in the center and spread out over the Succotash.

Warm a large ovenproof nonstick sauté pan over medium heat. Add a little oil to the pan. When the oil is fairly hot, place one tortilla with Succotash and cheese in the pan, filling side up. Top with thinly sliced cured meats of your choosing. Place an empty tortilla on top and press down a bit to meld it with the cheese. When the bottom tortilla is nicely colored, carefully turn the quesadilla over and put the pan in the oven.

When the cheese has melted, take pan out of the oven and place the quesadilla on a cutting board. Dab off any excess oil from both sides. Let it rest for about 1 minute so the cheese can set. Cut it into quarters.

Repeat to make another quesadilla. Transfer to plates and serve.

Note: A *charcutier* is a person who makes—you guessed it—charcuterie. During an interview for my column, "Kitchen Conversations," I learned more about charcuterie from Chef Ferdinand Metz, who was the long-standing president of the Culinary Institute of America. Check it out on the website *The Daily Meal*, if you like to read about the real lives of our chefs and all kinds of folks involved with cuisine.

Serving suggestion: We are in the brunch chapter, so if you like, serve an egg on top of your quesadillas—it works beautifully! And offer a drizzle of Red Chimichurri (page 226) if you have a mind to.

My Big Fat Smile of a Salad

WITH YOGURT DRESSING, LAMB CHOPS, AND POMEGRANATE

What the Greek salad has become is what happens to so many dishes that have reached iconic status in broader America—something sadly diminished from the creators' original. Did you know that the original version called for a "hidden" portion of potato salad? Greek salad was perfected in Tarpon Springs by a proud immigrant named Lou Pappas, who was part of the wave of Greek immigrants responsible for bringing the sponge-diving industry to the United States. I hope he would like my "brunch" version.

This recipe requires a large platter, or you can serve the roasted lamb on a side plate and pass it.

Give yourself enough time to assemble the rather long list of ingredients that comprise this celebratory salad. Many parts can be made and/or set up well in advance of plating your final dish. The lamb aspect of this dish needs to be timed right. We have a "hot and cold" meal here, so you want to have the salad almost ready when you go to cook the lamb. After the lamb comes out of the oven and while it rests, you can assemble the salad on the platter.

Serves 6

Note: You will notice I haven't provided specific quantities for many of the ingredients in this dish. When you make a "Party Platter," there can be a great deal of play in the type and amount of ingredients you and your guests may want. In fact, instead of composing the salad on a platter, some folks might like to set out all of the ingredients much like a salad bar and let the guests have at it themselves!

Upland cress and watercress are not actually related, but they both have a peppery quality and either one will be great here.

If you're using the more authentic and deeply flavored olives that still contain the pits, warn your guests.

For the lamb:

6 "double-cut" lamb chops, evenly portioned and trimmed

1 tablespoon olive oil

Leaves from a few sprigs fresh rosemary

Kosher salt and cracked black pepper

Peanut or vegetable oil, if needed

⅓ cup Dijon or Creole mustard, or more as needed

½ cup plain unseasoned breadcrumbs (panko or fresh)

Prepare the lamb for cooking: Arrange the chops on a platter about 1 hour before you wish to cook them. Drizzle with the oil. Scatter the rosemary over and season with salt and pepper. Set aside while you prepare the other salad elements.

For the potato salad:

6 new potatoes, scrubbed

¼ cup finely chopped fresh parsley

½ cup thinly sliced scallions, white parts mainly

½ cup mayonnaise

1 teaspoon Dijon or Creole mustard

1 tablespoon fresh-squeezed lemon juice

Kosher salt and cracked black pepper

Make the potato salad: Cook the unpeeled potatoes in unsalted water until tender, about 20 minutes. Let cool until you can handle them. Peel and dice the potatoes (you should have about 2 cups), placing them in a bowl.

In another bowl, combine the parsley, scallions, mayonnaise, mustard, and lemon juice. Add to the potatoes; mix well. Add salt and pepper to taste. Mix and set aside. If making this in advance, cover and refrigerate for up to 1 day, but remove the mixture from the fridge about 15 minutes before proceeding so you're not serving it fridge-cold.

continued ➜

For the Greek yogurt salad dressing:

½ cup olive juice from a jar of olives

1½ cups plain Greek yogurt

½ cup red wine vinegar

¼ cup fresh-squeezed lemon juice

¼ cup honey

1 tablespoon garlic powder

½ tablespoon onion powder

1 tablespoon chopped fresh oregano

2 tablespoons Dijon mustard

2 teaspoons kosher salt, or more if needed

1 teaspoon cracked black pepper, or more if needed

¼ teaspoon crushed red pepper

1½ cups extra-virgin olive oil

Make the Greek yogurt salad dressing: Put everything except the oil in a blender and blend until smooth. With the motor running, stream in the oil. Season with more salt and black pepper if needed. Set aside.

For the salad:

1 small head romaine lettuce (we like the crisp hearts), cleaned and cut into shreds

Kale or arugula leaves, torn if large

Upland cress or watercress

1 to 2 ripe tomatoes, cut into wedges

1 cucumber, peeled and cut into bite-size pieces

Avocado wedges (cut at the last moment)

½ to ¾ cup crumbled feta cheese, or more as desired

1 red or yellow bell pepper, stemmed, seeded, and cut into rings

2 beets, cooked, peeled, and sliced or cubed

Greek olives (we used a combination of Kalamata and Sevillane)

Pickled peppadews or other pickled peppers, drained and cut into bite-size pieces

3 to 4 radishes, thinly sliced

½ cup pomegranate arils, or more as desired

Make the salad: Start by covering the center area of a large platter with the romaine and torn kale and drizzle with some of the salad dressing. Now mound the cool potato salad in the center and top with the cress.

Next, alternate tomatoes and cucumbers around the salad. Add the avocado. Scatter the cheese on top of the salad. Place bell pepper rings and beets on the platter as you like.

Place olives, peppadews, and radishes around the edge. Garnish with the pomegranate arils. Drizzle or spoon some of the extra salad dressing around. Set the platter aside while you cook the lamb.

Finish the lamb: When you are ready to cook, preheat the oven to 425 degrees.

Heat a large, heavy sauté pan over medium-high heat. Add the chops and cook, turning over as needed with tongs, until evenly browned on both sides and just pink inside. If they render a lot of lamb fat, pour it out and carefully discard it. (Add a bit of peanut oil to promote a good sear on the lamb if needed.) Remove the chops to a rack set on a rimmed baking sheet. Brush the chops lightly with mustard on both sides and the edges. Top with the breadcrumbs, place the chops back in the skillet, and put the skillet in the oven for about 2 minutes. Remove and keep warm. Do not let the lamb overcook, as it is best at medium-rare—I like it to be 125 to 128 degrees on an instant-read thermometer, knowing the temperature will "ride up" as they sit.

Finally, place the warm chops around the perimeter of the salad platter and serve.

Eggs "In a Sunshine State of Mind"

There is more than one theory of how Eggs Benedict got its name. My preferred story tells of a gent, one Lemuel Benedict, a Wall Street broker, who was suffering from a hangover in 1894 and ordered "some buttered toast, crisp bacon, two poached eggs, and a *hooker* of hollandaise sauce" at the Waldorf Hotel in New York. I am not sure where the hooker got its name, but I've loved Eggs Benny since I first tasted it. And since this one has an edge of sweetness, we like to serve it with a countering side of something with a savory character. Hard to beat bacon.

Serves 4 to 8, depending on appetites

For the Sauce Maltaise:

1 cup fresh-squeezed blood orange juice, cooked in a small heavy saucepan until reduced by half

Sriracha Hollandaise (page 231; *omit the sriracha sauce*)

A few drops of hot sauce (optional)

Make the Sauce Maltaise: Whisk just enough of the warm reduced blood orange juice into the hollandaise to give it a citrus tang but not to allow it to become too "loose." The amount will vary, but start with about 3 tablespoons. Add the hot sauce, if using. Reserve any leftover reduced juice for another time. (It can be frozen.) Set the Sauce Maltaise aside in a warm place.

For finishing the dish:

Grits, 'Snips, and Chips (page 158; chips are optional here), kept warm

8 eggs, poached and kept warm

8 slices bacon, cooked as you like

Orange slices or wedges

Finish the dish: Place the Grits, 'Snips, and Chips in warm pasta bowls. Top with the poached eggs. Top the eggs with the Sauce Maltaise. Add the bacon strips. Garnish with the orange slices.

Fully Loaded Cracked Conch Po' Boy

In truth, conch is not in fish markets anymore, so I'm quite comfortable suggesting you make this sandwich with a fillet of fish or a line of shrimp. Should the day come when conch is in your shopping cart, however, you will be ready to go back to the original. Just don't let the delay prevent you from making a po' boy of some sort! Do note that conch is farm raised in a few places and can be had with an internet search and shipping. It will come frozen, but conch, when *properly* frozen, comes right back to life when defrosted overnight in the fridge. A properly frozen piece of fish is better than one never frozen but left out on the boat too long!

Makes 1 sandwich

For the conch:

½ cup all-purpose flour

Kosher salt and cracked black pepper

1 egg

¼ cup cornmeal

5 ounces conch, pounded until thin (or a thin fillet of your choice of fresh fish, or 4 or 5 medium-size shrimp)

Canola or peanut oil

For the sandwich:

1 (10- to 12-inch) section of Cuban or French bread

Comeback Sauce (page 233) or mayonnaise

Creole mustard (optional)

Pickles

Tomato slices

1 cup shredded lettuce

Make the conch: Season the flour with some salt and pepper and put it in a bowl. In another bowl, mix the egg well with 2 tablespoons water. In a third bowl, mix the cornmeal with a bit more salt and pepper.

Dredge the conch (or other seafood) in the seasoned flour, then the egg mixture, then the cornmeal. In a sauté pan or cast-iron skillet, heat ⅛ to ¼ inch of oil over medium heat. Add the conch and fry until golden on both sides and cooked through, just a few minutes per side. Drain on paper towels for a moment.

Make the sandwich: Split the bread horizontally about three quarters of the way through, leaving it hinged. Toast it if you like. We like.

Spread Comeback Sauce on the inside of the bottom portion of the bread. Spread mustard on the inside of the top portion. Place the pickles and tomatoes on the bottom portion of the bread. Top with the lettuce, then the fried conch.

For the Fully Loaded Zone: If you have stood in line at a great neighborhood sandwich place, you can visualize the array of things one can put on a sandwich or sub. Let that be an inspiration and starting point! Me? I'm smearing Korean gochujang like my chef-friend Edward Lee likely would.

Flora-Bama White *Mojo* BBQ'd Grouper Sandwich

It seems counterintuitive to use mayo when grilling, but as I developed the recipe I realized just how *smart* it is. This is made "Flora-Bama" by the marriage of classic *mojo* with a traditional white BBQ sauce, a.k.a. "Alabama" BBQ sauce.

A lot of fun is had at the border between our two states, but the hyphenated "Capital of Fun" would be the Flora-Bama Lounge, made famous in song and film. Around since the mid-1960s, the lounge popularized the now-famous mullet-tossing contest. This event has been taken up by a good number of bars in our state. Hit the highways and wander to find them.

Serves 4

For the white *mojo* BBQ sauce:

1 cup mayonnaise

1 tablespoon Creole mustard

2 cloves garlic, minced

½ teaspoon cracked black pepper

¼ cup apple cider vinegar

¼ teaspoon kosher salt

¼ teaspoon smoked pimentón

1½ to 2 teaspoons horseradish sauce

1 tablespoon agave sweetener

Hot sauce to taste

½ cup Classic Sour Orange *Mojo* (page 222)

Make the white *mojo* BBQ sauce: Whisk all the ingredients together in a bowl. Allow to marry for at least 1 hour before using; refrigerate if making the sauce more than an hour in advance.

For the sandwiches:

4 (5-ounce) portions grouper or firm white fish of your choice

Kosher salt and cracked black pepper

Oil to "anoint" the grill

4 burger-type buns

Make the sandwiches: Heat up an outdoor grill to medium-high heat. Season the fish with some salt and pepper. Oil the grill grate. When hot, place the fish on the grill. Begin basting with the BBQ sauce when the fish is about halfway cooked. Fish is more delicate than meat, and your most delicate tools are your fingers! Simply push your forefinger into the flesh of the fish as it cooks to check doneness. You will get the hang of noticing when it moves from being kind of dead/mushy (raw) to springy and nicely cooked. When it is moving toward that springy state, liberally brush on the fine sauce you've made.

Toast the buns when the fish is just about cooked and well sauced. Place the fish on the toasted buns and serve.

Steadman's Boatyard Grilled Citrus and Soy Fish Tacos

When we lived in Key West in the early 1970s I walked home from my job in Old Town to a place we rented in New Town. I'd pass over a bridge that was part of the Key West Bight, and nearby was a very faded wooden barnlike building that housed some of the vessels of Steadman's Boatyard (since renamed "Spencer's"). Little grills and smokers could be seen in use at Steadman's, and smelling the fragrance of fresh fish wafting up to the apex of the bridge made me hungry. It still does. Boatyard need not be in walking distance.

Serves 4 (2 tacos per person)

Note: Many fish tacos call for battered and fried fish. This one is a touch lighter.

For the fish:

4 (5- to 6-ounce) portions fresh fish such as grouper, mahi, or small jack fish (skin-on is fine) if you are so lucky

¾ cup olive oil

½ cup soy sauce

Juice of 1 orange

Juice of 1 lemon

Juice of 1 lime

6 whole black peppercorns, toasted

¼ bulb fennel, thinly sliced

½ red onion, thinly sliced

4 to 6 cloves garlic, thinly sliced

6 tablespoons thinly sliced rounds of fresh ginger

For the tacos:

8 corn tortillas

Peanut or vegetable oil

Accoutrements: avocado, shredded lettuce or a nice coleslaw you like, chiles, diced tomatoes, or whatever else you wish—go for it

Make the fish: Combine all the ingredients and marinate the fish for 15 to 30 minutes. (Do watch the time, as soy can overpower fish if left any longer.)

Heat up an outdoor grill (or a grill pan). Rub the grill grate with a lightly oiled clean towel. Put the fish on the grate and cook until just cooked through. (The time will vary with the thickness of the portions.) Remove from the grill and let rest on a side plate.

Make the tacos: Fry the corn tortillas in a sauté pan with a slick of oil until soft and fill them with the fish and any other accoutrements you like. Serve flat style or folded-over style. Your tacos, your call.

The "No Mas Embargo" Cuban Sandwich

The movie *Chef* revealed the rich rewards of a Cuban sandwich to many folks all over the world. I know that right after seeing the flick we had to have a *Cubano* very quickly! The keys to success in making this sandwich are not hard, but the first one does take a bit of time. The pork needs *mojo* to marinate, and then after a proper marinating session, slow roasting. *Mojo* is essential to making a Cuban the soulful sandwich it is. The second whammy is the *pressing* of the sandwich. If you don't have a sandwich press, you can make one—see the Notes below.

Serves 1

1 (8-inch) section of Cuban bread or other light, airy hoagie-style bread

6 tablespoons butter, very well softened or melted outright

Your favorite mustard (traditionally a simple yellow variety is used)

3 or more slices Bourbon *Mojo* Roasted Pork (page 132; see Notes for substitutions)

3 ounces sweet deli ham, sliced

Classic Sour Orange *Mojo* (page 222; optional)

2½ ounces Swiss or Jarlsberg cheese, sliced

Pickle slices

Begin heating up your sandwich press.

Cut the bread horizontally in half. Spread some butter on the interior cut sides. Heat a skillet over medium heat and toast the bread's insides evenly.

Working on a cutting board, lay the toasted Cuban bread cut side up. Spread a *thin* layer of mustard on the cut sides of the bread from end to end.

Heat the pork and ham slices in the same skillet with a bit more butter to warm and crisp them and add a bit of that buttery goodness. We like to spoon some Classic Sour Orange *Mojo* on the meats now.

Layer the slices of pork, then the ham, and then the cheese on the bottom bread half. It is important to have the cheese cover the meats completely so that when the cheese melts it "enrobes" them. Top with some pickle slices (not too many or the sandwich could get wet; more pickles can be served on the side if you want) and then replace the top half of bread.

Brush the butter all over the outside of the bread. Press the sandwich in the hot sandwich press. When the cheese is nice and melty and both sides are flat, crispy, and hot (5 to 6 minutes), your sandwich is ready to slice, which is done traditionally on an *extreme* bias . . . pinky *extended.*

Serve with more *mojo*, if you went that route.

Notes: The classic Cuban sandwich is made in that wonderful contrap-tion known as a "sandwich press." If you do not have one, it is easy to approximate. Place the assembled, buttered sandwich in a nonstick, empty skillet. Wrap a clean brick with foil and place it on top to press the sandwich down. Every part of this sandwich is already cooked, but we want to crisp it and get the cheese nice and gooey. When the cheese is peeking out from the bread, turn the sandwich over and crisp the other side. If a brick is not handy, just find something heatproof and heavy. Many kitchen supply stores sell sandwich weight tools as well.

Cuba's light, airy bread (called "pan de agua") makes the "eggshell ef-fect" so damn good when the sandwich is pressed. "Sturdier" breads will not have this ideal texture. If the term "eggshell effect" seems mysteri-ous, take a look at the bread once you cook it—the ideal Cuban bread will crack the way an egg does when you hard-cook it and then start tapping your spoon on the shell.

A simpler version that is still better than many: Make the Classic Sour Orange *Mojo* (page 222) and marinate a pork tenderloin in it for a few hours. Cook and slice it up, and you will have the all-important *mojo* fla-vors without the long cooking time of the Bourbon *Mojo* Roasted Pork.

5

IN A FUSION
STATE OF MIND

Cooking in a
World of Change

Roasted Oysters

WITH SRIRACHA HOLLANDAISE AND QUICK PICKLED SHALLOTS

Roasted oysters were a treat that Emeril first revealed to me when we would visit with him in New Orleans years back. He was an extraordinary guide to the Crescent City, and we never knew what was next—but it was always delicious. We brought the roasting idea back home to Florida, and this is one of the results. You might wonder why the oysters are called "Roasted" versus "Grilled." Me too. But, hey . . . when in NOLA you let the good times roll, by any and all means.

Makes 24 oysters

For the pickled shallots:

1½ cups peeled shallots

1 tablespoon sugar

1½ teaspoons kosher salt

½ teaspoon cracked black pepper

½ cup rice vinegar

For the oysters:

24 oysters (any variety; fresh is key), carefully shucked just before you are ready to cook, on the half shell

Sriracha Hollandaise (page 231)

Make the pickled shallots: Thinly slice the shallots crosswise, against the grain like an onion for a hamburger. (You can do the slicing with a knife or a mandoline.) Break up the shallot rings to separate them. Put the shallots in a bowl and sprinkle with the sugar, salt, and pepper. ("Drift" the dry spices through your fingers over the shallots and mix them in. This distributes the spices before the liquid does and helps the shallots weep a bit, which softens them and gets the sugar well into the structure of the shallots.) Add the vinegar and let macerate for about 30 minutes and up to 90 minutes at room temperature. When ready to use, you can drain off the pickling liquid if you wish and save it for one more use.

The flavors of the pickled shallots become more balanced if you allow to rest for a few hours or cover and refrigerate them overnight. (They will keep for a day or so, covered in the refrigerator, if you have any left over.)

Make the oysters: Heat a charcoal outdoor grill to medium-high. (Charcoal is ideal because it promotes a smoky quality.) Carefully place the oysters in their shell on the grill grate, shell side down to keep the oyster liquor in the shell so it flavors the oysters as they cook. When the oysters have begun to curl (usually 3 to 4 minutes), transfer them to serving plates. If there is too much of the liquid still on the oysters, pour it into a cup and save it for another use. This liquid amount can vary a good deal, so you need to judge that. We want to have a nice coating of the Sriracha Hollandaise, which will not be possible with an overly "wet" oyster.

Spoon on the Sriracha Hollandaise—the amount per oyster is up to you. You want to taste the natural flavors of the oyster, so let that be the one guide in regards to "how much." Top with the shallots. Be sparing with them, too. Serve immediately.

Note: I would advise making a menu that gets "double duty" out of the charcoal on the grill that is only used briefly for the oysters. Juicy steaks could be good following the seafood here.

Golden Corn "Hoe Cakes"

WITH SWEET-HOT PEPPER JELLY AND CHICHARRÓN CRUMBLES

The wordplay possible in the title of this dish could easily serve as one of those waggish quickie allusions in a Shakespearean comedy. Yet corn, as a historical ingredient, probably contributed more than any other in the Puritan settlers' efforts to keep from starving in the New World—thanks to Native Americans, especially the Powhatans' long cultivation. Indians also introduced the technique of corn roasted in the ashes of fires, which was raved about by the newly arrived. The pepper jelly here is just like the one my mother used to make; at home, we had it with cornbread. One *porktastic* trip to a Latin American café in Miami as a young adult made me a devotee of chicharrónes. It was my knees that crumbled then.

Serves 4 to 6

2 cups fresh corn kernels

½ cup diced sweet onion

1 jalapeño chile, seeded and minced

⅓ cup milk

1 egg, beaten

1 teaspoon sugar

½ teaspoon baking powder

½ teaspoon salt, plus more for seasoning the chicharrón crumbles

¼ teaspoon cracked black pepper

½ cup yellow cornmeal

½ cup all-purpose flour

Peanut or vegetable oil for pan-frying

Chicharrón crumbles (see Notes)

Sweet-Hot Pepper Jelly (page 215), at room temperature or warm

Ground cayenne to taste

Fresh lime juice to taste

Put the corn in a bowl and add the onion, jalapeño, milk, egg, sugar, baking powder, ½ teaspoon salt, and pepper to the bowl and mix well. Fold in the cornmeal and flour. Transfer to a food processor and pulse to combine. Turn it out into a clean bowl.

Heat a slick of the oil in a large nonstick skillet over medium heat. Working in batches, spoon the batter into the pan like big "silver dollar" pancakes and cook until golden brown, about 2 minutes per side. Drain on paper towels. (The cooked hoe cakes may be kept warm in a low oven if need be.)

Reheat the chicharrón crumbles in a low oven, around 225 degrees, for 15 to 20 minutes. Halfway through the warming time, take them out and finely chop them, then return them to the oven.

Stack the hoe cakes on serving plates; I like a little stack of three of them for each serving. Top with the Sweet-Hot Pepper Jelly. Season the chicharrón crumbles with salt, cayenne, and lime juice and scatter them over the hoe cakes. Serve.

Note: We buy chicharrónes from Latin markets. If you are hard pressed to find one near you, bacon crumbles will be fine too. Chicharrónes are a combo of textures that go from succulent, outrageous "fattiness" to crunchy as all get-out.

Serving suggestion: Sour cream or *cotija* cheese adds a nice dimension of tang to this dish.

"Galbi" Marinated and Grilled Royal Red Shrimp
WITH NICARAGUAN *GALLO PINTO*

Whether one likes or dislikes the term *fusion*, it *is* the word most used when describing the collage of different cultures and foods not allied before. Sometimes one amazing person can be a catalyst for you. Roy Choi from L.A. has been a master at fusion cooking. After a fascinating yin-yang youth as his parents moved from poverty to doing pretty damn well, Roy rocked back and forth with experiences that included a span in a military high school to teaching English back in Korea to an epochal moment when Emeril "spoke to me right through the television set as I sat watching *The Essence of Emeril*." The young cook soon started making his wild-for-the-times Korean tacos and selling them while roaming Southern California's concrete highways and byways. He had opened up a new Pandora's Box and it was a *beauty*. The secret world of Korean food was behind a veil that had shielded cuisines like Thai and even Japanese in America until not so long ago. Chefs started to hit the late-night spots in "K Towns" and seek flavors that they don't cook all day and night. We moved from butter, cream, and demi-glace to gochujang, kimchi, and bulgogi with the zeal of the newly saved, and it was inevitable that we would begin to twist our menus in Korean ways. Here I have a dish that begins in Korea and finishes in Nicaragua.

Gallo pinto means "spotted rooster." Found in the cuisines of Nicaragua and Costa Rica, it is making fast inroads in the United States. Throughout Latin America, dishes featuring rice and beans abound. *Moros y Cristianos* are famed in Cuba and elsewhere, and Panama and El Salvador have *casamiento* as their prize of this genre.

Serves 4

For the shrimp:

24 very large shrimp (Royal Red if you can get them, but any good shrimp will work), peeled and deveined

"Galbi" Marinade (page 222)

Vegetable oil for the grill grate

For the *gallo pinto*:

3 tablespoons canola oil

3 tablespoons extra-virgin olive oil

3 cloves garlic, minced

1 sweet onion, peeled and chopped

1 red bell pepper or poblano chile, seeded and diced

Kosher salt and cracked black pepper

1 teaspoon freshly ground cumin

1 tablespoon Worcestershire sauce (or Lizano, a Caribbean sauce, if you can find it)

1½ cups canned small black or red beans, drained

1 cup Chicken Stock (page 237)

2 cups cooked long-grain white rice

Chopped fresh herbs (optional)

Marinate the shrimp: Combine the shrimp and marinade and toss well to coat. Cover and chill in the refrigerator for 1 hour or up to 6 hours.

Meanwhile, make the *gallo pinto*: Heat the two oils in a large, heavy pan over medium-high heat. Add the garlic and stir until nicely fragrant. Add the onion and bell pepper and cook for 3 to 4 minutes (we are just extracting the flavors of the vegetables, not cooking them until they break down). Season with some salt and pepper and stir in the cumin. Stir in the Worcestershire sauce, the beans, and the stock. Bring to a boil, then lower the heat to medium-low and simmer until heated through. We want a fairly "stiff" mixture versus a "soupy" one.

Stir the cooked rice into the beans and allow to just heat through. Many families make this part in advance and reheat it. Adjust the seasoning to your preference. (If you want fresh herbs in it, this would be the time to add them.) Set aside, covered to keep warm.

Heat an outdoor grill to medium-high. Lightly oil the grill grate. Drain the shrimp in a colander to remove all the excess marinade.

When the meal is close at hand, put the shrimp on the grill; with the sugar in the "galbi," the shrimp could easily burn, so keep an eye on them and turn a few times. They will cook in just 2 to 3 minutes.

Spoon the warm *gallo pinto* onto the base of four serving plates. Top with the grilled shrimp and serve.

Serving suggestion: Add a side of kimchi and some wedges of lime, if you like.

Note: It is best to make the rice the day before and have it cooled completely. (And it's always nice to divide up the prep work.) I often add some braising greens that we find at our nearby farmers' markets. *Gallo pinto* is also heavenly served on its own or with a cooked egg of your fancy on top.

On Fusion Cooking

Nearly thirty years ago I wrote the words above while sitting in a small, unpainted wooden building in Key West, our southernmost city of our southernmost of the contiguous forty-eight states. The building had most recently housed a women's hair parlor. It was an incongruous place to awaken new ideas . . . but when the Muse touches us we go for the ride.

When I wrote *On Fusion Cooking* in 1988, I did so as a means to understand where I thought I should take my own personal cooking. I was not seeking to navigate a route for others. But as luck would have it, as I leaned away from conventional cuisine and craned forward like a voyager in the bow of a ship heading into the wind, I read the words of the French philosopher-historian Jean-François Revel. It was his seminal work, *Culture and Cuisine: A Journey Through the History of Food,* that helped me to focus my spyglass on the cuisine that America would soon be belly-deep in.

A book arrived at our home last month. I ordered it out of curiosity for the title, *The Way We Cook,* as well as respect for the authorship behind it (*Saveur*). A beautiful John Thorne quote helps lead it off: *"To Cook is to lay hands on the body of the World."*

While reading this book I got hungry. The images in it are irresistible. One of my former chefs had given us some biscuits and homemade butter the day before, after a fine lunch in his care featuring fried catfish and a lamb belly BLT. I tasted the biscuit straight from the bag and worried that it seemed a little bland, but my faith in this chef is high so I didn't give up. I fired up the toaster oven and let a biscuit heat while the home-churned butter tempered on the stone counter beside the wooden knife block.

I retrieved my coffee, and when the timer bell dinged, I pulled the now toasty biscuit out and carefully sliced it in half laterally, taking care with the delicate crumbly texture. I dabbed the butter, noting its salt as I licked my thumb. The butter relaxed into and along the biscuit's crenellations. I took a bite. The oven's warmth had ignited the biscuit's arc of possibilities.

And the butter itself offered an even greater revelation. All over again I was reminded of what power lies in homemade things. The butter was at once sweet with a knife's edge of salt. Then it conveyed a faint murmur of funkiness, finally intimating cheese depths. It was as if eating butter on biscuits before this had been like skimming along on the surface of

"To Cook is to lay hands on the body of the World."

a placid lake in a quiet skiff—and then, for the first time—plunging an oar into the water and touching a sandy, earthy bottom a few meters below me. My perception was enlarged by this expanded realization of what butter *should* be.

After lingering over the *Saveur* book's images, I studied its list of recipes. Here I saw Fusion within the framework of Tradition, which always gives it her very best chance of being revelatory, as well as delicious—the most important quality of all! I praise the world that contains the craftsmen and craftswomen who tend to traditions. (I am one of them, much of the time, in my commitment to properly made food.) I don't often like food that requires explanations or needs quotation marks around its descriptions. I love the artisanal foods. Food that is what it *says* it is cannot be forsaken.

I order classic French fries in a Parisian bistro and know that potatoes were not cooked in France until the seventeenth century. I notice "Calabrian Ricotta with Coffee Mousse" on a menu in a café in Florence and think of the ships that first carried coffee beans to Venice in the sixteenth century, not to mention the Muslim traders with the methodology to make the coffee. I lust for the taste of pork from a Guatemalan food truck in Los Angeles and remember that no pork existed in that Central American land prior to the Columbian food exchange

between the Old and New Worlds in the fifteenth century. Thus our much-extolled notion of authenticity is a thoroughly modern construct. And fusion, far from being a new(ish) idea, has been part of a culinary continuum, well, *forever*.

> "From my point of view, the future of our cuisine lies in Fusion."
> —Libby H. O'Connell, Chief Historian at the History Channel

Nikkei Shrimp with Ají Amarillo
ON CHAUFA FRIED RICE

Nikkei refers to the fusion of the foods of Peru and Japan, which commenced with the arrival of the first Japanese in Peru during the late nineteenth century. One of the young stars of the contemporary Peruvian Nikkei is Mitsuharu Tsumura, who operates an internationally renowned restaurant named "Maido." He has performed at the famed Mistura gastronomic events in Peru, where he exalts fusion cooking. In Miami we have the young and talented Diego Oka doing his take on Nikkei. We watched him teach at the Culinary Institute of America's World of Flavors conference and were very impressed. It's the ají amarillo that represents the Peruvian influence here.

Chifa is a word that refers to the fusion of foods of Peru and China. *Chaufa* refers to a category of rice dishes as, say, *paella* can be a host of rice-based dishes. Arroz Chaufa is also known as "Chinese rice." In fact, *chifa*'s etymology comes from the Cantonese for "to eat rice." Why this matters so much in Florida is that Florida is the birthplace of this term *fusion* and one of the incubators for so many of these culinary hyphenations. I recognized it and named it "fusion" in the late 1980s out of wonder, excitement for what we could explore, and also respect—a reverential marriage between fitting soul mates. Showcasing a dish that exemplifies fusion with the historical clarity of Peruvian history is my way of paying homage to those pioneers. But it is also—and this matters deeply—very, very tasty.

Serves 4 as an appetizer or 2 as an entrée

Chaufa Fried Rice (page 172)

2 tablespoons canola oil

1 serrano or other chile, seeded if desired, minced

1 shallot, thinly sliced

12 large shrimp, peeled, deveined, and cut into bite-size pieces

1 cup thinly sliced shiitake mushroom caps (stems can be saved for stocks)

2 teaspoons ají amarillo puree

Soy sauce (optional)

Bring the Chaufa Fried Rice to room temperature.

Heat a wok over medium-high heat. Add the oil and then the chile and shallots. Cook until fragrant. Add the shrimp. Stir-fry for a moment. Add the shiitakes and ají amarillo and cook until the mushrooms are tender. Add the prepared Chaufa Fried Rice and stir-fry until heated through. Serve in warm bowls with soy sauce on the side.

Serving suggestion: This can be garnished with a wide variety of herbs, greens, avocados, and tomatoes.

Note: Ají amarillo sauce can be ordered via Amazon but also may found in Latin grocery stores around America.

Bacon-Speckled Hush Puppies, Chicken Liver Butter, and Asian Spice Syrup

When I was asked to join some other James Beard Award–winning chefs in New York City and cook at a dinner benefiting my great friend Charlie Trotter's educational foundation, I submitted this recipe as my contribution to our cocktail nosh. I was sure that James Beard himself would have no problem with such a casual creation at a soiree named in his honor, due to his all-embracing love of American regional foods.

Florida cookery has a long history of respecting its locally sourced ingredients; in animal husbandry, *respect* is a term that means that when livestock and poultry are harvested, all parts are treasured and used—snout to tail, beak to feet. Chicken livers, all too often, are organs left behind. We use them here in a way that is as creamy and delicious as it is conscientious.

Makes 16 hush puppies

For the chicken liver butter:

1 pound chicken livers

½ cup milk

½ cup (1 stick) unsalted butter, softened, divided

Kosher salt and cracked black pepper

1 shallot, minced

2 to 3 tablespoons brandy

6 tablespoons heavy cream

1 tablespoon combined chopped fresh oregano, thyme, and mint

1 to 2 tablespoons prepared mustard (optional)

Make the chicken liver butter: Trim the livers of their connective sinews. Place in a bowl, add milk to cover, and set aside for 30 minutes.

Drain the livers well, then place on paper towels and blot away all liquid. (This promotes faster sautéing, which helps avoid overcooking—a wise precaution, as overcooked chicken livers are not nearly as tender as medium-rare ones.)

Melt one third of the butter in a skillet over medium-high heat. Season the livers with salt and pepper. When the butter starts to foam, place the livers in the skillet (cook in batches to avoid crowding them) and sauté quickly, turning once, until lightly crisped on the outside. Remove to a plate as soon as they are cooked.

When all the livers are cooked and removed to the plate, add the shallot to the pan and stir. When just softened, add the brandy and shake the skillet. As soon as the liquid thickens, pour it over the seared livers.

Transfer the liver mixture, the remaining butter, and the cream to a food processor and pulse until just smooth. Add the herbs and mustard (if using). Pulse again. Adjust the seasoning with salt and pepper as needed. Pass the liver mixture through a fine-mesh sieve into a bowl. (This is the step that makes the dish buttery-smooth!) Transfer to a clean glass or ceramic bowl and let cool to room temperature. Cover with plastic wrap and chill in the refrigerator until needed.

For the Asian spice syrup:

7 tablespoons sake

5 tablespoons tamari or soy sauce

7 tablespoons rice vinegar

1 cup sugar

1 tablespoon minced fresh ginger

2 cloves garlic, thinly sliced

1 teaspoon seeded and minced Scotch bonnet chile

Make the Asian spice syrup: Combine all the ingredients in a nonreactive saucepan and cook until reduced to a honey-like consistency, 6 to 10 minutes. If you'd like, strain the sauce to remove the solids for a smoother consistency.

To serve, break the Bacon-Speckled Hush Puppies open, smear the insides with chicken liver butter, and drizzle with the syrup.

For serving:

Bacon-Speckled Hush Puppies (page 239)

Choripán Dogs
WITH CHIMICHURRI, TATER CHIPS, AND A VIETNAMESE PICKLE PARTY

The portmanteau *choripán* is easily understood, as it weds the words *chorizo* and *pan* (the Spanish word for "bread"). When the sausage is split down the middle it is referred to as a *mariposa*, Spanish for "butterfly." We are fortunate to live near a great small artisanal butcher shop named Proper Sausages, so we source ours from there most often. We outfit our *choripán* with a good chimichurri, classic in many parts of the Americas, but we also "fuse" things by serving up the pickles we learned to love from Vietnamese cookery. The great bridges in cuisine cross over even deep waters with amazing ease when they do so with the help of the most common culinary heartthrobs like sausages and pickles.

Store-bought kettle-style potato chips are not a total defeat if you don't have a mandoline or the desire to fry your own chips!

Serves 4 to 6

For the Vietnamese pickle party:

12 ounces carrots, peeled and cut into matchstick pieces

8 ounces daikon radish, peeled and cut into matchstick pieces

4 ounces jicama, peeled and cut into matchstick pieces

1 tablespoon kosher salt, or more to taste

2 teaspoons plus ¼ cup sugar, or more to taste

About 3 tablespoons hot water

½ cup plus 2 tablespoons apple cider vinegar

1 tablespoon crushed red pepper, or more to taste

¼ cup fresh cilantro leaves, roughly chopped (optional)

Make the Vietnamese pickle party: Put the carrots, daikon, jicama, salt, and 2 teaspoons of the sugar in a bowl and allow to marinate and "weep" for about 15 minutes. Don't go much longer, or the salt tends to remain in the vegetables and we don't want that.

Meanwhile, put ¼ cup sugar in a bowl. Add the hot water and stir to dissolve.

Drain the weeping vegetable mixture, rinse it quickly in cold water, and blot dry with paper towels—or, if you have one, spin in a salad spinner—to remove all the liquid that would otherwise dilute the pickling liquid.

Put the vinegar, sugar water, crushed red pepper, and cilantro (if using) in a bowl large enough to hold the vegetables. Add the vegetables and toss well. Taste and adjust the seasoning if needed. Refrigerate, covered, until cold. (The pickles will keep in the refrigerator for up to a month *if* you have not consumed them before that!)

continued ➜

For the homemade potato chips:

2 large Idaho potatoes, scrubbed, skins left on

Peanut or canola oil for deep-frying

Kosher salt

Make the homemade potato chips: Thinly slice the potatoes with a mandoline. Put them in a large bowl and cover with a generous amount of cool water to rinse them. Drain in a colander, rinse, and cover again with cold water. Drain them well and allow to dry for a few minutes on a mat of paper towels or clean cotton towels.

In a heavy pot or a Dutch oven, heat 1 inch of oil to about 360 degrees. (If you don't have a deep-frying thermometer, try one chip and see if the cooking is nice and even and hot enough but not burning. It will bubble due to the water still within the potato.) Fry the chips in batches until nicely colored and crispy. Carefully remove them with a slotted spoon or a wire mesh skimmer. Drain on dry paper towels and sprinkle the chips with salt while they are still hot and glistening with the sheen of the cooking oil. Set aside.

For the *choripán*:

4 to 6 (6-inch) lengths of chorizo (or sausage of your choice), 1 per person; if the sausage casing is plastic, remove it

4 to 6 (6-inch) lengths of Cuban bread or 1 hoagie roll, sliced lengthwise and toasted just before serving

Red Chimichurri (page 226)

Mayonnaise (optional)

Make the *choripán*: Heat an outdoor grill to medium-high (or, grill lacking, heat a heavy skillet over medium heat). Put the chorizo on the grill grate and cook, turning occasionally, until cooked through; the internal temperature should be at least 145 degrees. (You can also finish the sausages in the oven if working inside; 350 degrees for about 10 minutes should do it.)

Drizzle the toasted bread with Red Chimichurri, as well as mayonnaise if desired. Mayonnaise adds richness, of course, and balances the spice and acidity some. Position the cooked sausage in the middle. Place some of the pickles over the sausage. Since the pickle is cool in temperature, do this at the last possible moment. Scatter a handful of the chips on the sausage too. Take a photo if you like. Get a drink. I'm having a *cocktail*. Grasp the "dog" firmly, lean over a plate . . . and savor.

Smoked Fish Dip on Corn Cakes
WITH CHARRED SCALLION–TOASTED ALMOND ROMESCO

I love how the sweetness of these corn cakes pairs with smoked fish. The fusion of old Florida dishes and the foodways of Spanish-descended Florida immigrants was an early part of my journey cooking "in the hyphens." Simply wandering the little bodegas and Hispanic grocery stores here brings me ideas. The "romesco" cousin sauce I've created to go along with the corn cakes is a recipe that would work with a wide variety of foods. Try it on grilled fish and meats of all kinds.

Serves 4

¾ cup yellow cornmeal

6 tablespoons all-purpose flour

1 tablespoon baking powder

Kosher salt and cracked black pepper

3 eggs, separated

1 cup milk

4 tablespoons butter, melted

1 tablespoon honey

A pinch of cream of tartar

1 cup corn, cooked until somewhat charred

Rendered bacon fat or peanut oil

Smoked Fish Dip (page 235)

Charred Scallion–Toasted Almond Romesco (page 230)

Combine the cornmeal, flour, baking powder, and 1 teaspoon salt and 1 teaspoon pepper, or more to taste, in a bowl.

In a separate bowl, whisk the egg yolks, milk, and melted butter together. Pour into the cornmeal mixture and stir to combine.

In a clean bowl, whip the egg whites together with the honey and cream of tartar to medium-stiff peaks. Fold into the batter. Season the corn with a little salt and pepper and fold it into the batter.

Heat some bacon fat in a sauté pan or on a griddle over medium heat. Add about ¼ cup of the batter. Check for browning on the bottom when you start to see pinholes appear on top. Flip it over and finish cooking. It is good to make a small one as a tester and see if you are happy with the level of salt and pepper. Season as desired and continue to cook the remaining batter. Keep the corn cakes warm in a low oven as you make them.

Spoon a nice amount of the Smoked Fish Dip on the base of four serving plates. Cover each with a corn cake. Spoon more dip on top, then top with a second corn cake. Add a trio of small dollops of Charred Scallion–Toasted Almond Romesco around the stack. Serve.

Serving suggestion: You can garnish the top of the corn cakes with sour cream and/or herbs as desired. Lemon wedges are welcome with almost any seafood as well.

6

ROCKIN' THE BOATS

Fish and Seafood

Black Grouper
WITH SPLIT-ROASTED TOMATOES, SWEET ONION "CREAM," AND CORN RELISH

We have been moving away from the reliance on a lot of cream and butter in our cooking in this new century, with welcome advances made possible by powerful blenders and an awareness of the offerings from within the Vegetable Kingdom. Flavor is found in plenty of places the more we explore them. Scarcity and awareness may be tough teachers in the beginning, but the resourceful cook can be bountifully rewarded. The world of vegetables dominates this dish.

Serves 2 as an entrée

For the sweet onion "cream":

2 sweet onions, with peels left on

¼ teaspoon kosher salt

1 tablespoon fresh-squeezed lemon juice

1 tablespoon extra-virgin olive oil

For the split-roasted tomatoes:

1 to 2 ripe, in-season tomatoes, cored (if they are small tomatoes, use 2 halves per person, and save any leftovers for another use)

Extra-virgin olive oil

Kosher salt and cracked black pepper

A few drops of sherry vinegar

1 teaspoon agave sweetener

For the grouper:

2 (5- to 6-ounce) grouper fillets

Kosher salt and cracked black pepper

2 tablespoons extra-virgin olive oil

For serving:

Corn Relish (page 215)

Make the sweet onion "cream": Preheat the oven to 400 degrees.

Place the onions in a baking dish and bake for 1 hour, or until the onions are quite soft to the touch. (Really more like dilapidated-looking!) Allow them to cool enough to handle, but proceed while still warm to get the most yield from them.

Cut off the ends of the onions and scoop out the onion puree that has formed in the interior. Place the puree in a blender and add the salt, lemon juice, and oil. Blend until smooth, then set aside. (The puree can be made in advance. Refrigerate if not using the same day and warm just before ready to serve.)

Make the split-roasted tomatoes: Preheat the oven to 275 degrees.

Slice the tomatoes in half and place cut side up in the middle of a small nonreactive rimmed baking sheet or baking dish. Brush with oil. Sprinkle with salt and pepper, the vinegar, and then the agave. Roast for 15 to 25 minutes, just until their skins begin to pull away. (Size and ripeness determine the cooking time, so pay heed to this.) Remove them from the oven and set aside, covered to keep warm.

Make the grouper: Season the fish fillets with salt and pepper. In a nonstick sauté pan over medium-high heat, warm the oil.

Add the fish and cook, turning once, until cooked through, 6 to 8 minutes total. Remove to a plate and cover the fish with a tent of aluminum foil to retain the heat.

Serve by placing a nice spoonful of the onion "cream" on the base of each of two serving plates. Top with a grouper fillet. Place a half tomato to one side of each fish fillet and spoon some of the Corn Relish on top of the fish.

Tea-Spiced Cast-Iron Spotted Sea Trout

WITH CAPERS, CUCUMBERS, MANGOS, AND BROWN BUTTER

Spotted or sea trout is one of those creatures that got a name without a true birthright. Perhaps some early fishmongers were trying to make it sexier or more sellable than its common name, drum. They had no need. It is fine as it is. But names get stuck. (The Mango Gang, anyone?) The spotted sea trout is a member of the drum family and widely fished in Florida. I began cooking salmon with the tea cure I use here, but because salmon is a fish we enjoy more when we are outside of Florida, these days I use sea trout. Feel free to adapt to any fish you like, as a wide range would be excellent cooked in this way. We all need to think "outside the boat" about what we prize for dinner!

Serves 4

For the smoked tea spice:

2 tablespoons Lapsang Souchong loose tea leaves, pulsed in a small food processor or very finely chopped

4 tablespoons sugar

2 teaspoons kosher salt

1 teaspoon cracked black pepper

Make the smoked tea spice: Mix all the ingredients together. (You will net more of the smoked tea spice than you need for this recipe, but leftovers keep a long time if tightly sealed and kept in a cool, dark spot.)

For the sea trout:

4 (6-ounce) fillets of sea trout, skin on

For the mango-caper-cucumber brown butter:

1 lemon

1 cup peeled and diced cucumber

Kosher salt

6 tablespoons butter, cut into three equal portions

1½ tablespoons small capers, drained and rinsed

1 cup diced fresh mango

To finish the dish:

Canola or other light oil

Make the fish: Lay the fish on a work board and season it on the skinless side of the fillets with 2 teaspoons of the smoked tea spice. Cover with plastic wrap and keep cold or cool for at least 1 hour.

Make the mango-caper-cucumber brown butter: Cut the rind and white pith away from the lemon. Remove the segments by slicing between the membranes; pick out the seeds. Cut half of the segments into ½-inch pieces. (Save the remaining lemon for another use.)

Sprinkle the cucumber with kosher salt and allow it to stand for about 20 minutes in a sieve to drain off the excess water. Rinse, pat dry, and set aside.

Heat a saucepan over medium heat. Add the butter and cook, stirring, until it turns a deep brown and smells nutty, 3 to 4 minutes. Your observations are more key than time on a clock. When the hazelnut smell and brown color have just arrived, remove the pan from the heat and stir in the lemon pieces, cucumber, capers, and mango; swirl the pan to combine. Keep the sauce warm.

Finish the dish: Preheat the oven to 400 degrees.

Heat a cast-iron pan: I start mine up to 10 minutes in advance oftentimes to really "set the heat." That doesn't mean to make it scorching hot—it means to have the heat steady and even. A cast-iron pan is a thick pan, and that is part of its power; it holds on to the heat when the food goes in it. But it has a better chance if properly heated.

Once hot, add enough oil to coat the bottom and lay in the seasoned fish. Cook until nicely browned on one side, then turn the fillets. Carefully drain off the excess oil. Transfer the skillet to the oven until the fish is just cooked through or done to your liking, 6 to 8 minutes.

Remove the fillets to serving plates and top with the brown butter sauce (or serve the sauce on the side). Serve immediately.

Flounder "à la Meunière," with Saltine Crackers

Some recipes rightfully last lifetimes—spanning generations and centuries—not because they are clever but rather because they are logical and beautiful. This is one of them. The delicate perfection of pristine fish is not something we have only recently discovered—maybe we should first thank the fishermen and -women of the world. The nearly innate understanding of a very few ingredients is the cornerstone of a preparation like a fish done "à la Meunière." The words themselves harken back to much earlier times, when town folk knew that the flour they used to make "the staff of life" often came from a local miller. This dish came along for me when I was just learning to cook and when American chefs were literally soaking in the history of classic French cuisine. I am indebted. (Minus the saltines...)

Serves 2

2 (5- to 6-ounce) fillets of flounder

½ cup whole milk

All-purpose flour for dredging (about 1 cup, but don't cut yourself short—the dish is named for this ingredient!)

Kosher salt and cracked black pepper

¼ cup (or slightly less) clarified butter (depends on the size of the pan)

2½ tablespoons whole butter

2 tablespoons freshly squeezed lemon juice, plus lemon wedges for serving if you'd like

½ cup chopped fresh parsley

¼ cup diced cucumber, peeled or not

½ cup (or more, if desired) saltine crackers, broken into crouton-size pieces

Place the fillets in the milk and let them soak for about 10 minutes. This step aids in giving the fish a nice color. Remove the fish from the milk and dredge it in the flour (discard the milk). Season the fish with some salt and pepper. When you are ready to cook, shake off all excess flour.

Heat a sauté pan over medium heat for a minute, then add the clarified butter. Gently place the floured fillets into the hot butter. Cook for 3 to 5 minutes, until there's a nice golden-brown color, then carefully flip it over. Cook for another 3 minutes, or until the second side is golden brown and the fish is just cooked through. (You can take a knife or a spatula and carefully "peek" into the interior to see if it is opaque, which it needs to be.) Remove from the pan and place the fish on a warm plate.

Discard the butter in the pan (but there's no need to clean out the pan). Quickly add the whole butter to the pan and swirl it around to melt. Cook the butter until it turns slightly brown. Then add the lemon juice and parsley. Shake the pan. Add the cucumbers.

Spoon the sauce over the fish. Scatter the crackers over the sauce. Serve with extra lemon on the side if you'd like.

Pompano and Fideo Noodle Stew
WITH ROSA'S "TWO WAY" TOMATO SAUCE

One way I learned about fideo—Spanish for "noodle"—was through the works of Anya Von Bremzen, José Andres, and Colman Andrews. Another was simply seeing them in the Latin markets and wondering how to cook them. Those two ways of learning about food have been my main routes in cuisine. It helps to be friendly and chat up the folks in the store about how they cook things too. That was especially true before we had writers like the aforementioned publishing and sharing their passions here in America. I like the unexpected manner of cooking the noodles here that is *not* by boiling them first, but rather by "toasting" them in olive oil and then cooking them in the sauce you are making. The result is like no other noodle.

Serves 4 to 6

¼ cup vegetable oil

3 slices good bacon, cut into 1-inch lengths

3 cloves garlic, minced, plus 2 cloves thinly sliced

1 serrano chile, minced (seeds may be left in if desired)

½ onion, diced

1 carrot, peeled and diced

½ bulb fennel, cored and diced (¾ cup)

Kosher salt and cracked black pepper

2 pounds scrubbed and debearded mussels

1 cup soft red wine (such as merlot, although I have used champagne if that was handy)

3 cups Rosa's "Two Way" Tomato Sauce (page 229)

1 (28-ounce) can whole tomatoes, pureed

8 ounces loose, dry fideo (or vermicelli) noodles

½ cup plus 2 tablespoons olive oil

2 tablespoons butter

12 ounces large shrimp, peeled and deveined, cut into bite-size pieces

2 pounds skin-on pompano fillets, cut into pieces 1 inch long (you can use bass or other fish as well, removing skin if you wish)

In a large rondeau pot (or Dutch oven), combine the vegetable oil and bacon. Cook over medium heat until the bacon is almost done. Add in the minced garlic, the chile, onion, carrot, and fennel and stir. Season with salt and pepper to taste and cook until softened, 8 to 10 minutes.

Add the mussels and wine. Turn up the heat to medium-high. Cover the pan with a tight-fitting lid and cook until the mussels steam open, 4 to 6 minutes. Using a slotted spoon, remove the mussels to a colander set over a bowl; discard any mussels that haven't opened. Put the Rosa's "Two-Way" Tomato Sauce and the pureed tomatoes in the pot and remove from the heat. Set the sauce and mussels aside.

In a large sauté pan over medium heat, cook the fideo noodles in the ½ cup olive oil. Toss and pull at them with tongs to shake them out of their bundles. Cook until nicely colored, about 8 minutes. Drain on paper towels for a moment, then stir them into the tomato sauce mixture. Place over low heat and cook, covered, until the noodles are soft to the bite. Add the mussels and the liquor from the bowl under the colander, stirring them into the noodles and tomato sauce. Cover and keep on very low heat so you don't overcook the mussels.

If your fish fillets are thick, preheat the oven to 350 degrees.

Heat another sauté pan over medium heat and coat the bottom with the remaining 2 tablespoons olive oil. Add the butter and increase the heat to medium-high. Add the garlic and cook for 20 seconds. Add the shrimp and fish. Cook until just cooked through, about 3 minutes. (Thicker fish, such as grouper, might take longer. Sear them first in the pan with the shrimp, then transfer to a baking sheet and finish in the oven.)

When the shrimp and fish are cooked, add them both to the stew. Season to taste. Gently stir. Heat the stew over medium heat and serve hot.

Serving suggestion: **Serve with some good, crusty garlic bread. If you need any more than this you are possibly jaded. So if you are, and you are like me, let me offer this further temptation: Smash some fine anchovies into some butter and slather it on your bread. Sit back and enjoy the broadest smile your face might be able to stretch into.**

Grilled Swordfish
WITH FERMENTED BLACK BEAN BUTTER AND MASHED YAMS

The verb *to barbecue* covers more ground for some than it does for others. For some it is a euphemism for "grilling" in general. For those of this faith, I think it also means "cooking while drinking a beer or a cocktail." I won't rain on their parade! Here we are doing so with a fish that had to be brought back from near extinction.

Serves 4

For the yams:

2 large sweet potatoes, peeled

Kosher salt

1 tablespoon butter, or more as desired

Cracked black pepper

For the fish:

4 (7- to 8-ounce) swordfish steaks, trimmed, set out at room temperature for 30 minutes

Olive oil to lightly coat the swordfish

Kosher salt and cracked black pepper

Vegetable oil to lightly "anoint" the grill

For serving:

Fermented Black Bean Butter (page 226)

Make the yams: Put the sweet potatoes in a pot with enough water to amply cover them. Salt the water and bring to a simmer. Cook until easily pierced with a thin-bladed knife, 15 to 20 minutes. Drain well. Mash them and add butter, salt, and pepper to taste. Keep warm while finishing the dish.

Make the fish: Rub the fish with a bit of olive oil and season with salt and pepper.

Heat an outdoor grill to fairly hot. Rub the grill grate with a lightly vegetable-oiled towel. Put the fish on the grill and cook for 3 to 4 minutes on the first side and 2 to 3 minutes on the second side. Transfer the swordfish to warm serving plates. Spoon some of the Fermented Black Bean Butter around the fish. Add a side of the yams and serve.

Hogfish Tempura
WITH COLONIAL
DRIVE DIPPING SAUCE

One of my favorite rockers was a guy named Lowell George. If Lowell's name is familiar but not *quite* within memory's cab ride, he was the lead guitarist and singer for the band Little Feat. He died young, like rockers sometimes do, but he imparted some wisdom in these lyrics: "Love is a perfect imperfection, sometimes happy, sometimes sad." Nothing is sad about this dish, but I find those first few words from George to be so true. Such it is with tempura. It looks imperfect. And that could throw you off when staring at a bowl of batter. But it is its very *oddness,* if you will, that creates tempura's capacity for crispy *perfection.* (Compliments to the song's writers as well, Paul Barrere and Tom Snow.)

Serves 4

1½ pounds well-trimmed hogfish (or other seafood such as shrimp)

Kosher salt and cracked black pepper

Canola or other oil for deep-frying

2 egg yolks

2 cups cold water

¼ cup ice cubes

2 cups cake flour, plus ½ to ¾ cup for dredging

Colonial Drive Dipping Sauce (page 233)

Cut the fish into wafers about the size of fat dominoes. This will allow quick and even cooking. Season with salt and pepper. Allow the fish to dry on paper towels until ready to fry. It is important to be sure your fish is blotted *very dry* before battering it and frying.

Bring the cooking oil to 360 degrees in a large pot. Have enough oil to *easily* submerge the fish, about 2 quarts. It is also key to maintain a steady temperature. Have the oil ready before you finish making the tempura batter, since time is of the essence.

In one bowl mix together the egg yolks, water, and ice cubes. (The icy temperature? It is to help reduce the development of gluten, which means crispier texture.) In another bowl, put the flour. When you are all set, and not a moment sooner, dump the flour into the wet mixture. Take four chopsticks and kind of "stab" the mix until a loose batter forms. Do not stir it at *all*. No circular motions. It is more an up-and-down motion with the chopsticks. It needs to be barely mixed and even a bit lumpy with streaks of the cake flour still showing.

Put the ½ to ¾ cup flour in a bowl or on a plate. Dredge the fish in the flour and then in the batter to coat each piece on both sides. Working in batches, carefully lower the fish into the hot oil. Cook for about 2 minutes on the first side and then, using a long spoon or other utensil, turn the fish onto the other side and cook

continued →

for about 2 more minutes. Raise or lower the heat to maintain that important temperature of 360 degrees. The seafood needs to be cooked through by the time it's golden on both sides. (We often "sacrifice" a piece as a "tester.")

Drain the fish on paper towels for a moment. Serve with the Colonial Drive Dipping Sauce in side bowls.

Serving suggestion: Serve with other Asian-style sauces if you'd like, instead of the Colonial Drive Dipping Sauce. Lemon wedges are nice with this fish too.

Upstate Soft-Shell Crabs
WITH "TOASTED" ORANGE JUS AND BACON-SPECKLED HUSH PUPPIES

While living in Key West, I had the great fortune to meet, cook for, and even hang out some with the essayist Jim Harrison. His *Men's Journal* column, "The Raw and the Cooked," was routinely cut out and sent to me by my dear friend and fellow Harrison admirer Charlie Trotter, and I remember one in particular in which Harrison wrote, "Since it is important to cook everything when it's absolutely fresh, we went through the *entire* container." (Recalling a box of seafood FedExed to him from Florida at the time.) He went on in his signature—which is to say, Rabelaisian— way, "I grilled an appetizer of baby-back pork ribs using Matouk's (a Caribbean fruit-based hot sauce). We moved on to soft-shell crabs *meunière*, then kebabs made from chunks of cobia (a rarely shipped Gulf fish) marinated in Mozambique *piripiri*." I believe Jim would love the crabs and delight in the bacon-speckled hush puppies. He'd probably wash it all down with flagons of white Burgundy.

Serves 4 as an appetizer or 2 as an entrée

For the soft-shell crabs:

¼ cup all-purpose flour

Kosher salt and cracked black pepper

4 jumbo soft-shell crabs, cleaned

2 tablespoons canola oil or peanut oil

1 tablespoon butter

For the "toasted" orange jus:

½ cup (1 stick) unsalted butter

1 shallot, finely diced

½ cup fresh-squeezed orange juice

½ teaspoon ground cayenne

2 tablespoons fresh-squeezed lemon juice

Kosher salt and cracked black pepper

For serving:

Bacon-Speckled Hush Puppies (page 239), made with 1 cup batter and 2 tablespoons diced cooked bacon

Make the soft-shell crabs: In a wide shallow bowl or pie plate, combine the flour with ½ teaspoon salt and ¼ teaspoon pepper. Dredge the crabs in the flour mixture to coat on both sides.

Heat the oil in a 12-inch cast-iron or nonstick skillet over medium-high heat until the oil is shimmering. Add the butter and allow it to melt.

Add the crabs, top side down. Cook, shaking the pan once or twice to keep the crabs from sticking, until browned, about 3 minutes. The crabs may pop and splatter, so stand back or use a splatter guard. With tongs, flip the crabs and cook until an instant-read thermometer inserted in the center reads about 145 degrees, 2 to 3 minutes more. Move to a plate, cover loosely with aluminum foil to keep warm, and set aside.

Make the "toasted" orange jus: Heat a small but heavy saucepan over medium heat. Add the butter and cook, swirling the pan a few times, until the butter foams. Add the shallot and cook until the butter is the color of pale hazelnuts, 3 to 4 minutes. Add the orange juice and cayenne and cook for 1 minute more. Add the lemon juice. Season with a little salt and pepper and stir.

Serve the crabs on warm plates with the "toasted" orange jus spooned over them. Serve the Bacon-Speckled Hush Puppies on the side in a basket with a liner.

Spiny Lobster on Mussel-Saffron Nage
WITH STEAMED SPINACH AND YUCA HASH BROWNS

The French phrase *à la nage* translates to "in the swim." The classic method refers to shellfish (usually) simmering gently in a flavorful broth. But cuisine always changes, and language reflects that as best it can. We now refer to a nage also as a sauce made from whisking butter into the aforementioned broth, once the broth is reduced down and concentrated enough to latch on to that butter. The result is delicious in any language.

Serves 4

For the mussel-saffron nage:

3 tablespoons unsalted butter

1 to 2 shallots, minced (about ⅓ cup)

1 jalapeño chile, seeded and minced

1 small fennel bulb, thinly sliced (1½ cups), fronds reserved

½ teaspoon saffron threads

1 star anise

1 bay leaf, broken

1½ cups dry white wine

1 cup Chicken Stock (page 237)

Kosher salt and cracked black pepper

3 pounds cleaned and debearded mussels

4 tablespoons cold butter, cut up

Start the mussel-saffron nage: In a heavy medium to large pot over medium-high heat, melt the butter. Add the shallots, jalapeño, and sliced fennel. Cook until somewhat tender and aromatic, 4 to 6 minutes. Add the saffron, star anise, and bay leaf. Let the saffron heat up a moment, then add the wine and stock. Season with a little salt and pepper. Bring to a simmer and cook for 4 to 5 minutes.

Add the mussels to the pot. Cover with a tight-fitting lid and steam the mussels until they open, about 5 minutes, shaking the pan occasionally so they cook evenly. Remove the mussels to a large bowl. Discard any mussels that did not open. Once just cool enough to handle, remove the mussels from their shells and set the mussels aside in a bowl. Discard the shells. Continue to cook the mussel cooking liquid until it is reduced by half, about 10 minutes. Strain it into a bowl through a fine-mesh sieve. (You should have about 2 cups.)

Transfer the 2 cups nage to a clean small, flat heavy saucepan. Bring to a boil again and cook to reduce to ½ cup of liquid. (Straining and then reducing the nage again in a clean pan results in a cleaner, more refined sauce.)

Wrap the cooked mussels up in an aluminum foil "pouch." Set aside.

For the lobster:

4 spiny lobster tails, split in half lengthwise, shells left on

Kosher salt and cracked black pepper

¼ cup clarified butter

For the spinach:

4 good-sized handfuls of spinach leaves

A glug of extra-virgin olive oil

Kosher salt and cracked black pepper

For serving:

Yuca Hash Browns (page 168)

2 lemons, cut in half crosswise

> *Note:* This can be made with a wide variety of seafood if spiny lobster are not in your area or you would like another type of fish or shellfish. If you want to make eating it a bit easier you can remove the lobster meat from its pretty shells before plating.

Make the lobster: Preheat the oven to 350 degrees.

Season the lobster meat with salt and pepper. Set aside.

Heat a nonstick skillet large enough to hold the lobsters over medium heat. Add the clarified butter. Cook the lobsters starting with the meaty side down and then turning them over a few times. When they are nicely colored, remove them to an oven-proof pan meat side up. Cook them in the oven until just cooked through, about 5 minutes. Remove the lobsters from the oven and cover to keep warm.

Warm the mussels in the oven in the foil package.

Make the spinach: Steam the spinach with the oil in a pan large enough to hold it. Season lightly with salt and pepper.

Finish the nage: With the heat on medium to medium-low; whisk in the butter bits until the butter is melted and incorporated.

To serve, put the Yuca Hash Browns to one edge of each serving plate. Put the lobsters in the middle of each plate. Spoon the nage upon them and then top with the warmed mussels and the steamed spinach. Garnish with the fennel fronds. Add the lemon halves for guests to squeeze as they wish.

7

BARNS, WALLOWS, COOPS

Meat and Poultry

"Doc Cohen's Tzimmes"
WITH BRISKET, CARROTS, SWEET POTATOES, AND PRUNES

This dish is a traditional Ashkenazi Jewish stew and features sweet in the forms of carrots, sweet potatoes, and (most typically) prunes. In the abundant and joyful cooking found in our wide-ranging Jewish populations in Florida, this dish is often part of a Rosh Hashanah table. I was a guest at one such celebration and determined to make it myself. We make the version that contains meat, although many do not. The word *tzimmes* or *tsimmes* is also a Yiddish expression for "making a fuss" over something. The holidays often allow for a bit more of a "fuss" and extravagance, which, we are learning, indulging in meat feasting should be.

Brisket is a cut of meat that more of us might enjoy cooking ourselves at home. My ever reliable copy of *The Complete Meat Book*, by Bruce Aidells and Denis Kelly, informs us that "the leaner portion (of brisket) is called the 'flat' and that we want to have the part that is fattier and contains 'the deckle point.' It is called the 'brisket front cut.'" Point well taken!

Serves 6 to 8

For the braise:

3½ pounds well-marbled, boneless beef brisket

2 tablespoons kosher salt

1½ tablespoons cracked black pepper

¼ cup olive oil

1 sweet onion, peeled and sliced

3 carrots, peeled and roughly chopped

1 head of garlic, cut in half

¾ cup red wine vinegar

2 quarts beef stock

Make the braise: Preheat the oven to 350 degrees. Place a rack in the center of the oven for a roast this large to cook as evenly as possible.

Pat the brisket dry and rub it all over with the salt and pepper.

Heat the oil in a large rondeau or heavy roasting pan over medium-high heat. If necessary, straddle the pan across two burners. Brown the brisket on both sides.

Remove the pan from the heat, then add half of the onion slices, all of the carrots, and the halved head of garlic to the pan and stir. Add the vinegar and stock to the pan. Return the beef to the pan. Cover the pan with heavy-duty aluminum foil and secure tightly. Braise the brisket in the oven for 2 hours.

Remove the pan from the oven. Lift the meat out and place the meat in a pan. Strain the braising liquid though a fine-mesh sieve into a bowl. Discard the spent vegetables. Let the braising liquid cool to room temperature, then refrigerate overnight. (Note: You do not need to add a cover to the braising liquid, as a "fat cap" will form overnight in your refrigerator and protect it.) Cover and refrigerate the meat overnight as well.

The next day, take the meat out of the refrigerator, unwrap it, and let it come to almost room temperature.

For the tzimmes:

1 sweet onion, peeled and somewhat thickly sliced

1 pound carrots, peeled and cut into sticks ¾ inch wide by 2¼ inches long

8 cloves garlic, peeled and left whole

3 tablespoons olive oil

2 sprigs fresh rosemary or oregano

½ tablespoon ground charnushka or caraway

A pinch of cracked black pepper

3 sweet potatoes

Kosher salt

1 cup pitted prunes

Note: **Charnushka is a spice often used in making Jewish rye bread. It adds another traditional element, though not specifically to tzimmes.**

Make the tzimmes: Preheat the oven to 300 degrees.

Remove and discard the "fat cap" from the strained and reserved braising liquid. (Note: Any milky liquid at the bottom is best discarded, as it will cloud your sauce.) Warm the liquid in a saucepan. Set aside.

In a bowl, combine the remaining onion, carrots, and garlic, breaking up the onion layers well.

Take the same braising pan, now cleaned, and put it back on the burners. Heat over medium to medium-high heat. (The goal is to give the vegetables a bit of color via caramelization, which varies from stove to stove.) Add the oil and scatter the onions, carrots, garlic, and rosemary in the oil and dust the vegetables with the charnushka and pepper. Cook the vegetables for about 10 minutes, stirring frequently.

Put the brisket on top of the vegetables. Add the warm braising liquid. Cover the pan with foil and roast in the oven for 1 hour.

Meanwhile, peel and cut the sweet potatoes into sixths, put them in a large pot, and cover with cold water. Add some salt. Bring to a simmer and cook until they are just easily pierced with a knife. Drain and set aside.

Add the prunes to the meat and return to the oven, covered, for about 45 minutes more.

Remove the pan from the oven.

Let the meat rest for another hour at this point.

When the meat is cool enough to handle, slice it into ¼- to ½-inch-thick pieces against the grain and arrange in overlapping "shingles" next to each other on a section of aluminum foil. Fold the foil shut. Scoop up the vegetables and sweet potatoes and place them in an ovenproof dish. Spoon a little bit of the braising liquid on them and season. Cover with foil or an ovenproof lid. Pour the remaining braising liquid through a strainer into a clean saucepan. Gently cook it until it is reduced to a nice coating consistency. Set aside.

continued ➔

Put the vegetables and sweet potatoes back in the warm oven. Give them about a 10-minute head start, then put the aluminum foil package of meat in the oven to warm. (Note that the "package" can sit on a pan to be safer, but the folded up foil treatment helps create a slightly steamy environment, which helps ensure moist meat.) When both are hot, remove them from the oven and spoon the vegetable mixture onto each plate or serve family style. The same can be done with the sliced meat.

Season again with salt and pepper over all. Serve with the reduced braising liquid.

Coffee-Rubbed T-Bone Steaks

Coffee culture in Florida has been certainly sped along (pun intended) by our big love of what is commonly referred to as "Cuban coffee." When we first started living in Key West, we quickly adopted the customs of the locals and brewed our morning jump-starter in what essentially was much like a sock. The different brewing technique immediately awakens one (here we go again) to other possibilities of the bean. Spice rubs, to wit. Another Florida feature in this dish is the beef. While not known as widely as it might be, Florida was the state where cattle were first introduced to North America. And though tourism has become much bigger than cattle, we are still among the top beef producers in the United States.

Yield depends on how many steaks you cook

T-bone steaks, at least 1 inch thick, with about ½ inch of fat intact along the edge (I like a steak that is 1½ pounds or a bit more, so it has the thickness to allow for a great char and also some juicy interior)

Per steak: 2 tablespoons Coffee Spice Rub (page 221)

Kosher salt and cracked black pepper

About 1 hour before cooking, place the steaks on a cutting board and cut some incisions into the meat. Rub the Coffee Rub into the slits and all over the steaks. Season with salt and pepper. Let stand for 1 hour.

Heat an outdoor grill to high.

Grill the steaks until nicely crisp on the outside and medium-rare on the inside, and about 120 degrees on an instant-read thermometer, about 4 minutes per side. Remove the steaks to a carving board and let rest for about 5 minutes.

Cut them along the bone and then cut the meat into slices crosswise to the bone. Serve.

Note: We prefer a T-bone to a porterhouse if presented with the option. Why? The T-bone comes from further down the loin and so avoids more of the tough gristle that runs through the strip side of the meat. The T-bone has a smaller amount of the filet mignon but enough for a "taste"; truly a filet is a better meal if you are making sauces like béarnaise. Are you? Well, then . . . happy to drop by!

Serving suggestion: We offer our Cauliflower in a "Cali" Way (page 163) often when we make this meal. But feel free to choose whatever you wish. Maybe for us it was a Juan Valdez inspiration.

"Oxtail Tuesdays"

There is a Cuban place near where we live that serves braised oxtails every Tuesday (listed under the Cuban term *rabo*). The portion is perhaps the reason some sidle up to the stools along the two counters, but for us it is sheer savory, powerful way they make them. One of my friends is a very fine young chef born in Thailand who now lives in Miami. (His name is very long, so everyone knows him as "Chef Bee.") He frequents that Cuban café like a religion has formed around those oxtails. And he always gets two orders to take back and share with his kitchen crew. I wonder if they add in any favored Thai spices when he gets to work? Oxtails can be made into many, many dishes and in many ways. Here is a base recipe to give you the platform to do just that.

Serves 6 to 8

¾ cup all-purpose flour

¼ cup curry powder

4 (or a bit more) pounds oxtail, cut into pieces 2 inches thick

Kosher salt and cracked black pepper

¼ cup peanut or vegetable oil

¼ cup olive oil

5 cloves garlic, minced

1 large onion, finely chopped

2 poblano peppers, seeded and diced

2 red bell peppers, seeded and diced

2 cups canned diced tomatoes with their juices

¼ cup pitted green olives, chopped

1 tablespoon thyme leaves, chopped

1 cup Madeira wine

1 cup red wine

¼ cup sherry vinegar

About 6 cups beef stock (enough to almost cover the oxtails)

Preheat the oven to 300 degrees.

Mix the flour with the curry powder. Dust the oxtails with the mixture. Season the oxtails with salt and black pepper. In a large heavy shallow pan or pot over medium-high heat, heat the peanut oil. Brown the oxtails on *all* sides. Transfer them to a platter and pour out the oil you seared the oxtails in.

Put the olive oil now in the same pot. Return to medium-high heat. Add the garlic, onion, poblanos, and bell peppers and cook until tender, 6 to 8 minutes. Add the tomatoes, olives, thyme, Madeira, and red wine and simmer until the liquid has reduced by about one quarter, about 10 minutes. Add the vinegar.

Return the oxtails to the same pot if it is large enough to hold them and the liquids. If not, move them to a large enough vessel or cook it in two pots. It is important to have a vessel with a heavy "cast" to it so that the temperature is kept low and steady . . . the way braises work best.

Add the stock. Bring to a simmer over medium heat. Skim off and discard any fat that rises to the top.

Cover the pot with aluminum foil or a tight-fitting lid and braise in the oven for 3 to 3½ hours, until the oxtails are very tender and the meat slides off the bones.

continued →

Remove the oxtails to a side pan. Strain the braising liquid, first through a large-holed strainer and then a medium-mesh sieve. Let cool to room temperature, then refrigerate until cold, preferably overnight. Cover and refrigerate the oxtails, as well.

The next day, remove the fat cap and discard it. Put the braising liquid in a pot and bring to a simmer. Degrease as needed. Cook until it is reduced to 4 cups. Set aside. The oxtails and braising liquid may be prepared to this point a few days in advance if you prefer.

The best way to reheat this dish is in a vessel shaped so as to keep the prepared sauce fully surrounding the oxtails, which helps keep the meat moist and the sauce from cooking down too much. I like to use casserole dishes that snugly fit around the bones. Use two if you need to (which is especially smart if you are just cooking for two and want leftovers). Preheat the oven to about 325 degrees. Cover the casserole dish well with aluminum foil or a tight lid. Moisture is your ally here. When the oxtails are simmering in the sauce, after 25 to 30 minutes, remove them and serve them with the sides you wish.

> *Note:* The curry is quite delicate here and can be replaced by cumin or a combination of spices if you prefer.
>
> *Serving suggestion:* The Haitian Pikliz Slaw (page 218) is an excellent go-with. Rice or noodles are also perfect.

Pork Stew with Raisins, Tamarind, Plantains, and Chiles

The foods of faraway India became a part of the history of Florida and the Caribbean long ago. The Florida peninsula is filled with dishes that move beyond the expectations one might have in such a mix of southern, Latin, and Caribbean populations. But the enjoyment of dishes that, like curry-based ones, cool us off makes perfect sense in our sunny state.

Serves 4

2½ cups diced pineapple

3 tablespoons plus 3 tablespoons apple cider vinegar

½ jalapeño chile, seeded (or not, if a spicier stew is desired)

1 pound boneless pork shoulder, cut into 1-inch cubes, all gristle and silverskin discarded, fat left on

6 cloves garlic, thinly sliced

1 tablespoon finely diced ginger

Kosher salt

10 whole black peppercorns

6 whole cloves

¼ teaspoon ground cinnamon

½ teaspoon sesame seeds

¼ teaspoon turmeric

5 dried chiles de árbol, stemmed, seeds kept in

1 teaspoon cumin seeds

½ sweet onion, diced

1 tablespoon raisins

1 tablespoon tamarind concentrate (bottled, typically)

2 tablespoons peanut oil, or more if needed

1 maduro (very ripe) plantain, cut into ½-inch-thick slices

2 cups Chicken Stock (page 237)

½ teaspoon sugar

Toss the pineapple with 3 tablespoons of the apple cider vinegar and jalapeño and set aside to marinate.

Toss the pork, garlic, ginger, and 2 teaspoons salt in a bowl until the pork is coated. Set aside.

Toast the peppercorns, cloves, cinnamon, sesame seeds, turmeric, dried chiles, and cumin in a dry skillet over medium-high heat until fragrant, about 1 minute. Transfer to a spice grinder and grind to a powder.

Transfer to a food processor. Add the onion, raisins, tamarind, and the remaining apple cider vinegar. Blend well.

Heat the oil over medium heat in a heavy saucepan. Cook the plantains in the oil on both sides until golden. Drain on paper towels. Add the pork to the pan and cook, turning occasionally, until lightly browned on all sides, about 2 minutes, taking care not to burn the garlic and ginger (reduce the heat as necessary). Add a touch more oil if needed.

Reduce the heat to low. Add the spice mixture and stir vigorously until fragrant. Add the stock and sugar. Cover and cook over medium heat until the pork is tender, about 1 hour, stirring from time to time. (I like a glass, see-through lid for chores like this one. It keeps the moisture in if the lid is well fitted and it lets us keep an eye on things.)

Return the plantains to the pan and add the marinated pineapple with its juices, too. Cook for another 8 to 10 minutes so the flavors are nicely developed. Season if needed. Serve hot.

Serving suggestion: The pork can be served with simple white rice or Trini Rice with Coconut Milk (page 171). Due to the elements within the stew I also like to top garnish this dish with toasted unsweetened coconut, crispy plantain chips, a few raisins, and a bit of chopped raw chiles.

On "New World Cuisine"

"I stole everything I ever heard. But
mostly I stole from the horns."
—Ella Fitzgerald

As soon as I was nineteen and old enough to do
what I wanted, I got myself to south Florida. I
took a couple of detours, to be sure: a brief stint
of college in Hawaii, manual labor in Colorado
and Kansas, and work as a short-order cook in
an Illinois diner, before I settled into cooking
and made my way back down to Key West for
good. It was the early 1970s and in south Florida
I was coming in contact with the cuisine of the
Caribbean and Latin America on a daily basis.

When I eventually decided to become a pro-
fessional chef, I naturally gravitated to classic
French cuisine—that was what one did back
then. In the 1970s, regional American cooking
had few proponents. (It would be ten years before Alice Waters and Paul Prudhomme kindled
that fire.) I didn't have the money to attend
cooking school, but I did have the will to be
self-taught. One by one I bought the books that
would form the foundation of my education.
I read them like a jailhouse lawyer, sensing
they were my only hope of escaping the rough
lives of the cooks I encountered during the wild
and wooly days and nights in the first kitchens
I knew.

Initially I was deeply influenced by France's
"three-star chefs"—Roger Vergé, Alain Chapel,
Alain Senderens, the Troisgros brothers. Yet my
day-to-day eating experience was of vibrant
New World flavors—West Indian chutneys and
Central American plantains, Bahamian conch
salad and Cuban steak à *la parrilla*—in the cafés

and open-air market stalls of Old Key West.
Slowly but surely the magic of those foods and
their special language came to define me as
a chef.

There was, in fact, a defining moment in my
decision to become the chef that I am today; it
was one morning in 1987, as I sat on the deck
behind Louie's Backyard.

At this point I'd cooked in a lot of *joints*, and
I use that word purposefully. I'd been frying
eggs and barbecuing ribs even as I was ventur-
ing into the Cuban and Bahamian shacks and
cafés around Key West for lunch or a *café con
leche*. By the '80s I had become a chef and I was
running Louie's, long considered one of the best
restaurants in Key West. Louie's is situated in a
spot where the Gulf of Mexico meets the Atlantic Ocean. I was studying a stack of cookbooks—
French, Middle Eastern, southwestern, Italian—
in pursuit of dishes for my menus, when
I looked up to see a sailboat drifting southward.
I too drifted with it for some time, wondering
where it might be going and what the sailors
would see, touch, and taste when they got
there.

And just like that, I realized that it was time
for me to put away my books on the dishes of
other places. It was one of those moments of
complete clarity: as much as I had drawn from
the wisdom and artistry of hundreds of years
of European cuisine, it was now time for me to
express where and what I was living, and that
was Florida. South Florida, in particular.

I thought about how North America's music
had evolved, how its literature and architecture
and dance were amalgamations of cultures

... West Indian chutneys and Central American plantains, Bahamian conch salad and Cuban steak *à la parrilla* ...

bumping up against one another. Key West was a place where Spanish, African, and Anglo influences converged, yet the foods we were eating (including at my own restaurant) seemed almost frozen in time. No one had yet imagined what kind of fusion cuisine might result if those Atlantic cultures were expressed in food the way the cuisines of New Orleans, California, and the American Southwest were products of the different peoples who inhabited them.

I urge you to get in front of a map of the Caribbean and Central and South America. Compare it to the United States. Think about how different "our" foods are, not only from our southern neighbors', but even region to region, state to state, and city to city. You can't help but be struck by how many food experiences there are to be had in the enormity of that complex geography. The Americas are guided culinarily by a vast range of histories and an ever-shifting present tense.

My moment of clarity then became one of resolve. I closed up my books and stashed my notes. The sailboat was beyond the horizon now. I could *feel* Cuba just ninety miles away. The answer had been around me all along. I ate

it and drank it almost every day. My new teachers were going to be in the cafés and homes of south Florida, not in the books of France.

In the following weeks and months I went back to some of the same joints I'd eaten in many times since I had settled in Key West in 1973. I went to a restaurant called B's and another called La Lechonera, to El Cacique and to some places that had no names at all. I sat on stools at counters and ordered the Cuban-Bahamian fare. I pestered cops and fishermen and housepainters and housewives about what they were having. Often I asked them if they wouldn't mind translating a menu item for me. I earned the suspicion of many a waitress as I quizzed her and took notes on a little spiral pad. It got very exciting; I felt like I was cracking a case! Or solving a puzzle. With each meal I envisioned how it was cooked, and how I would adapt it to the things I loved from my own life experiences.

continued →

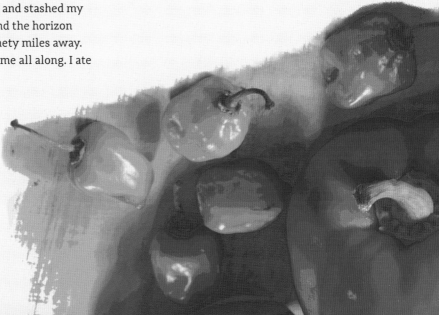

Less than a year after my epiphany on the deck, my friend and partner Proal Perry and I opened up an addition to Louie's Backyard. It was on the second story. I wanted an informal restaurant. I was offering then-unheard-of constructions like "*Mojo* Marinated and Roasted Chicken with Saffron Rice and Rioja Essence" and "Seared Tenderloin of Beef on a Bed of Crispy *Vaca Frita*" and "Grilled Florida Snapper with *Mojo Verde* and Plantain Curls." Diners at Louie's would come up when they heard I was now cooking at the Café, eye the menu, and typically head right back down the stairs to the more "cosmopolitan" food I had created in the original restaurant. Before they departed, however, they offered their opinions, and for a long while they went like this: "What, are you *crazy*? I'm not paying twenty bucks for black beans and yellow rice."

That was then, and we not only survived, but in the words of William Faulkner, we *prevailed*.

My dishes are not "authentic" dishes. I use history as a logical point of entry, but I cook with twenty-first-century openness. The best analogy I can think of is how the musician Ry Cooder approached his work with the Cuban musicians in the beautiful *Buena Vista Social Club*. Mr. Cooder is a talent who admires talent. He respected those men and women so much that he went down to their world to make great music. He played *with* them. That's how I like to feel about my approach to Caribbean and Latin cuisine. I'm not simply playing their music; we're making music together.

Happily, America's foods, eating habits, and cooking methods have evolved and diversified more in the last 25 years than in the previous 175. Think back to the 1970s and the shelves of any midsize city's supermarket. Most stores catered to what could be called the meat and potatoes diet. Simplicity dominated the menus of the day; variety was virtually nonexistent. Radicchio, arugula, and fresh herbs were unheard of in American cooking. No meat, fish, or produce was imported from abroad. Witness the same shelves today, filled with exotic foods, spices, and ingredients from the earth's far corners: salmon from Chile, prawns from Ecuador, steaks from Argentina, wild mushrooms from Italy, lamb from New Zealand, rare cheeses from France. The list is nearly endless.

This revolution in our food habits is even more dramatic when it comes to eating out. And I am not talking about sophisticated, world-class restaurants in major cities like New York, Chicago, and San Francisco. In inexpensive snack foods—what is now called the "fast" food movement—that phenomenon is startling. My friend Luis Zalamea told me a story that I find intriguing. In his prep-school days, a sophisticated classmate took him to the Italian district fringing Greenwich Village to a hole-in-the-wall food stand, the only place in New York where you could sample a new delicacy just introduced from Naples: pizza. To think that in little more than fifty years pizza has become one of the most popular foods in the world, with sales in the billions of dollars per year, and yet to recall its humble beginnings in America is to fathom the food revolution in this country. Similarly, Mexican cuisine has made itself a part of the quotidian American diet. *Antojitos*—Mexican snacks or appetizers such as tacos, enchiladas, burritos, and nachos—are readily available in take-out chains and inexpensive, family-friendly restaurants all over the United States. But the popularity of this type of Mexican fare is a double-edged sword, because it eclipses both the indigenous cuisine of Mexico as well as a more refined type of Mexican cuisine with a strong French influence from the period in the nineteenth century when Mexico was ruled by the Habsburg emperor Maximilian I. (It's even rare in Mexico, where it can be sampled only in aristocratic households and very few restaurants.) In the last two decades a talented group of Mexican chefs has attempted to revive the country's French-accented cuisine, as well as some of the exquisite dishes formerly served only to Aztec emperors. But these have been isolated efforts, lost in the powerful mainstream of the popular cookery I have already mentioned.

You begin to see how to speak of the cuisine of the New World in generic terms would be like reducing France's many unique culinary traditions to "French cooking." The pillars of New World cuisine, as it is known, are in pre-Columbian cultures, especially those of Peru and Mexico; in Africa, particularly in the Caribbean, Brazil, and southern United States; in Asia and the Pacific throughout the Americas to a subtler yet important extent; and, of course, in Europe.

Brazil is certainly an epicenter of New World cuisine, divided (like ancient Gaul) into three parts: the indigenous tribes, the African slaves, and the Europeans who subjugated them. Peru is another nexus of New World foods, blessed as it is with a vertical geography, from its coastline, supplied by the Humboldt Current with abundant fish and seafood, to the tropical fruits of the Amazon Basin jungles, to the tubers of its snow-capped peaks. These unique features resulted in a varied and opulent cuisine dating back at least six thousand years. Peruvian cuisine is like a wide channel fed by many tributaries: pre-Incan and Incan, European (Spain, Italy, France), plus Polynesian, Chinese, and Japanese.

The language and vocabulary of this cuisine is not one most of the readers of this book will have grown up with, but that is part of its allure. I find delicious the very sounds of these words: *ah-cahr-ah-zhay, shee-sheem, mo-ho, chi-fa*. To prepare for the pronunciation of many of these words you may want to drink a *mojito* first. My Spanish-speaking friends kindly congratulate me for even trying some of these words as they gently prompt me to get them right. That's all I'm asking of you. Just take it one day at a time and let the pleasure of these foods connect you to the New World of Latin American and Caribbean cooking.

Rhum and Pepper Painted Pork Belly
WITH MANGO-LIME COULIS

When I created a fish dish in the 1990s using the Rhum and Pepper Paint, it so got the attention of James Beard Award–winning writer Alan Richman that he claimed it to be one of the "Top 25" of the twentieth century. With hopes that you will like the paint in a new forum, I have joined it with meaty, fatty pork belly—a celebratory partnership. The refreshment of mango was also in that earlier creation. Like a good dance, decades can pass but a strong pairing goes on. *Saturday Night Fever* begat *Pulp Fiction*.

Note that the pork has to be marinated for two days before cooking to take in the Rhum and Pepper Paint.

Serves 10 to 12

3 pounds fresh pork belly, skin removed

2 cups Rhum and Pepper Paint (page 220)

¼ cup rendered bacon fat or canola oil

Mango-Lime Coulis (page 214)

Fresh-squeezed lime juice, if needed

Take the pork belly and lay it on a cutting board. Prick it in many, many places on both sides with an ice pick or fork but just puncture the *surface* of the skinned belly. Brush the "paint" all over the pork belly with a pastry brush (or just dip and rub it all over).

Set the pork on a rack for about 10 minutes to drain off excess paint.

Meanwhile, heat the bacon fat in a heavy pot over medium heat. Do not let it start smoking; just before it gets to that point, add the pork belly, laying it down carefully away from you. Cook, turning several times, until both sides are nicely browned.

Remove the pork belly from the pot and it set aside. Pour off the fat from the pot.

Preheat the oven to 375 degrees.

Transfer the pork, skinned side up, to a clean rack set over an aluminum foil–lined baking sheet or roasting pan. (This aids in cleanup.) Cover the pork with more foil.

Cook on the center oven rack until an instant-read thermometer inserted into the thickest part reads 145 degrees, about 1 hour. Remove the foil and return the pork to the oven for about 5 minutes to add a nice glossy exterior look to the roast. Remove it to a board to rest for 8 to 10 minutes.

When almost ready to serve, gently warm up the coulis. Feel free to squeeze a bit more lime in it if the flavor has become subdued.

Cut the pork into small rectangles and put each on a serving plate draped with some of the Mango-Lime Coulis. Serve.

Bourbon *Mojo* Roasted Pork

When Bourbon and *mojo* meet, it is as if the great Kentucky-born Cassius Clay/Muhammad Ali were taking on Cuban pugilism's near-mythical Teófilo Stevenson in some mighty match between deeply steeped cultural forces. Yet here an embrace, not a fight, results. This is not a pork roast you are trying to keep medium-rare or medium. The final internal temperature of the pork here will be well above the now "approved" 145 degrees we like for many pork dishes. This is *lechón asado* by another name, or *pulled pork* by another. The long cooking time inclines some folks to cook it overnight; in the end, it is more than worth the wait.

Serves 6 to 8 with leftovers

1 (7- to 8-pound) bone-in, skin-on pork shoulder roast

1 cup bourbon (this is *not* the time to pull out your treasured Pappy Van Winkle)

2 cups Classic Sour Orange *Mojo* (page 222)

2 sweet onions, peeled and sliced

Kosher salt and cracked black pepper

Notes: I like to baste the pork as it cooks. It requires some effort to pull that big hunk of pork out of the pan, retrieve the fatty-boozy liquid, and then pour it over, but it amps up the flavor so I want to mention it.

The pork we are using is alternatively called a pork butt or a pork shoulder, though in the United States the word *shoulder* more typically means the blade bone will still be present. We like the bone left in as it protects the moisture and hence the flavor.

Serving suggestion: I like it as is with Caramelized Pineapple Salsa (page 224) spooned over it. Candied Sweet Potatoes (page 165) would also be a fitting partner.

Remove the rind from the pork roast—the tough part (the hide) that is just above the fat. Take care to *leave ¼ inch of fat* intact, as it adds great flavor.

Score the fat (but not the meat) all over in a cross-hatch pattern. Pierce the meat with a small knife in about 30 places to help the marinade attain best effect.

Combine the bourbon and Classic Sour Orange *Mojo*.

Place the pork in a very large bowl (or a very large "food grade" plastic bag) and coat it all over with the bourbon mixture. Marinate in the refrigerator for 1 to 3 days, turning the pork over every day.

Remove the pork from the refrigerator at least 2 hours before you want to cook it.

Preheat the oven to 400 degrees.

Pull the pork out of the marinade and put it on a platter to allow all of the excess marinade to drain off. Discard the marinade. Scatter the onions in the bottom of a deep roasting pan. Add about 1 quart water to the roasting pan too. If you have a roasting rack, set that up over the onions. (You can effect a roasting rack with rolled-up aluminum foil to help keep the meat off the bottom of the pan.) Season the pork with salt and pepper all over and place it over the onions, fat side up.

Roast for about 45 minutes, then lower the oven temperature to 315 degrees and cook for 6 to 7 hours, until an instant-read thermometer inserted into the thickest part of the meat reads 180 degrees.

Transfer the pork to a cutting board with a catch basin and tent with aluminum foil. Let rest for 20 to 30 minutes before slicing. You will be able to slice about 6 "steaks" before the bone causes you to need to "assemble" portions. The small meat bits can also be made into all manner of other dishes. (Save the bone and freeze it for a bean or other soup one day.)

Pork Chops
with Lemonade

We love lemonade all over the South. In the great movie *Steel Magnolias*, lemonade is referred to as "the white wine of the South." (Perhaps true for some, but I know *I'm* not skipping *my* wine for it!) The lemonade in this case is going to make us a nice glaze for our brined and juicy pork chops. A rocking chair on a big breezy porch would be my idea of a perfect ending to a beautiful dinner. And a reprise of that movie for an added touch.

Serves 4

For the lemon reduction:

2 cups fresh-squeezed lemon juice

1 cup sugar

For the lemonade-soy glaze:

2 tablespoons soy sauce or tamari

2 cloves garlic, thinly sliced

½ tablespoon fresh thyme leaves

1 teaspoon ground cayenne

1 tablespoon dark toasted sesame oil

For the pork chops:

3 cups water

¼ cup apple cider vinegar

5 tablespoons firmly packed brown sugar

6 allspice berries

½ teaspoon crushed red pepper

1 dried chipotle chile, stem removed but seeds left in

1 tablespoon kosher salt, plus more for seasoning

1 tablespoon cracked black pepper

4 bone-in pork chops, about 1 inch thick (preferably from a great farm)

Vegetable or canola oil for the grill pan

Make the lemon reduction: Put the lemon juice and sugar in a blender and blend. Transfer to a heavy saucepan and cook over medium heat until reduced to about 1 cup.

Make the lemonade-soy glaze: Combine all the ingredients with the lemon reduction. If the glaze is a bit too sticky, whisk in a few drops of hot water. We want it the consistency of honey. Set aside.

Make the pork chops: In a bowl, combine 3 cups water, the vinegar, brown sugar, allspice, crushed red pepper, dried chipotle, and the 1 tablespoon salt. Stir until the sugar and salt dissolve.

Place the pork chops in a large sealable plastic bag and pour in the brine. Seal and refrigerate for 6 hours or overnight.

About 30 minutes before you plan to begin grilling, remove the chops from the refrigerator. Discard the brine, rinse the chops *briefly* in cold water, and pat dry with paper towels.

Preheat the oven to 425 degrees.

Season the chops with a bit more salt and the black pepper.

Heat a grill pan on the stove top over medium-high heat. Lightly oil it. Sear and partially cook two of the chops on the grill pan. When they are nicely colored on both sides, place them on a rack set over a baking pan. Repeat with the remaining two chops. Put the chops in the oven and roast for about 20 minutes, until they register 140 degrees on an instant-read thermometer.

Remove from the oven and add about 1 tablespoon of the lemonade-soy glaze to the top of each chop, spooning it on evenly. Return the pan to the oven for about 4 minutes. Remove and let the chops rest for 5 minutes before serving.

Note: If you'd like to get a little fancy, microplane or zest lemon across the chops just before serving. Scatter fresh thyme leaves over them too, if you like.

"After Church" Ham, Mac 'n' Cheese, and Coca-Cola Collards

Universal comfort foods join in a single dish here. If you add in the Pickled Roasted Gingered Beets (page 216), you would be prequalified for a genuine southern meat-and-three meal. The meat-and-three party is one of endless innovation tied to tradition at some juncture. Life in these United States is like that.

When families were larger than today's typically are, a whole ham would likely be the ham you'd be serving. And afternoons, often after church was over, would be leisurely ones around a loaded supper table. If you have the mouths to feed, please proceed with a whole ham. But if you want a meal that won't be Mark Twain's definition of eternity—"two people and a ham"—then a ham steak is your new and smaller friend.

We often will simply mix Mac 'n' Cheese and Coca-Cola Collards together in a single casserole and warm them in the oven before serving family-style.

Serves 4

1½ pounds ham steaks
(about 6 ounces per guest)

Cracked black pepper

3 tablespoons butter

½ Scotch bonnet or other chile, seeded and minced

½ sweet onion, thinly sliced

2 tablespoons light rum

½ pineapple, peeled, cored, and finely diced

1 cup pure pineapple or apple juice (from a juice bar or home juiced)

Kosher salt and black pepper

Mac 'n' Cheese (page 160), warmed

Coca-Cola Collards (page 161), warmed

Season the ham steaks with some black pepper (salt is already at play in the ham's cure). In a large skillet, working in batches if needed, heat the butter over medium-high heat until melted. Add the ham in a single layer and cook until a bit of color appears, turning to brown both sides; this will take 9 to 10 minutes total, but most of the cooking should be done on the first side. Gently remove to a platter or baking dish.

Add the chile and onion to the skillet you cooked the ham in and turn up the heat. When the onion is soft (allow 5 minutes, stirring from time to time), carefully add the rum and deglaze the pan. Add the pineapple and the juice and simmer until the pineapple is soft, about 10 minutes. Season with salt and black pepper to taste. (Salt will be more needed than pepper at this juncture. It might seem counterintuitive to add salt to fruit, but that is exactly the spice needed to balance things out.)

When just a bit of the liquid remains, turn the heat to very low. Slip the ham steaks into the skillet and cover. Don't allow the liquid to boil. You only want to warm the meat up.

Serve the warm side dishes on the side in casseroles and spoon the ham and its sauce on a platter to pass. Like church.

Chicken-Fried Veal Steak

WITH TOMATO GRAVY, TORN GREENS, AVOCADO, AND SOUR CREAM

The most famous way of doing a "chicken-fried" dish is with beefsteak, but the technique can be applied to a vast number of items. Alligator would make perfect sense if you were to line up a source. I've gone with veal, and that method of breading and shallow pan-frying the meat took me back to a dish I learned long ago while following Italian masters like Giuliano Bugialli and Marcella Hazen. The straight "steak" route often calls for a gravy of some kind, and I wanted to keep that tradition, as it is beloved here in the South. But I like to involve more vegetables, fruits (avocado in this case), and greens, which I think elevate the dish. It emulates the *costolette di vitello* lessons I received long ago. We southerners love Italy too.

Serves 4

For the tomato gravy:

3 tablespoons rendered bacon fat

1 cup finely chopped sweet onion

1 tablespoon minced jalapeño chile

2 cloves garlic, minced

2 tablespoons all-purpose flour

½ cup Chicken Stock (page 237), warmed

2 cups diced tomatoes (if using good canned tomatoes, drain off the liquid)

1 teaspoon fresh thyme leaves, roughly chopped

1 tablespoon Dijon mustard

Kosher salt and cracked black pepper

1 cup whole milk, warmed

2 teaspoons red wine vinegar

Make the tomato gravy: Heat the bacon fat in a large skillet over medium heat. Add the onion, jalapeño, and garlic and cook, stirring occasionally, for about 5 minutes. Sprinkle the flour over the onion mixture and cook, stirring constantly, for another 5 minutes.

Add the warm stock and bring just to a simmer. Add the tomatoes, thyme, mustard, and salt and pepper to taste. Return to a simmer. Add the milk and bring to a light boil; lower the heat to a simmer and cook, stirring often, for 2 minutes.

Add the vinegar. Season to taste. Puree this mixture in a blender; it is not necessary to strain it. Keep it warm in a clean saucepan while you cook the veal.

For the chicken-fried veal:

¾ cup all-purpose flour

1 tablespoon kosher salt

1 tablespoon cracked black pepper

1 teaspoon pimentón
(or good-quality paprika)

2 cups organic buttermilk

2 eggs, beaten

4 cups panko breadcrumbs, processed a bit smaller if desired (this helps the crumbs to adhere better)

1½ pounds veal scallopine, cut into 4 sections, pounded *thin*

Peanut or vegetable oil

¼ cup Parmesan cheese grated at warm room temperature (optional but it adds some umami notes)

For serving:

1 ripe avocado, peeled, pitted, and cut into cubes (optional)

2 handfuls of mixed lettuces and greens, cut into ribbons (chiffonade)

¼ sweet or red onion, thinly sliced

Our House Vinaigrette (page 225) or other favorite vinaigrette

Kosher salt and cracked black pepper

Sour cream

Make the chicken-fried veal: Preheat the oven to 350 degrees.

In a shallow dish, combine the flour, salt, pepper, and pimentón.

In another dish, whisk the buttermilk and eggs together.

In a third dish, lay in the panko crumbs.

Bread the veal by dipping first in the flour, then the buttermilk mixture, and then the panko.

Heat a large heavy skillet over medium heat and add about ¼ inch of oil. Add the veal to the hot oil (the oil should come about one third of the way up the veal) and cook until golden brown and cooked through, about 3 minutes per side, adjusting the heat as needed for a golden brown color. Place the veal on an ovenproof pan. Scatter the cheese, if using, over the veal. Keep warm in the oven while you prepare the plates. (If you take longer than expected, lower the oven or turn it off so as not to dry out the meat.)

Put the avocado, lettuces, and onion in a mixing bowl. Add enough of Our House Vinaigrette to lightly dress them. Season with salt and pepper if needed. Set aside.

Place a nice amount of the tomato gravy at the base of each plate. Spoon on some sour cream for added richness and some bright "color" at one point on the plate. Top the tomato gravy with the veal. Mound the lettuce mixture over the hot veal and serve quickly. When you work with two contrasting temperatures, speedy is the best way to go.

Lamb Vindaloo

Vindaloo was one of those words I felt was quite firmly positioned within the realm of Indian food. But upon study I came to learn that it started in the same land as adobos—Portugal—where marinating food in a *vinha-d'alho*—a mixture of vinegar with crushed garlic and seasonings that flavor and tenderize—was popular. The term *vinha-d'alho* in fact points directly at the presence of garlic (*alho* in Portuguese). In the 1600s, the Portuguese were busy discovering new lands, and Goa became a favored place with them. The Goans were a mix of Hindus and Catholics, but they were also much more capable of eating chiles than the folks from Portugal, so vindaloos were adapted in India before making their way back to the New World in a transformed state. The transformation continues . . . but a hefty dose of garlic remains intact in this simple paste for rubbing on a section of beef, chicken, pork, and even fish before cooking it. Here we do it with deep, delicious lamb.

Serves 6 to 8

For the vindaloo paste:

8 dried guajillo chiles, stemmed, cut open, and scraped of any seeds

1 tablespoon cumin seeds

½ tablespoon whole black peppercorns

¾ cup distilled white vinegar

6 tablespoons chopped peeled fresh ginger

6 cloves garlic, peeled and chopped

1 cinnamon stick

4 whole cloves

⅛ teaspoon ground cayenne

1 star anise

¼ teaspoon turmeric

1 teaspoon kosher salt

½ cup fresh-squeezed orange juice

Make the vindaloo paste: In a somewhat wide saucepan, toast the dried chiles, cumin seeds, and peppercorns over medium heat, turning the chiles until pliable and the cumin is fragrant, about 6 minutes. Add ⅓ cup water, the vinegar, ginger, garlic, cinnamon stick, cloves, cayenne, star anise, turmeric, and salt. Bring just to a boil. Turn off the heat.

Let stand until the chiles are soft, about 30 minutes. Discard the cinnamon stick and star anise. Transfer the chile mixture to a blender, add the orange juice, and puree to a smooth paste.

For the lamb:

2 pounds boneless lamb shoulder, cleaned of all silverskin and sinew, cut into 1-inch pieces

¼ cup canola oil

2 tablespoons unsalted butter

1 onion, diced

6 to 8 scallions, white and green parts, finely chopped

3 cloves garlic, minced

2 tablespoons fresh oregano leaves, chopped

1 Scotch bonnet chile, seeded and minced

1½ cups white wine

2 cups Chicken Stock (page 237) or lamb stock if you have it

14 ounces small waxy potatoes, cut into quarters

2 large carrots, peeled, halved lengthwise, and cut into ½-inch-thick half moons

14 ounces calabaza or butternut squash, peeled, seeded, and cut into large cubes

Kosher salt and cracked black pepper

Make the lamb: Preheat the oven to 350 degrees.

Rub the lamb pieces evenly with ½ cup of the vindaloo paste (save the rest in the freezer for next time). Cover and refrigerate for 4 hours or overnight.

Heat the oil in a large ovenproof skillet over medium heat. Drain the lamb and sear it, in batches, in the skillet for about 10 minutes, until lightly browned all over. Using a slotted spoon, transfer the meat to a clean bowl; leave the cooking juices in the skillet. (When working in batches you will likely need to add a bit more fat or oil to the pan as the first batch tends to soak it up. Add just enough to promote searing.)

Melt the butter in the pan and, working quickly, add the onion, scallions, garlic, oregano, and chile. Cook, stirring, for about 2 minutes.

Return all of the lamb to the pan and stir to coat well. Scrape up the browned bits from the bottom of the pan to keep all of the great flavor. Add the wine. Scrape the pan bottom again; the alcohol in the wine helps release the spice bits. Add the stock and bring to a simmer. Cook, uncovered, for 15 minutes.

Add the potatoes, carrots, and squash and season with salt and pepper to taste. Stir.

Cover the pan, place in the oven, and bake, stirring every 30 minutes or so, for 2 to 2½ hours, or until the meat is beginning to fall apart and the potatoes are tender.

Skim any oil off the top of the stew. Season again as desired. Serve.

Note: We have been getting lamb for many years from our friends John and Sukey Jamison at Jamison Farm out of Latrobe, Pennsylvania. To net the 2 pounds cleaned lamb you will need to buy about 2½ pounds.

Spatchcocked Chicken *Piri Piri*

Portuguese sailors were likely to have been the first to successfully map Florida, as documented in what historians and cartographers know as the Cantino planisphere. (A planisphere is a type of star charting device.) *Piri piri* is Swahili for "pepper pepper," and the chiles are thought to have been carried by Portuguese sailors leaving African colonies. So let us have power in *piri piri*, and let history rest a bit.

Serves 2 to 4

For the *piri piri*:

2 tablespoons bourbon

3 tablespoons extra-virgin olive oil

1 to 2 *piri piri* chiles, or 1 Scotch bonnet chile, seeded and minced

4 cloves garlic, minced

1 tablespoon smoked pimentón

¾ cup diced sweet onion

1 red bell pepper, diced

Kosher salt and cracked black pepper

Grated zest and juice of 1 lemon

½ cup loosely packed fresh Italian parsley leaves

For the chicken:

1 (3½-pound) best-quality chicken

Kosher salt and cracked black pepper

2 tablespoons olive oil or (even better) duck fat

Make the *piri piri*: Put a small saucepan on the stove and heat it over medium heat. Carefully add the bourbon and ignite it with a long match. Shake the pan as the alcohol burns off. Set aside.

Heat the oil in another saucepan over medium heat until it is quite warm. Add the chiles and garlic and stir for a moment. Add the pimentón. Stir. Add the onion and bell pepper. Add a bit of salt and pepper. Cook for about 8 minutes, stirring. Take care to scrape the bottom of the pan with a wooden spoon to keep the pimentón from sticking. (Our flat-edged wooden spoon is the favorite tool here.) We want the bell pepper to be fairly soft. Remove from the heat and let cool a bit.

Scrape the mixture into a blender or food processor. Add the lemon zest and juice, parsley, and bourbon and blend until smooth. Check for seasoning. Put the *piri piri* in a clean container. Cover and refrigerate until ready to use, up to 2 weeks.

Make the chicken: Preheat the oven to 350 degrees.

Cut the wing tips off the chicken and save them for stock. Use kitchen shears to cut out the backbone and save it for stock too. Using your hands, flatten the chicken. Cut out the keel bone and add it to the stock bones. Towel off any bits of remaining organ meat that might be left from the butcher shop and discard them.

Season the chicken all over with salt and pepper and then rub with the oil.

Wrap a clean heavy brick with aluminum foil. (We didn't have one so we used our Mexican *molcajete*, a heavy mortar. We simply made a square of foil and used it as a barrier between the bird and the *molcajete*.)

Heat a cast-iron pan (or other heavy skillet) large enough to hold the chicken flat over medium heat.

Place the chicken *skin side down* in your pan and weigh it down with the brick. Steadily brown/char the chicken on the skin side for about 20 minutes. Do not allow it to burn; adjust the heat as needed. Turn the chicken over and cook for about 15 more minutes, until slightly charred and golden on that side, too.

Remove the bird to a cutting board. Coat the chicken on the skin side with the *piri piri*; you may not need it all (save the rest in the refrigerator for another use). Put the chicken on a wire rack with a rimmed baking sheet under it.

Place it in the heated oven and cook for 10 to 15 minutes, until an instant-read thermometer reads 165 degrees. Set aside to rest for about 5 minutes.

Cut the chicken into pieces and serve.

Chicken and Rice Pilau with Pigeon Peas, Raisins, and Green Olives

If any constancy has been established in cuisine it has *not* been via this dish. Pilau adapts to ingredient changes and shifting of cultural gears due to the comforting, steady hands of the two main ingredients in this one-pot stew. It is perhaps, along with its Spanish cousin, arroz con pollo, the most emblematic of all Florida dishes. Add some shrimp if you have a mind to and you will probably earn unanimous support.

The first time I had this dish was during a classic college spring-break road trip. I joined a friend to crash at his parents' house in Jacksonville Beach. It took nearly a full twenty-four hours by Greyhound bus from central Illinois to reach our destination, where luckily we were allowed admittance to a church supper despite our long-haired look. (Even framing earnest faces, long hair was no way to ease the locals in 1971.) But we somehow charmed them, and we sat at a picnic table with fragrant plates of pilau, which soothed *all* participants. Two years later I was living in Key West and enjoying the dish's Cuban cousin just as much. Here is but one way to make this iconic Florida meal.

Serves 6 to 8

BASIC PIGEON PEAS

The famous dish Hoppin' John may actually be named for these peas. "A pigeon," when said with a certain accent, makes me think this is the case. What is certain is that pigeon peas are a great way to feed many folks from all over.

Makes about 2 cups

1 cup dried pigeon peas

1 bay leaf, broken

Kosher salt

Go over the pigeon peas to check for any small stones. Rinse them briefly and then soak in about 3 cups water overnight.

The next day, drain and place them in a medium pot with the bay leaf, cover with water, and simmer until tender, about 35 minutes.

Drain and discard any remaining liquid and the bay leaf. Season with salt to taste. Serve. These may be made a day or so in advance and kept in the refrigerator, or frozen for another time.

2 tablespoons butter

3 tablespoons light olive oil

3 cloves garlic, minced

½ to 1 Scotch bonnet chile, seeded and minced (datil chile peppers from the St. Augustine area would be great here if you can get them)

8 bone-in, skin-on chicken thighs (preferably free range, kosher, organic)

Kosher salt and cracked black pepper

1 large carrot, peeled and diced

1 poblano pepper, diced

½ sweet onion, diced

1 tablespoon smoked pimentón

2 tablespoons fresh thyme leaves, chopped; or 3 tablespoons chopped fresh basil or other subtler herbs

1 cup long-grain white rice, well rinsed and drained

1 cup unsweetened coconut milk

2 tablespoons apple cider vinegar

2 cups Chicken Stock (page 237), warmed

1 cup canned diced tomatoes with their liquid

½ cup raisins

2 tablespoons chopped fresh Italian parsley

¼ to ½ cup green olives, pitted and chopped (use less if you like a more subdued olive taste)

½ cup Basic Pigeon Peas (page 144; optional), warmed

¼ cup pickled peppadews (optional), chopped

In a large sauté pan, heat the butter and oil over medium heat until the butter melts. Add the garlic and chile and cook until quite fragrant.

Season the chicken with salt and pepper and add it to the pan. Sear on all sides, turning. Turn up the heat a bit to brown it as you do this (allow about 12 minutes).

Remove the browned chicken to a clean baking pan or dish and cover to keep warm. Scrape the loose bits of meat that might have grabbed the bottom of the pan. There is a lot of flavor there, so we want to keep it. I have a flat-bottomed wooden spoon that I love for this job. Leave those bits in the pan to become part of the overall flavor profile.

Add the carrot, poblano, onion, and pimentón. Season with a bit more salt and pepper. Sauté over high heat to remove the water from the vegetables, stirring, until the vegetables become slightly tender, about 4 to 5 minutes.

Add the thyme, rice, coconut milk, vinegar, stock, and half of the tomatoes. Stir.

When the mixture is just beginning to simmer, return the chicken to the pan, skin side up.

Lower the heat and cover with a tight-fitting lid. (If you don't have one that fits, use aluminum foil.) It is also important to be sure the heat is low so that the chicken is not subjected to anything close to boiling temperature. This also allows the rice to gently cook. Gently push the wooden spoon around the bottom of the pan one or more times during this cooking to prevent the rice from sticking and scorching. Cook about 20 minutes, or until the chicken reads about 140 degrees on an instant-read thermometer. There is more time on the stove ahead, so fear not: The chicken will be fully cooked by the end.

Add the raisins, parsley, olives, and the remaining tomatoes to the rice mixture. Stir gently. Season one more time to taste.

Cover and cook for about 15 more minutes, until the internal temperature of the chicken is about 160 degrees. (It will ride up in temperature after you remove it from the heat.) Serve or set aside, covered to keep warm, for up to 30 minutes before serving.

Notes: Since datil chiles are often hard to find, we like to offer a bottled datil chile hot sauce as a table condiment.

Recipes for this dish often call for a whole cut-up chicken. For a braise, though, we prefer all dark meat to keep things really moist.

"Koreatown" Fried Chicken

Koreatowns are not as big in Florida as in some states—but give it time. Korean chefs and home cooks are already offering dynamic twists on the ever-evolving axes of what I have long termed "New World cuisine." We make this chicken dish with an Eastern soy-based marinade and then we juke back to America with a buttermilk brine that then connects with a flour dredge to get that all-important crispiness of fried chickens everywhere.

Serves 2 to 4

¾ cup soy sauce

2 tablespoons sugar

½ cup ponzu

6 tablespoons Asian Spice Syrup (page 95), plus more for drizzling

¼ cup minced garlic

¼ cup finely chopped fresh ginger

1 high-quality chicken, cleaned and cut up into 8 to 10 pieces

About 2½ cups buttermilk (enough to submerge the chicken)

About 3 cups all-purpose flour (I would rather have plenty of flour than not enough when I dredge)

Vegetable, canola, or peanut oil for shallow-frying

Mix the soy sauce, sugar, ponzu, Asian Spice Syrup, garlic, and ginger in a bowl with a whisk to dissolve the sugar. Add the chicken pieces, cover, and put in the refrigerator to marinate overnight (if possible) or about 6 hours. When ready to cook, drain off and discard the marinade.

Place the chicken in the buttermilk and allow to soak for at least 4 hours or up to overnight in the refrigerator.

Put the flour in a large bowl or pan with enough room to work. Lift the chicken out of the buttermilk, letting the excess drip through a colander into the sink. Discard the buttermilk.

One piece at a time, dredge the chicken: Place it in the flour and push it around in the flour to evenly coat. (I like the word *dredge* in that it conveys a sense of deeply and thoroughly coating the chicken.) Put the chicken on a plate or, even better, a wire rack to allow air to circulate around the chicken, which helps make it more crispy. This can be done ahead of time and the chicken kept refrigerated. Sprinkle on a bit more flour just before frying, especially if any "balding spots" appear just before adding the chicken pieces to the hot oil.

When you are ready to cook, heat 1 inch of oil in a deep-fryer or 12-inch frying pan to 375 degrees.

When the oil is ready, add the chicken with tongs, *skin side down to start*. Drop the chicken away from you as you do this—and gently please. Start with the larger pieces. The oil temperature will drop. It ideally will be at 315 to 325 degrees *throughout* the cooking process. To start cooking, cover the pan with a splatter screen if you have one. (I favor the splatter screen method over

continued →

a non-see-through lid; I am more secure knowing I can keep my eye on hot bubbling fat!) Do not crowd the bird. Cook in two batches if need be. Many home kitchen stoves can't maintain a high enough heat, so working in two batches is a way to solve that. The oil needs to be able to swirl around the bird as she cooks. If cooking in batches, keep batch 1 in a warm oven on a wire rack as you cook batch 2.

Cook for about 20 minutes, turning the pieces after the first 5 minutes and thereafter from time to time. Remove the chicken when it has reached a deep golden brown and an interior temperature of 165 degrees on an instant-read thermometer. Place on a wire rack set up with a pan underneath to catch any oil drips until ready to serve. It's best to let the chicken sit for about 10 minutes after frying so that it reaches a good resting interior temperature as well as texture. Serve hot, drizzled with more Asian Spice Syrup.

Notes: For this recipe you may notice we do not season the dredging flour. The soy marinade and the Asian Spice Syrup we drizzle at the end supply *plenty* of flavor.

If you have bacon drippings you can flavor the oil by using a ratio of about ⅓ cup bacon fat to 2 cups oil.

The kind of frying here is termed "shallow-frying," which differs from deep-frying because the chicken "peeks" above the fat burbling away. The key to great frying is a steady temperature. You need to start high, for as soon as you drop that chicken in, the temperature drops sharply but should settle into the zone that makes for even cooking . . . as long as you keep the dial tuned to the right place. An instant-read thermometer is the tool you need here. Don't make the mistake of sticking the thermometer in the meat over and over, though, as it denatures the crust. The crispy crust is a marker of great fried chicken. The primary marinade with its dramatic power is what makes this a chicken to remember.

Serving suggestion: Drizzle some more Asian Spice Syrup on the chicken as it rests. (Warm it up some first.) You could also top with some chopped up thinly sliced scallions, torn cilantro, and a minced chile, or put them in the syrup at the last minute. The Corn Relish (page 215) is but one of a number of side items in the book to consider adding to the plate. It provides a note of sweetness to play against the soy, as well as acidity, which is welcome in the midst of chicken, skin, and deep-frying.

Chipotle BBQ Chicken

WITH NOT FRIED SWEET POTATO FRIES AND CARAMELIZED PINEAPPLE AND RAW TOMATO SALSA

I am looking forward to the great Orlando chef, our friend John Rivers, doing a version of this dish for the crowds that come to his fun chicken restaurant named "Coop." (I am sure the place would be even *more* jammed, though!) We work with two of our favorite effects here: the smoky heat of chipotles and the deeper sweetness of caramelization in luscious pineapple. There are American classics that fly above many others, and this bird is one of them. If I had to pick a "final day" it would feature a lot of blues music, the writing of Annie Dillard as well as *Mystery Train* by Greil Marcus, and a meal of barbeque like this. Just don't rush me to the door quite yet. I want to eat more.

Serves 4

1 (3½-pound) chicken, cut up into 8 or 10 pieces

Kosher salt and cracked black pepper

Chipotle BBQ Sauce (page 228)

Caramelized Pineapple Salsa (page 224)

Not Fried Sweet Potato Fries (page 164)

Season the chicken with salt and pepper and set it aside in the refrigerator uncovered for at least 1 hour and up to 3 hours to dry out the skin a bit. (This would be a good time to make the salsa if you haven't already.)

Heat an outdoor grill to medium, with a steady fire. Put the chicken on the grill grate, skin side down. When it is about halfway cooked, begin to baste it with the Chipotle BBQ Sauce. Continue cooking, turning and painting the bird, until it is not quite 165 degrees in the thigh meat. Remove from the grill and let rest for a few minutes.

Serve the chicken with the Caramelized Pineapple Salsa and the Not Fried Sweet Potato Fries alongside.

Barbeque's First State

There are few culinary subjects I can think of that stir such rabid debate—from Texas to Memphis to the Carolinas and back down to the Caribbean and South America—as the "true origins" of barbeque. Here's how I see it unfolding: Once upon a time at the dawn of humankind, small family circles and larger tribal structures evolved. Men, primarily, became the hunters, and women made what the men caught and killed edible by cooking it. From this hypothesis, we can logically assume the first pit-masters were probably *women*. (How's that for one?) The American journalist and author Waverly Root stated that cooking in this fashion was "so natural under primitive circumstances that it would practically invent itself everywhere, especially in societies accustomed to living outdoors most of the time."

The Caribe Indians, native to the island of Hispaniola, taught Spanish invaders how to use green wood lattices lashed to a framework for cooking meat over a smoldering fire; they called it *barbacoa*—or what we now know as *barbecue* or *barbeque*. A staple of the local diet was the wild hog. The Indians called the animals *boucan*, a word that eventually came to be applied to the lawless, seafaring islanders—or buccaneers.

The point often missed is that when talking about the noun *barbeque*, the discussion usually swirls around its New World origins as described by a sixteenth-century Spanish explorer, whereas the verb *to barbeque*, as an act, has been practiced since antiquity. Homer's *Iliad* mentions "spits" and "five-pronged forks" for roasting oxen, which were "basted with salt and wine."

The word *barbacoa* has been traced back to the Taino Indian dialect. (The now-extinct Tainos were a branch of the larger Arawak American Indian group.) The earliest appearance of *barbacoa* in print in Europe can be found in the *Summario de la historia natural o De la natural historia de las Indies*, by the Spaniard Gonzalo Fernández De Oviedo y Valdés following his travels in what is now Florida in the early 1500s.

In the New World, cooking outdoors persisted well into the modern era. In fact, this was the state of cooking throughout the Caribbean and Florida before the advent of air-conditioning. And the detached southern kitchen, an architectural feature ubiquitous to the plantations of the South, was developed not only to prevent the all-too-common kitchen fires from spreading to main living quarters but also as a way of maintaining social and deeper boundaries. My second job was in a kitchen in Key West that had a detached barbeque pit area. The man who taught me how to cook meat over fire was a black gentleman who

He had learned to cook in the time-honored method of his ancestry…

went by the moniker Bicycle Sammy. He had learned to cook in the time-honored method of his ancestry, which, in most opinions, is the one that matters. (The way I see it, barbeque has done, and continues to do, more to bridge the divides of the past than any amount of speechifying.)

Say what you want about beef and bar-beque—but in Florida, it is pig meat that we squeal over. And while it might be our "inside voices" squealing, make no mistake, it is primal, porcine pleasure we set up the fires for! Some theorize that roasted pig was another one of history's happenstances that rewrote the game plan for our edible preferences. It has been said that in ancient times, an accidental fire on a pig farm in China engendered the pleasures of well-flamed porkers. And here in Florida, the so-called Chinese Box has become the totem for many a backyard barbeque. Marketed under the name Caja China ("Chinese Box" in Spanish), this wonderful grill is responsible for countless meals across the state. I've even exported a few Caja Chinas to Los Angeles and presided over some wildly popular pork parties on Sunset Strip—proving yet again that all the world over, nothin' says lovin' like pork from a coal-burnin' oven!

Roasted Duck with Sorghum and Benne Seed Gastrique

Sorghum? Benne seeds? Some eyebrows raised when I mentioned our creating this dish via my Facebook page. Louis Osteen, my longtime chef-friend and Pillar of Southern Cooking, wrote in from his restaurant in South Carolina when he saw my posted photo of this dish to kiddingly ask, "Little Low Country creepin' in there, Norman?" I laughed and wrote him back, "Louis! Florida is the state of cultural bridges. We like the 'flow' from all directions!"

This dish pays homage to a slightly more distant past than many of mine. But I will not deny our multiculturalism from the distant or the near. Flavor is my "boss" and "scripture."

Serves 2 with leftovers

For the duck:

1 (4- to 5-pound) duck, rinsed and patted dry, giblets removed and saved for another use

3 tablespoons Escabeche Spice Rub (page 220)

1 orange, cut in half

1 long sprig fresh rosemary

1 head garlic, cut in half

For the sorghum and benne seed gastrique:

½ poblano or other chile, seeded and diced

2 shallots, diced

3 cups fresh-squeezed orange juice

⅓ cup fresh-squeezed lemon juice

½ cup sherry vinegar

½ cup sorghum syrup

1 tablespoon smoked pimentón

½ teaspoon kosher salt

½ teaspoon cracked black pepper

1 tablespoon soy sauce

1 tablespoon benne seeds (aka sesame seeds), lightly toasted in a dry skillet (I like organic ones for deep flavor)

¾ cup Chicken Stock (page 237; optional)

Note: The gastrique can be made a day or two in advance with the spice-rubbed duck and also kept refrigerated.

Start the duck: Remove the excess fat from the bird as well as some of the skin flap near the neck area. Take a sharp knife and prick the skin all over—but only skin deep. Rub the Escabeche Spice Rub all over the duck as well as inside the cavity. Place the orange, rosemary, and garlic in the duck's cavity. Tie the legs together with butcher's twine. Place on a rack set in a roasting pan and refrigerate uncovered for 1 to 2 days. (Leaving the duck uncovered helps promote a crispy skin.)

Make the sorghum and benne seed gastrique: In a heavy saucepan, combine the poblano, shallots, orange and lemon juices, vinegar, sorghum, pimentón, salt, and pepper and bring to a boil. Reduce the heat to a simmer and cook for about 20 minutes. Let cool for about 5 minutes, then strain through a medium-mesh sieve.

Add the soy sauce and benne seeds and set aside. (If more "meatiness" is desired, add the stock.)

Finish the duck: Take the spice-rubbed duck out of the refrigerator a few hours before you are ready to cook.

Preheat the oven to 350 degrees.

Roast the duck on the rack in the pan for 1½ to 2 hours, turning it over every 30 minutes and also removing the duck fat from the roasting pan. (This step will be much needed the first and possibly second time, when the fat is flowing. The duck fat that accumulates can be saved for other cooking projects.)

When the duck is close to temperature (about 130 degrees when measured with an instant-read thermometer deep in the thigh), reheat the gastrique. When the gastrique is thick enough to coat a spoon, take the duck out and baste it with the gastrique 8 to 12 times. Return the duck to the oven and baste about every 15 minutes, turning to cover the entire bird. Cook until the temperature reaches 165 degrees. Remove the duck from the oven and let rest, underneath tented aluminum foil, for about 10 minutes.

When ready to serve, cut the backbone off the duck using poultry shears. Remove the legs and cut away the thighs. Place on a warm platter. Slice the breast meat and add it to the warm platter. Serve with the remaining gastrique alongside in a bowl.

Cornbread-Stuffed Quail

WITH STRAWBERRY-ANCHO-GUAVA JAM AND SWEET AND SOUR PARSNIPS

One of the great honors I've had was to represent the state of Florida at the 2015 Milan Expo for American Food 2.0. The group of chefs selected—known as the United States' "Culinary Dream Team"—all are recognized by the James Beard Foundation and/or the International Culinary Center and are also members of the American Chef Corps, an initiative launched by the U.S. Department of State to elevate the role of culinary engagement in America's formal and public diplomacy efforts. This who's-who of chefs included Daniel Humm, Mary Sue Milliken, Hugh Acheson, and David Kinch. One of the courses we cooked featured this dish, and I loved seeing our Italian chef counterparts taste the "jam" with which we glazed our fat, cornbread-stuffed quail. Eye-popping smiles are a universal language.

Serves 4 as an entrée (2 quail per person), or 8 as an appetizer (1 quail per person)

For the stuffing:

½ cup currants

⅓ cup port wine

14 Corn Sticks (page 241), or 13 ounces cornbread, cut and/or broken into bite-size pieces

3 tablespoons butter

2 tablespoons olive oil

1 clove garlic, minced

½ poblano pepper, seeded and finely diced

2 ears corn, kernels cut off the cob

Kosher salt and cracked black pepper

½ cup diced red onion

1 cup diced fennel

½ cup diced red bell pepper

1 tablespoon chopped fresh sage leaves

1 cup toasted shelled unsalted pistachios, roughly chopped

½ cup organic white miso

Make the stuffing: Soak the currants in the port for about 30 minutes.

Put the broken-up 14 Corn Sticks in a large mixing bowl.

Heat a large skillet and add some of the butter and oil. When the butter has melted, add the garlic and poblano. Stir well. Add the corn. Season with salt and pepper and cook over medium-high heat until the corn is lightly browned, about 5 minutes. Add this to the 14 Corn Sticks. Stir well.

Put the remaining butter and oil in the skillet and place over medium heat. When the butter melts, add the onion, fennel, and bell pepper. Season with salt and pepper and cook until lightly browned, 6 to 8 minutes. Add to the cornbread along with the sage.

Drain the port off the currants into a small skillet and cook over medium-high heat until reduced to a consistency thick enough to coat the currants. Now coat them. Add the pistachios and currants to the cornbread mixture. "Rub" in the miso. Mix all together. Season to taste (miso adds some salt, so taste before adding more) and set aside.

For the quail:

8 quail, semi-boneless, lightly rinsed from the package and dried with paper towels

2 tablespoons butter, softened

Kosher salt and cracked black pepper

Canola oil

For serving:

Strawberry-Ancho-Guava Jam (page 227)

Sweet and Sour Parsnips (page 158) or another side of your choice

Make the quail: Preheat the oven to 400 degrees.

Stuff the quail with the stuffing. Tie the legs together. Smear the butter around the outside of the quail. Season them with a bit of salt and pepper. Set aside. (This can be done a few hours ahead of time; cover and refrigerate the quail, then remove them from the fridge about 30 minutes before cooking.)

Heat a heavy ovenproof skillet large enough to fit all of the quail over medium heat. When the pan is hot, add oil to coat the bottom of the pan and add quails, one by one, breast side down. Brown them on all sides. Drain off and reserve the excess oil and place the birds breast side up in the skillet in the oven.

After 4 to 5 minutes, remove the skillet from the oven and baste the quail with the fat from the skillet to promote a crisp skin. Remove any excess fat again. Dab the birds with a dry towel, which will help the sauce adhere. Spoon and brush some of the Strawberry-Ancho-Guava Jam on them. Return to the oven and cook until nicely colored, about 8 minutes. Serve more of the jam on the side. Serve on warm plates or a communal platter with the Sweet and Sour Parsnips.

> *Notes:* Quail can be ordered online. D'Artagnan is an excellent source for all manner of specialty items. Cornish game hen is a fine substitute, though you'll have to cook them longer. For simplicity in eating, the *semi-boneless* quail are a good choice and what we use.
>
> Don't feel you need to make the 14 Corn Sticks to make this stuffing. Any simple good cornbread from your own favorite recipe will be fine.

8

'N' THREES

Side Dishes

Sweet and Sour Parsnips

When I pick up parsnips in markets, some fellow shoppers actually stop and ask me, "How do you prepare them?" They are as easy to prepare as the ubiquitous carrot and often a notch sweeter. For that reason they take well to the lift of acidity in our "sweet and sour" dish here.

Serves 4

1½ pounds peeled parsnips

3 tablespoons olive oil

1 tablespoon extra-virgin olive oil

1 tablespoon butter

1½ tablespoons sugar

1 teaspoon ground cumin

Kosher salt and cracked black pepper

¼ cup balsamic vinegar

1 tablespoon grated lemon zest

Cut the parsnips into largish "logs," about 2¼ inches long and ½ inch thick. Being slightly uneven is okay. Charming, in fact.

Heat the olive oils and butter in an 11-inch skillet over medium heat. Add the parsnips. Stir to coat with the fats and cook, covered, shaking and stirring from time to time, until the parsnips are glossy and easily pierced with the tip of knife, 8 to 10 minutes.

Add the sugar, cumin, and salt and pepper to taste. Cook, uncovered, for 5 minutes, stirring from time to time.

Drain or blot off the excess oil and discard it. Add the vinegar. Put the lid back on the pan. Cook, stirring, for 5 minutes.

Remove from the heat and add the lemon zest. Serve, or transfer to a casserole dish and place in a low oven or off to the side until ready to serve.

> *Serving suggestion*: This is a fine side dish for many occasions. We use it in our Cornbread-Stuffed Quail with Strawberry-Ancho-Guava Jam and Sweet and Sour Parsnips (page 154).

Grits, 'Snips, and Chips

It was the whiteness and sweetness of parsnips that inspired me to join them with the whiteness and nurturing goodness of grits. They also are sweet like carrots, so with the garnish of some salted chips we have a fine triad of balance. Parsnips need to be more widely enjoyed! If you have not yet fallen for them, once you peel them and note their fragrance you will see why I think so. The chips? They just look great on top of the kind of bland landscape of grits. Then couple that with the contrast in textures and it all makes sense. And if food doesn't make sense I don't keep coming back to it.

Serves 6 to 8

For the parsnips:

8 ounces parsnips, peeled and diced (about 1½ cups)

1 cup heavy cream

1 cup whole milk

2½ tablespoons kosher salt

For the grits:

2 teaspoons kosher salt

2 tablespoons unsalted butter

1 cup stone-ground white grits

½ cup whole milk, warmed

For serving:

Crushed-up best-quality store-bought potato chips or homemade

Grated Parmesan cheese (optional)

Make the parsnips: Put the parsnips in a heavy saucepan and bring to simmer with the cream, milk, and salt. Take care to stir and be sure the parsnips don't "grab" the bottom—with starchy roots such as these, it is possible and simply stirring takes care of that. When the parsnips are soft, after 10 to 15 minutes, remove from the heat and drain the cream off into a bowl. Put the parsnips and 1 cup of the reserved cream in a blender and puree until smooth. Set aside, covered to keep warm. Reserve the remaining "parsnip-enriched liquid" for reheating the grits if needed.

Make the grits: Bring 4 cups water, the salt, and 1 tablespoon of the butter to a boil in a 3- to 4-quart heavy saucepan. Add the grits rather gradually, stirring constantly with a wooden spoon. Once the grits are all in the water, reduce the heat and cook at a bare simmer, covered, stirring frequently, until the water is absorbed and the grits are thickened, about 15 minutes.

Stir in the milk and the remaining 1 tablespoon butter and simmer, stirring to keep grits from sticking to bottom of pan, until the liquid is absorbed, about 10 minutes.

Fold in the parsnip puree. Season with salt if needed. Set aside in a bain marie, covered, if you're not quite ready to serve. If needed, stir in a little of the reserved parsnip cooking liquid to loosen the grits.

To serve, spoon the hot grits into serving dishes. Top with the chips. Add cheese if you'd like. Serve.

Note: I have made "chips," more aptly named *crisps*, with parsnips. They are a fine garnish if you want to take that step and move away from the ease of a store-bought bag of chips. To make them, create strips of the parsnips with a vegetable peeler or use a mandoline, shaving them into thin wafers as you would for potato chips. Rinse in cold water. Drain them well and then spin dry in a salad spinner. Set up a deep-fryer with immaculate oil and heat the oil to 350 degrees. Add the parsnips, taking care, as they do hold on to some water. If the oil ever comes up quickly, push the fryer pan off the heat until the oil subsides. Cook until you see they are nicely browned. Take a wire strainer and lift them into a bowl lined with paper towels. Season with a bit of salt and pepper. Of course, you could also make homemade potato chips for this recipe too.

Mac 'n' Cheese

It is probable and even *reasonable* to wonder why we include a recipe for mac 'n' cheese when there are so many in the world. But as ours fits so beautifully when actually mixed into *our* collard greens recipe we didn't want to err on the side of such practical thinking. It is also a nice and simple version of the classic dish without the collards.

Serves 4 to 6

For the cheese sauce:

1 cup shredded Manchego cheese

1 cup shredded white cheddar cheese or other similar cheese

1 teaspoon Dijon mustard

Kosher salt and cracked black pepper

1¼ cups whole milk

1¼ cups heavy cream

3 tablespoons rendered bacon fat or olive oil

½ to 1 jalapeño chile, seeded and minced

1½ tablespoons all-purpose flour

For the macaroni:

8 ounces elbow macaroni

Make the cheese sauce: Put the cheeses, mustard, and 1 teaspoon salt and 1 teaspoon pepper, or more to taste, in a large bowl.

Combine the milk and cream in one saucepan, bring to a simmer, and then keep it warm.

Heat the bacon fat in a large heavy saucepan over medium heat. Add the jalapeño and cook until softened. Add the flour, whisking well, and cook for about 3 minutes.

Add the warm milk and cream slowly in a few stages. This helps allow the dairy to assimilate into the newly formed roux. Bring to a boil and cook, whisking, for 5 more minutes to cook out the raw flour. Strain this creamy mixture though a fine-meshed sieve into the cheese mixture. Stir all together to melt the cheeses and combine well. Set aside while you cook the pasta.

Make the macaroni: Cook the macaroni in a large pot of rapidly boiling salted water until al dente. Drain, but do not rinse it. Mix the macaroni with the creamy cheese sauce. Taste for seasoning and serve.

> *Note*: If you want to make this into a gratin kind of dish you can scrape it into lightly buttered individual baking dishes (or one large one), top with breadcrumbs and grated Parmesan cheese, and bake in a 350-degree oven until bubbling and crusty, 15 to 20 minutes. But creamy and simple is good too.

Coca-Cola Collards

Coca-Cola, as most everyone knows, was invented in the South. Dr. John S. Pemberton, a former Confederate colonel wounded in the Civil War, became addicted to morphine and began a quest to find a substitute for the dangerous opiate. His first version was Dr. Tuggle's Compound Syrup of Globe Flower. Some many years later he took a syrup he made to his neighborhood pharmacy and mixed it with carbonated water. That was one hell of an "*aha*" moment! Using Coke in savory cooking has been going on for nearly as long.

Serves 6 to 8

¾ cup finely diced bacon

2 tablespoons olive oil

1 sweet onion, thinly sliced

6 cloves garlic, minced

2 teaspoons crushed red pepper

¾ cup dark brown sugar

6 tablespoons balsamic vinegar

1 tablespoon Creole mustard

2 pounds cleaned (stems removed) collard greens, cut into 2-inch pieces

2 cups Chicken Stock (page 237)

1 (28-ounce) can whole tomatoes

1 quart Mexican Coke (preferred for the nature of the sugar in that type)

A sachet containing 1 bunch fresh thyme, 12 whole black peppercorns, and 1 broken bay leaf

Kosher salt and cracked black pepper

Note: When we combine this with our Mac 'n' Cheese we call it the "Mac Daddy."

Cook the bacon in a large pot over medium heat with the oil. When the bacon is fairly crisp, add the onion, garlic, and crushed red pepper and cook for about 3 minutes. Add the brown sugar, vinegar, and mustard and cook, stirring, until the onion is very soft and browned, about 10 minutes.

Add the collard greens and allow to wilt for about 5 minutes. Add the stock, tomatoes, Coke, and sachet. Reduce heat and simmer for about 1 hour, until the collards are tender.

Drain the greens in a colander set over a saucepan, add the sachet to the liquid, and cook the liquids over medium-high heat until it reaches a "clinging" consistency, 20 to 30 minutes. Season with salt and pepper to taste. Strain over the greens. Serve hot.

Miso BBQ Carrots

Another name for this Asian-styled barbeque could be "Fifth Taste," in that it is made with miso paste. Miso is a powerful umami connector! So get your BBQ pals over and teach them something new about that ancient and lovable outdoor "sport."

Serves 4 to 6

For the miso BBQ sauce:

2 cups fresh-squeezed orange juice, cooked until reduced to about ¼ cup syrup, cooled somewhat

½ cup Koshi miso paste (we use Marukome Boy Koshi Smooth Paste)

2 tablespoons dark toasted sesame oil

1 tablespoon soy sauce

½ cup kecap manis (sweet soy sauce)

1½ teaspoons minced garlic

2 tablespoons minced ginger

2 tablespoons apple cider vinegar or rice vinegar

2 tablespoons honey

1 tablespoon *nuoc mam pha san* (a mixed fish sauce; optional)

½ teaspoon *yuzu kosho* paste (optional; it adds spice and citrus power)

Make the miso BBQ sauce: Whisk all of the ingredients together very well. Adjust the seasonings as desired.

For the carrots:

2 tablespoons butter

2 tablespoons olive oil

1 scant cup thinly sliced shallots

Kosher salt and cracked black pepper

3 cups peeled and sliced carrots (cut on a bias; 5 or 6 carrots)

Note: You will only need about ¼ cup of the BBQ sauce for this particular recipe, but the untouched part is capable of lasting a month or more in the fridge. It can be used for more batches of this side dish or as a glaze on a host of things you would love a bit of an "exotic" BBQ flavor on.

Make the carrots: Melt 1 tablespoon of the butter with 1 tablespoon of the oil in a 7-inch-wide sauté pan over medium-high heat. (Choose a pan that is not so large that the vegetables will potentially overcaramelize but also not so small that they will be too crowded and oversteam.) Add the shallots and stir well but only *once* to evenly coat them. Lower the heat to medium and cook until the shallots are caramelized evenly. Stir only a bit again. Season lightly with salt and pepper to taste.

Remove the shallots to a plate or bowl. Do not clean out the sauté pan. Add the remaining 1 tablespoon oil and 1 tablespoon butter, as well as the carrots. Cook the carrots over medium heat, stirring only a bit, for 5 to 7 minutes. Season them lightly, then put a lid on the pan to help soften the carrots somewhat. Cook for about 5 more minutes.

Add ¼ cup of the miso BBQ sauce (save the rest for another use; see Note) and stir. Let the carrots glaze and heat for about 2 minutes. Return the shallots to the pan. Taste and season to your preference. Serve hot.

Cauliflower in a "Cali" Way

The Colombian population has been growing steadily in south Florida. Understanding the subtleties in variations of Latin cuisine has taken me time, having not been born of those lands, but the trail has been a very tasty one! One stop here is *chorreada* or *chorreadas*, a very melodic word that Colombian people use for a cheese sauce. It sort of means "flowing," so we play with that in the reference to Santiago de Cali, which is the world capital of salsa music. In Colombia the more common items that are coated in this delicious way are potatoes. I like it with them but I also like it with a vegetable that adores cheese. This one.

Serves 4

3½ cups small cauliflower florets

Olive oil, just to lightly coat the cauliflower

Kosher salt and cracked black pepper

3 tablespoons butter

½ sweet onion, diced

½ cup diced ripe or canned tomatoes (drained if canned)

⅔ cup heavy cream

5 ounces Swiss cheese, shredded

Preheat the oven to 350 degrees.

Put the cauliflower in a mixing bowl, season with the oil and salt and pepper to taste, then transfer to a nonstick baking pan. When the oven is ready, roast the cauliflower for 10 to 15 minutes, until the florets are just soft to the bite. Set aside.

While the cauliflower is roasting, make the sauce: Melt the butter in a large sauté pan over medium heat. When it foams a bit, add the onion and cook until lightly browned on the edges, about 8 minutes. Add the tomatoes and heat through.

Add the cream and bring to a simmer. Season with a little salt and pepper. Stir in the cheese. Allow to melt and cook for another 3 minutes, stirring constantly.

Add the cauliflower and either serve or set aside until you are ready (heat through just before serving).

Not Fried Sweet Potato Fries

This is a simple recipe, but it does require careful monitoring. When you cook with butter-coated foods, the temperatures and cooking times will vary. So while we do ask for 30 minutes of cooking time, you need to keep a watchful eye. Butter is a harsh mistress! But . . . she has proven charms.

Serves 4

½ cup (1 stick) unsalted butter

2 cloves garlic, minced

2 teaspoons Escabeche Spice Rub (page 220)

2 sweet potatoes, peeled, cut into somewhat thin sticks (like you would for French fries)

1 teaspoon ground dried ancho chile

Kosher (or other coarse) salt

Preheat the oven to 450 degrees.

Melt the butter. Discard the foam as it rises to the top. Add the garlic, Escabeche Spice Rub, and ground chile to the melted butter. Stir well.

In a large bowl, toss the sweet potatoes in the butter mixture. Put them on a baking sheet lined with parchment paper or aluminum foil and bake for about 30 minutes, shaking the pan halfway through, until the fries are nicely colored on the edges. Cooking times can vary, so keep an eye on the sweet potatoes.

Remove from the oven. Season with salt to taste and allow to sit in the pan for about 5 minutes to come to full flavor and texture. Serve.

> *Note*: In dishes like this, where the spice plays a starring role, it's especially important that your spices be fresh and of the highest quality. I'd suggest purchasing spices with the same arduous circumspection one would employ when purchasing fish or meats.

Candied Sweet Potatoes

I read Ralph Ellison's monumental book *Invisible Man* while I was a young cook during a dreamy spell of time back in Key West. The writer recalls buying sweet potatoes, a term now used nearly interchangeably with yams, from a street vendor's cart in Harlem and how it propelled him back to memories of his youth and cooking the honeyed spud in the fireplace. He wrote of having them with pork roast, in a "pocket of dough," and even cold. One of the other ways he had them was candied. I set about to make my own version from that day immersed in Ellison's rich words. It is worthwhile getting sorghum in your pantry if you have not had it before. It makes the dish distinctly southern in flavor.

Serves 4

2 to 3 sweet potatoes (about 1¾ pounds), peeled and cut lengthwise into planks

Kosher salt and cracked black pepper

⅓ cup firmly packed brown sugar

⅓ cup sorghum syrup

¼ cup water

3 tablespoons butter, plus more for the casserole dish

1 teaspoon vanilla extract

¼ cup pecans, toasted and roughly chopped

Grated zest of ½ orange

Preheat the oven to 350 degrees.

Put the sweet potatoes in a large, wide pan and cover with salted water. Bring to a boil, then lower the heat just a bit. Cook until barely soft, 15 to 20 minutes. Remove them from the water and allow them to drain well. Blot off all the water with a clean towel.

Arrange the planks slightly overlapping in a buttered baking dish. Season with salt and pepper.

Combine the brown sugar, sorghum, water, and butter in a saucepan. Bring to a boil, then lower the heat and simmer for 5 minutes, stirring occasionally, making sure not to burn the syrup. Add the vanilla.

Pour this syrup over the sweet potatoes and place the dish in the oven. Pull them out after 15 minutes and baste a few times. Top with the pecans and orange zest and return to the oven. Bake for another 15 minutes, basting occasionally. Serve hot.

Note: There are many varieties of sweet potatoes in the markets. Explore and taste. The Japanese ones look blander but are actually packed with natural sweetness.

The Blackest of Beans

Only recently did I find out I actually liked *canned* black beans. They are a convenience food I have now allowed in. For a chef, that is not often the case, control freaks that we often are. If I loved having black beans before, you might know that now I can have them even more often, and without either twenty-four hours' notice or a pressure cooker. The reason they become "blackest" is due to the uncommon second step of draining the beans kind of midway and reducing the newly created "bean broth" to a divine and dark syrup of sorts that ultimately goes back into the beans.

Makes 2¾ cups; serves 6 to 10

4 tablespoons butter

3 tablespoons vegetable oil

2 ounces bacon, finely diced (about ½ cup; optional)

4 cloves garlic, minced

1 to 2 jalapeño chiles, seeded and diced (about ¼ cup)

½ sweet onion, peeled and finely diced

1 dried chipotle chile, split in half, stem discarded but seeds left in

1 tablespoon toasted and ground cumin seeds

½ tablespoon toasted and ground black peppercorns

1 bay leaf, broken

½ cup sherry vinegar

½ (750-ml) bottle dry sherry or white wine

2 cups drained but not rinsed canned black beans

4 cups Chicken Stock (page 237) or vegetable stock

Kosher salt and cracked black pepper

Heat a large rondeau or Dutch oven over medium heat. Add the butter and oil. When the butter stops foaming, add the bacon and cook until the fat has rendered. Add the garlic and jalapeños and cook, stirring, for 30 seconds or until very fragrant.

Add the onion, dried chipotle, cumin, black pepper, and bay leaf and cook until nicely aromatic, 5 to 8 minutes.

Add the vinegar and wine. Simmer for a few minutes, allowing the liquid to reduce by over half.

Add the beans. Stir to coat. Stir in the stock and bring to a *brief* boil. (Canned beans are already cooked, so we are just pulling the starches out before the next step.) Skim off any impurities that come to the surface.

Drain the beans, reserving the cooking liquid. Season the beans with salt and pepper to taste. Discard the bay leaf. Set the beans aside.

Put the bean liquid back in the cooking pan and bring the liquid to a high simmer. Cook for about 20 minutes, keeping a close eye on it toward the end, until about 1 cup remains. Pour the liquid over the beans and set aside to cool a bit before serving.

Fried Okra

I didn't grow up with okra, and I know some folks have not crossed over into the okra-loving camp *yet*. That is a shame, as you might have been told. When it is as crisp and fresh as this there is absolutely no problem with the feared texture some bring up in conversation. But I will say that the planning should be such that, moments after the crispy fried pods are drained on paper towels, they are in the guests' hands or on their forks. When I posted a picture of them online cooked to a golden hue and garnished with the very *non*traditional Korean seaweed I happened to have on hand, there was lot of positive reaction! So I offer them as a snack, a side, or a garnish just to show this southern staple's versatility.

Serves 8 to 12

¼ cup buttermilk

Kosher salt and cracked black pepper

1 pound fresh, firm okra, stems trimmed off

½ cup all-purpose flour

6 tablespoons stone-ground yellow cornmeal

½ teaspoon ground cayenne

Canola oil for frying

In a large bowl, stir together the buttermilk and 1 teaspoon salt and 1 teaspoon black pepper, or more to taste. Add the okra to the buttermilk mixture and set aside to soak for 15 minutes.

In a large bowl, combine the flour, cornmeal, 1½ teaspoons salt, the cayenne, and ½ teaspoon black pepper.

Drain the okra in a colander and discard the buttermilk mixture.

Working in batches, dredge the okra in the flour mixture, coating evenly. Shake off excess flour and transfer the okra to a nonstick baking sheet.

Heat 1 inch of oil in a heavy pot to 350 degrees. Working in batches, fry the okra (do not crowd the pot), turning the pods occasionally until golden brown, about 4 minutes. The sounds of the water in the okra cooking out is normal. Using a wire basket or a slotted spoon, transfer the fried okra to a paper towel–lined pan. Serve hot.

Serving suggestion: Serve with your favorite hot sauce if serving the okra as a side. I like it with shredded Korean seaweed on top too.

Yuca Hash Browns

It is an easy thing to add in bits of porky treats to these shredded cakes, but we have left them simple in order to go with foods vegetarians can enjoy too. The nutty almost-chestnut tones of yuca differentiate them from potatoes in subtle ways. They crisp up really well. These hash browns have also found their way on top of grilled burgers in our kitchens. There is a Cuban love called a "frita burger," which is a burger topped with skinny French fries. That was the jumping-off point for this baby. But with eggs over them or as a side to a fish or meat dish, they are going to be a steady friend to you, I am pretty certain.

Serves 8

2½ pounds yuca, peeled and cut into 1-inch pieces

Kosher salt and cracked black pepper

Clarified butter or olive oil or a combination

Put the yuca in cold, salted water and bring to a simmer. Cook the yuca until it is just easily pierced with a knife. This happens faster than potatoes—about 5 minutes will do it. Drain and spread the yuca out on a large pan to cool with space separating the yuca pieces. When cool enough to handle, rub the yuca through the large holes of a box grater. Discard any hard or "woody" parts that are a normal part of yuca but not something you want to eat. Gather into a bowl or simply leave it on your cutting board and season with some salt and pepper to taste.

Put the yuca on a nonstick 9-by-13-inch baking sheet and form into one big rectangular "cake." Divide into 8 equal rectangles about 3 by 2½ inches. Use a rubber spatula to gently guide or force them into more compact rectangles. Tamp down with your fingers, too. Once you have 8 fairly neat rectangles, top them with one piece of plastic wrap, aluminum foil, or parchment paper. Place another pan of the same size on top and push down gently.

Place in the freezer for about 30 minutes to help them bond. You can prepare these a day in advance.

Heat a nonstick griddle or pan over medium to medium-high heat and add enough clarified butter to coat the pan and then some. You want enough to add the crispy crunchy factor that makes hash browns so damn addictive. (You can add some more butter halfway through if you aren't sure, and that is fine.) Add the frozen hash brown rectangles and cook on a steady heat until crisp and golden on both sides. This can be done in batches, keeping the cooked ones in a low oven until ready to serve. The cooking time is more of a "crisping time" in that the yuca was precooked. Allow 10 to 15 minutes total to get them hot all the way through and crisp on the outside. Serve hot.

Succotash

The Narragansett Indian word *sohquttahhash*, rendered more simply today as *succotash*, refers to "broken corn kernels." Corn is an essential ingredient in succotash, but as any gardener can tell you, this dish extends a warm welcome to many vegetables. I use it on a quesadilla (page 71) in this book, but it is fine as a stand-alone dish too.

Serves 10 to 12 as a side dish (with leftovers)

¼ cup olive oil

3 tablespoons unsalted butter

1 jalapeño, seeded (if desired) and minced

2 cloves garlic, minced

½ sweet onion, diced

2 red bell peppers, diced

2 medium zucchini, chopped

2 cups blanched fresh field peas, black-eyed peas, butter beans, or crowder peas

2 cups fresh corn kernels

Kosher salt and cracked black pepper

¾ cup Chicken Stock (page 237) or vegetable stock

1 tablespoon coarsely chopped fresh tarragon

1 tablespoon finely chopped fresh thyme leaves

1 cup diced heirloom or other high-quality tomatoes

In a large, flat sauté pan, heat the oil and butter over medium-high heat. Add the jalapeño, garlic, and onion. Cook, stirring occasionally, for 6 to 8 minutes, until the onion is showing a touch of color at the edges.

Add the bell peppers, zucchini, field peas, and corn. Season with salt and pepper. Cook over medium to medium-high heat, stirring occasionally, until the vegetables are tender, about 10 minutes.

Add the stock, tarragon, and thyme. Bring to a high simmer, then remove from the heat and fold in the tomato. Taste for seasoning. Serve hot.

Coleslaw

The fact is we do love fried food in Florida. Technique is the salvation of foods properly fried, and coleslaw is the perfect matrimonial partner of said foods.

Makes 2½ cups; serves 6 to 10

¼ head green cabbage, cored and very finely shredded with a knife or a mandoline

2 to 3 radishes, shredded

1 large or 2 small carrots, peeled and grated on the large holes of a grater

¼ teaspoon fennel seeds, toasted and finely ground

¼ teaspoon ground cayenne

1 tablespoon kosher salt

1 teaspoon cracked black pepper

4 tablespoons sugar

4 tablespoons distilled white vinegar

½ cup mayonnaise, or more if desired (we use Duke's)

Combine the cabbage, radishes, and carrot in a bowl. In a cup, combine the fennel, cayenne, salt, black pepper, and 3 tablespoons of the sugar and add to the cabbage mixture. Pour 3 tablespoons of the vinegar over the mixture and stir; let sit for 10 to 15 minutes. This macerates the vegetables and pulls out some of the water.

Drain off and discard the resulting liquid from the cabbage mixture. Fold in the mayonnaise. Add the remaining 1 tablespoon sugar and 1 tablespoon vinegar. Season again to taste. Mix well and chill until ready to serve.

Trini Rice with Coconut Milk

Trini refers to the good people of Trinidad. The gifts of West Indian cookery were early and welcome components of Florida living. One taste and you will know why.

Makes about 2 quarts, enough for a party side dish

For the rice:

2 tablespoons butter

2 tablespoons olive oil

3 cloves garlic, thinly sliced

1 carrot, peeled and finely diced

½ poblano pepper, finely diced

1 red bell pepper, finely diced

½ sweet onion, finely diced

Kosher salt and cracked black pepper

2 tablespoons fresh thyme leaves, chopped

1 cup long-grain white rice, well rinsed and drained

1 cup unsweetened coconut milk

1 cup Chicken Stock (page 237)

2 tomatoes, peeled, seeded, and diced (or canned diced tomatoes, drained)

For the garnish:

1 cup dried currants

¼ cup chopped fresh culantro, tough stems at the base discarded

1 cup green olives, pitted and chopped

1 cup cooked Basic Pigeon Peas (page 144), at room temperature

Make the rice: In a large heavy-bottomed saucepan, heat the butter and oil over medium heat until the butter is melted. Add the garlic and cook until quite fragrant. Add the carrot, poblano, bell pepper, and onion. Season with salt and pepper to taste. Sauté over high heat to remove the water from the vegetables, about 5 minutes, stirring, until the vegetables become slightly tender.

Add the thyme, rice, coconut milk, stock, and half of the tomatoes, and season a bit. Bring to a simmer, then lower the heat and place a lid on the pan that fits well. Cook for about 20 minutes, until you see large holes in the rice mixture and just a little liquid remains. Remove from the heat but leave the lid on. Set aside for about 5 minutes.

Make the garnish: Bring 1 cup water to a boil and pour over the currants in a heatproof bowl. Set aside for a few minutes to plump them up. Drain the currants and discard the water.

Add the currants to the rice mixture with the culantro, olives, the remaining tomatoes, and the pigeon peas. Season one more time to taste. Serve.

> **Notes:** Culantro is similar in flavor to Italian parsley.
> This can be made in advance and gently reheated in a covered baking dish in a 300-degree oven.

Chaufa Fried Rice

This rice dish has a fascinating history, as you can read on page 93. In addition to the shrimp dish, it goes well with other meals too.

Makes 3½ cups

1 tablespoon canola oil

5 ounces hot or mild Italian sausage, casings removed, meat broken up

1 cup chopped onion

1 Scotch bonnet or Thai or other hot chile, seeded and minced

1½ teaspoons minced fresh ginger

4 scallions, thinly sliced into rings

2 tablespoons minced garlic

1 kaffir lime leaf

2 cups cooked jasmine or basmati rice (see box)

1 tablespoon sesame oil

3 tablespoons mirin (sweet rice wine)

1 tablespoon fish sauce

1 tablespoon rice vinegar

½ to 1 tablespoon sambal oelek or sriracha

2 eggs, cooked "scrambled style," cooled completely, and then chopped

¾ cup small cauliflower florets, blanched or roasted until just tender

1 tablespoon chopped fresh Thai or Italian basil leaves

1 tablespoon chopped fresh cilantro leaves

1 tablespoon chopped fresh mint leaves

Soy sauce

Heat a wok over medium-high heat and add the canola oil. Add the sausage and stir-fry for 1 minute, or until just about cooked through. Add the onion and cook until softened. Add the chile, ginger, scallions, and garlic. Stir well.

Add the kaffir lime leaf and the rice. Stir, shake, and turn the rice until it is hot.

Add the sesame oil and continue to stir-fry. Add the mirin, fish sauce, rice vinegar, and sambal oelek, continuing to stir over the heat. Add the scrambled egg, the cauliflower, and herbs. Stir-fry for 1 more minute. Add the soy sauce to taste and stir well. Serve hot.

TO COOK RICE

1 cup jasmine or basmati rice

A large pinch of kosher salt

Wash the rice well: Put it in a large bowl, fill with room-temperature water, and sweep your hand through the grains. The water will get cloudy. Pour off the water through a fine-mesh sieve and then dump the rice back into the bowl. Repeat this washing step until the water runs clear (three rinses are common).

When the rice is washed, fill up the bowl with water one more time and let the rice soak for 30 minutes.

Drain the rice. Pour 1¾ cups water in a medium-size saucepan, add the salt, and bring to a boil.

Add the rice. Stir a few times. When the water comes back to a full boil, quickly turn the heat down as low as it can go and cover with a tight-fitting lid. (I like a clear glass one if possible to keep an eye on things.) Cook for 15 minutes. Remove from the heat and let the rice sit for 5 minutes.

Remove the lid and fluff up the rice with a fork. Serve, or let cool and refrigerate until ready to use. The rice may be made one day in advance of making the full recipe of Chaufa Fried Rice.

Note: Thai basil, unlike Italian or Genovese, basil, has purple stems and buds as well as a sharper, bolder flavor that displays anise-like notes.

Thai Fried Rice

Once again it's best *not* to assume when history names a food something that it originated there. Such is the case with "Thai Fried Rice." The Chinese lay rightful claim to it. The Chinese cannot lay claim to inventing nonstick pans in the twentieth century (at least not to my knowledge!), so while a metal wok is the most "authentic" pan for this recipe, a regular nonstick pan can make a fine way to cook the mélange of grains, vegetables, and various aromatics.

Serves 10 to 12

2½ tablespoons Thai fish sauce

1 tablespoon soy sauce

2 tablespoons dark brown sugar

1 teaspoon crushed red pepper

1½ teaspoons cracked black pepper, or more to taste

4 tablespoons canola oil

3 tablespoons butter

2 cloves garlic, thinly sliced

1 tablespoon minced fresh ginger

1 cup diced red onion

1 red bell pepper, julienned, strips cut in half crosswise

10 shiitake mushroom caps, sliced

4 cups cooked jasmine rice (page 172), preferably leftover and refrigerated

2 cups very thinly sliced red cabbage

½ cup thinly sliced scallions

1 cup bean sprouts

1 tomato, peeled, seeded, and chopped

1 tablespoon chopped fresh cilantro leaves

Kosher salt

3 eggs, cooked "scrambled style"

Combine the fish sauce, soy sauce, brown sugar, crushed red pepper, and black pepper in a small bowl. Set aside.

Heat 2 tablespoons of the oil and the butter in a large sauté pan over medium-high heat. When the butter is melted, add the garlic and ginger and cook, stirring well, until fragrant. Add the onion, bell pepper, and mushrooms and cook until the mushrooms are soft, about 5 minutes, stirring occasionally. Add the cooked rice and stir.

Stir in the fish sauce mixture to coat the rice and set aside.

Heat the remaining 2 tablespoons oil in a very large pan or wok over medium-high heat until very hot. Add the cabbage, scallions, and bean sprouts and cook until the cabbage starts to wilt, about 3 minutes.

Add the tomato and cilantro. Season with salt and pepper to taste, stir, and cook for 1 minute. Stir in the rice mixture, along with the scrambled egg.

Serve hot, or set aside in a warm place until ready to serve.

> *Note:* The best fried rice is made with rice that is (a) leftover and (b) somewhat dry. The rice's texture is more protected when those characteristics are kept inviolate.

9

THE SWEET FLEET

Desserts

Key Lime Beignets

The world has many recipes for Key lime pie. In fact, a great one is in our previous cookbook, *My Key West Kitchen.* Our son and coauthor of that cookbook asked if we could do a recipe he vowed would be "as good if not better." Strong words. He was joined in these efforts by our superb pastry chef Gloriann Rivera from our restaurant in Mount Dora whom I imagine will write her own cookbook one day.

Serves 6

Preheat the oven to 200 degrees. Butter and flour a baking sheet.

For the French meringue drops:

4 egg whites

⅛ teaspoon cream of tartar

Pinch of salt

2¼ cups confectioners' sugar

Make the French meringue drops: Whip the egg whites until foamy. Add the cream of tartar and pinch of salt, then sprinkle in the sugar a little at a time, while continuing to whip at medium speed. Increase the speed to high once all of the sugar is in and whip to medium peaks. Once done, transfer the meringue to a plastic piping bag and cut off the end to about the diameter of the handle of a wooden kitchen spoon, then pipe the meringue from one end of the pan to the other, in an S-like pattern, snaking all the way from one end of the pan to the other, filling it up entirely.

Bake for 30 minutes, then check to see if it is dry and crispy. It should come off the paper easily. If not, just put it back in until it is, 15 more minutes at most. Turn off the oven and let it stay in there until you can handle the pan with your bare hands. Loosen it from the baking sheet, and allow it to cool completely before storing in an airtight container at room temperature. Crack or chop up into pieces when getting ready to make the beignets.

For the Key lime curd:

1½ cups sugar

Grated zest of 7 Key limes

1½ cups Key lime juice

6 eggs

4 egg yolks

6 ounces butter

Make the Key lime curd: Put the sugar, zest, juice, eggs, and yolks in a bowl over a pot of simmering water. Whisk occasionally until the mixture heats up. As the liquid gets hotter, whisk more frequently until it begins to thicken, then whisk continuously. Cook until a ribbon of curd can be seen to remain on the surface of the curd. Then, remove from the heat and whisk in the butter a piece at a time. Push through a sieve into a bowl. Cover the surface with plastic wrap to avoid forming a skin, and wrap the top of the bowl. Place in the fridge until well chilled.

For the beignets:

¾ cup whole milk

¼ cup granulated sugar

1¼-ounce envelope (2¼ teaspoons) dry yeast

1½ cups buttermilk, room temperature

2 tablespoons vegetable shortening

1 pound bread flour

18 graham crackers, cracked into pieces

1½ teaspoons ground cinnamon

1 teaspoon mace

1 teaspoon salt

Vegetable or canola oil for deep-frying

Confectioners' sugar

Make the beignets: Bring the milk to 110 degrees, add 1 teaspoon of sugar, and then add the yeast to bloom. Wait 10 minutes. Pour the milk into a mixing bowl and add buttermilk, shortening, and the rest of the sugar, whisking to dissolve.

Meanwhile, put the flour, graham crackers, spices, and salt in a food processor and blend well.

In a mixer add all your wet ingredients and little by little start adding the dry ingredients.

Let the mixture rest covered, at room temperature, until double in size, about one hour.

Heat a pot of oil to 350 degrees. Fry the beignets a few at a time. Fry until golden brown, then flip until bottom is also golden brown. Transfer to a rack, or paper towel-lined plate to drain and cool slightly before dusting with confectioners' sugar.

Put the lime curd in individual ramekins or small mason jars and use it as a dipping sauce. Crush up the French meringue drops and scatter them over the warm beignets. Serve.

Note: The meringue drops and curd may be made up days in advance.

Mama's Zucchini Bread Layer Cake

WITH SPICED TAMARIND JELLY AND RAINBOW CARROT–CREAM CHEESE FROSTING

Like many backyard gardeners, our mother had a bountiful harvest of zucchini. So much so that she began to make zucchini bread, which, of course, I preferred to the sautéed variety back then. I slathered mine with cream cheese after giving it a good toasting. I brought in "special forces" when creating this cake by enlisting her grandson—our son, Justin—to bring this recipe to a level we felt would impress the lady for whom we name this sweet marvel.

Serves 10–12

For the spiced tamarind jelly:

14 ounces tamarind pulp (we use El Sembrador–brand frozen pulp)

½ cup apple jelly

3 tablespoons Pickapeppa sauce

For the zucchini bread:

½ cup golden raisins

1 cup spiced rum

2¼ cups all-purpose flour

1¼ teaspoons baking soda

½ teaspoon baking powder

1 teaspoon ground cinnamon

½ teaspoon grated nutmeg

½ teaspoon kosher salt

2 eggs

1½ cups sugar

⅔ cup canola oil

2 teaspoons vanilla bean paste

1½ cups grated zucchini

¾ cup crushed pineapple, drained

½ cup finely diced candied ginger

For the rainbow carrot–cream cheese frosting:

1½ cups coarsely grated rainbow carrots

Grated zest of 3 lemons

1 tablespoon granulated sugar

1 pound cream cheese

1 cup (2 sticks) butter, softened

2 teaspoons vanilla extract

2 cups confectioners' sugar

Make the spiced tamarind jelly: Put the tamarind pulp in a pot and boil for 30 minutes to reduce. Remove from the heat and stir in the jelly and Pickapeppa sauce. Return to the heat and simmer for another 15 minutes. Pour into a jelly jar with a lid, and let cool to room temperature before placing in the refrigerator to store.

Make the zucchini bread: Preheat a convection oven to 325 degrees, low fan, or a regular oven to 350 degrees. Grease three 9-inch round cake pans and line the bottoms with parchment paper.

Put the raisins in a small saucepan and cover with the rum. Bring to a simmer, then remove from the heat and set aside to plump and cool.

In a medium bowl, whisk the flour, baking soda, baking powder, cinnamon, nutmeg, and salt.

In a large bowl, whisk the eggs and sugar until light and fluffy. Stir in the oil and vanilla, then stir in the zucchini, pineapple, ginger, and the raisins with the rum.

Make a well in the flour mixture, pour in the zucchini mixture, and stir to incorporate.

Pour into the prepared pans and bake, rotating for even color, for about 35 minutes, until an inserted toothpick comes out clean. Set on wire racks to cool, then wrap in plastic and chill in the refrigerator for 2 hours.

Make the rainbow carrot–cream cheese frosting: Toss the carrots with the lemon zest and granulated sugar in a bowl. Set aside.

Put the cream cheese in the bowl of an electric mixer and beat to soften. Beat in the butter, scrape down, and beat until smooth. Stir in the vanilla and confectioners' sugar. Remove the bowl from the mixer and fold in the carrots.

Once the cakes have chilled, trim the top of each cake to create a level surface. Place the first cake layer on a cake stand or serving plate. Spread frosting on top with an offset spatula. Place a second cake layer on top, frost it, top with the third layer, and frost the top and sides of the cake. When the sides and top are smooth, use the tip of the spatula to create grooves in the frosting if you'd like.

Tropical Fruit
Cholados

Cholados are "theater food" for children of *all* ages! It is best to make them one at a time, so they are not for a formal dinner but more birthday-party fare. Admittedly you will need an ice-shaver—but they are available in stores for much less money than a blender, and something that gets children to eat a lot more fruit is money well spent, we think. Feel free to switch up the fruit as you like. This dish originates in South America, but once our Colombian-born chef Camilo Velasco made us some *cholados*, we thought it belongs anywhere the fruit is beautiful.

4 cholados

Lots of shaved ice

1 cup grenadine syrup

4 large fresh strawberries, hulled and quartered

1 banana, peeled and cut into ¼-inch rounds

1 mango, peeled, pitted, and cut into long spears

6 ounces peeled and cored ripe pineapple, cut into long spears

¾ cup sweetened condensed milk

We like to serve these in wide-mouth mason jars with long spoons and straws. Have all the fruits, the grenadine syrup, and sweetened condensed milk ready to go. As the note above indicates, shave just enough ice for *one cholado at a time*, and work fast!

Pack each mason jar halfway with shaved ice and drizzle 2 tablespoons of the grenadine syrup over the ice in a circular motion, making sure to spread it evenly. Add one quarter of the strawberry slices and one quarter of the banana slices.

Fill the jar with more shaved ice, leaving about ½ inch of space to the rim, and pour another 2 tablespoons of the grenadine syrup evenly over the ice. Place a few mango and pineapple spears in the jar sticking halfway out of the lip of jar.

Drizzle some sweetened condensed milk over the fruit into each of the mason jars.

Serve with a long spoon and a straw.

Cinnamon Brioche Sticky Buns
AND PLANT CITY STRAWBERRY MILKSHAKES

Some farmstands in Florida offer a stunning combination of fresh-picked fruit as well as some *very* fine baked goods, such as the buns found at Knaus Berry Farm in Homestead. If Homestead is a bit far for you, we wanted to create a version that you could make in your home. And Plant City is famed for the luscious strawberries grown nearby; the annual Strawberry Fest there is a must-do! Wherever you live, you can likely find a place not far from you where, at the right time of the year, you can score some beautiful berries for the shake below.

Makes 6 *large* **sticky buns**

For the brioche dough:

3½ cups bread flour, plus more for the work surface

4 teaspoons instant yeast

¼ cup sugar

½ cup whole milk, scalded and cooled to warm

4 eggs

1 tablespoon kosher salt

1 cup (2 sticks) unsalted butter, cut into pieces and softened

For the filling:

4 tablespoons unsalted butter

2 tablespoons unsulphured molasses

1 tablespoon ground cinnamon

¾ teaspoon ground cardamom

1 cup light brown sugar

A pinch of kosher salt

½ cup chopped toasted pecans

For the sticky mix:

½ cup (1 stick) unsalted butter

1 cup packed light brown sugar

6 tablespoons unsulphured molasses

½ teaspoon kosher salt

¼ teaspoon cracked black pepper

1 cup chopped toasted pecans

Make the brioche dough: Measure the flour into a medium-size bowl. Whisk in the yeast, then the sugar.

Put the milk and eggs in the bowl of a stand mixer and whisk together by hand. Add the flour mixture on top, attach the bowl to the mixer, and using the dough hook, mix on low to incorporate all of the ingredients.

Turn up to medium and mix to develop, about 4 minutes. Turn the mixer down to low, set a timer for 30 minutes, and begin adding the butter in pieces steadily. When all the butter is in and the 30 minutes are up, scrape down the bowl to make sure nothing is sticking to the sides or bottom, then resume mixing on medium speed for another 10 minutes.

Meanwhile, grease a bowl for proofing the dough and set nearby. When the 10 minutes are up, transfer the dough to the greased bowl, cover with plastic wrap, and proof for 1 hour at room temperature. Gently punch the dough down. Using a bowl scraper, loosen the dough from the sides of the bowl, and fold the outsides into the middle. Flip the dough over in the bowl and rewrap with plastic. Place in the refrigerator overnight (at least 8 hours).

Make the filling: Melt the butter with the molasses, cinnamon, and cardamom. Put the brown sugar in the mixer with the salt. Pour the butter mixture into the mixer while beating on medium. Add the pecans and mix to combine. Set aside.

Make the sticky mix: Melt the butter in a saucepan, then add the brown sugar and molasses. Bring to a simmer, then whisk in the salt, pepper, and ½ cup of the pecans. Pour the mixture into the bottom of a 10-by-8-inch baking dish and set aside to cool.

continued →

Finish the sticky buns: Remove the dough from the refrigerator and dust your work surface with flour.

Using a bowl scraper or spatula, loosen the dough from the bowl and turn it over onto the work surface.

Press and roll the dough out to a 12-inch square, flouring as needed to avoid sticking. Leaving a 1-inch border of dough around the edges, and a 2-inch border at the nearest edge, scatter the filling over the surface of the dough. Scatter the reserved ½ cup pecans over the filling.

Place a small dish of water nearby. Starting at the edge of the rectangle farthest from you, roll the dough toward you a few inches at a time, starting at the left and moving right, until you reach the edge nearest you. Seal the roll completely by using the water as an adhesive, and pinch the roll closed. Once the seal is formed, flour the seal and work surface to avoid sticking. Line a baking sheet with parchment. Lifting under both sides, transfer the roll to the baking sheet, place plastic wrap over it, and chill again before proceeding, about 30 minutes.

Note: If the milkshake is not in the plan, Greek yogurt on the buns is also a nice way to roll.

After the log has chilled, remove from the fridge and make gentle marks on the log to use as guides for portioning six equal pieces by first marking the middle and then each half into thirds. Cut the roll into six portions and transfer them cut sides up to the baking pan with the sticky mix, spacing them evenly apart. Cover the pan with plastic and set aside to proof in a warm place until doubled in size, about 1 hour.

Preheat a conventional oven to 400 degrees. When the rolls are nicely proofed, remove the plastic and wrap the pan with aluminum foil. Bake for 15 minutes, then remove the foil and bake for another 20 minutes. The internal temperature should read 190 degrees when finished. Let cool for 20 to 30 minutes, then invert onto a serving dish.

For the Plant City strawberry milkshakes:

3 pints fresh strawberries, hulled

½ cup sugar

6 ounces premium vanilla ice cream

3 cups whole milk

While the unbaked buns are chilling, make the Plant City strawberry milkshakes: Cut the strawberries in half and toss with the sugar. Cover with plastic wrap and allow to macerate for a few hours if possible to allow the juices to come out and transform the fruit.

When ready to serve, put the strawberries and their syrup, the ice cream, and milk in a blender and blend until smooth. Pour and serve immediately with warm or room-temperature sticky buns.

Orange-Pistachio Thumbprint Cookies

WITH CANDIED GINGER–PAPAYA JELLY

Family traditions come to the fore here with these easy-to-make cookies. We are big cookie bakers each year at Christmas. Make these, and see if you will want to bring them to a holiday party, or simply stuff them in your bag and take them to work for a bumped-up coffee break!

Makes 24 cookies

For the candied ginger–papaya jelly:

14 ounces ripe papaya, diced

2 tablespoons sugar

3 tablespoons fresh-squeezed lemon juice

½ cup finely diced candied ginger

For the cookies:

¾ cup (1½ sticks) butter

½ cup confectioners' sugar, plus more for dusting

Grated zest of 1 orange

¼ teaspoon orange oil

1¾ cups all-purpose flour

½ cup toasted pistachios, finely chopped

Grated lime zest

Make the candied ginger–papaya jelly: Put the papaya in a small saucepan and stir in the sugar and lemon juice. Boil to *au sec* (until almost dry), about 12 minutes. Stir in the candied ginger and simmer for 1 minute. Remove to a jelly jar and set aside to cool.

Make the cookies: Preheat a convection oven to 350 degrees or a regular oven to 375 degrees.

In the bowl of an electric mixer, cream the butter with the confectioners' sugar, orange zest, and orange oil until light and fluffy. Stop the mixer and scrape down the bowl. Mix in the flour and then the pistachios. Scoop and shape the dough into balls, place ½ inch apart on ungreased baking sheets, and make an indent in each one with your thumb.

Bake for 20 minutes, then remove to racks to cool completely. Once cool, roll in confectioners' sugar and fill each with a spoon-ful of the jelly and finish by grating lime zest over the tops of the cookies.

Once the jelly has been applied, serve the same day. The cookies without the jelly will keep in an airtight container for about 2 weeks.

Bananas for Stephen Foster

Stephen Foster wrote "Oh Susanna" when he was just twenty-one years old, and it was one among many songs of his that dished up idealized race relations of the time dressed in nostalgia. I wonder what Foster would compose if he tasted the "Plantains in Temptation Sauce" that we learned to cook from Venezuelans transplanted to Florida.

Serves 4

For the hot chocolate:

1½ cups whole milk

1½ cups unsweetened coconut milk

½ cup dark brown sugar

2 tablespoons unsweetened cocoa powder

¼ teaspoon kosher salt

2 ounces bittersweet chocolate, chopped (we use 65% Ecuador)

For the hoe cakes:

2 cups fresh corn kernels

½ cup diced pineapple or mango

⅓ cup milk

1 egg, beaten

1 teaspoon sugar

½ teaspoon baking powder

½ teaspoon kosher salt

¼ teaspoon ground black pepper

½ cup yellow cornmeal

½ cup all-purpose flour

Peanut or vegetable oil for pan-frying

For the bananas:

1 tablespoon virgin coconut oil

⅓ cup dark brown sugar

3 tablespoons guava jelly

¼ teaspoon ground cayenne

¼ teaspoon kosher salt

¼ teaspoon black pepper

¼ cup unsweetened coconut milk

3 ripe bananas

Make the hot chocolate: Bring the two milks to a scald in a heavy saucepan, then whisk in the brown sugar, cocoa powder, and salt until dissolved. Bring to a simmer, then pour over the chopped chocolate in a heatproof bowl. Let stand for 2 minutes, then whisk until smooth. Pour back into the pan and set aside. (If necessary, reheat the hot chocolate to serve.)

Make the hoe cakes: Put the corn in a bowl. Add the pineapple, milk, egg, sugar, baking powder, salt, and pepper and mix well. Fold in the cornmeal and flour.

Transfer the mixture to a food processor and pulse until smooth. Turn out into a clean bowl or other container.

Heat a generous slick of oil in a large nonstick skillet over medium heat. Spoon the batter into the skillet in silver-dollar-size pancakes and cook until golden brown, about 2 minutes per side. Transfer to paper towels. (These may be kept warm in a low oven if need be while you finish the prep.) Set aside.

Make the bananas: Heat a pan over medium-high heat. Add the coconut oil, brown sugar, guava jelly, cayenne, salt, black pepper, and coconut milk and stir. Peel and split the bananas. Once the sauce is bubbling, add the bananas. Spoon the hot caramel over the bananas or turn the bananas gently, to cook evenly. Cook until the bananas are soft but still hold their shape.

Serve the bananas on top of the hot hoe cakes. Serve the hot chocolate in mugs alongside. Feel free to add strong spirits to this.

Legacy School

The new generation cooking today is doing precisely what all have done, but faster and with an Esperanto of global vocabularies supplied by a new definition of *Amazon* and its flood of ingredients never seen before. I was brought up in a different age, but my mother and grandmother valued education so highly that, despite my youthful tendencies, their wisdom won the day. But I had to travel my own personal road before the lost highway got lights. Even at twenty-one, I had no idea what I wanted to be "when I grew up"; I was adrift, so I tried many jobs. They included concrete sprayer in a Kansas feed lot, shoeless flower seller on the streets of Honolulu, tree trimmer, carny, Ball jar factory worker, and hot tar roofer. After getting fired from that last one, in desperation I turned to the newspaper ads for some new hope. I scanned the choices my future might hold and turned this one up: "Short-order cook. No experience necessary, $3.50 an hour."

Over the years my teachers became the folks I stood on hot lines with in kitchens from Colorado to Illinois to Florida. When you don't know how to cook and you've had no formal training, you need to learn from everyone around you who can save you time . . . and even pain. They were at work to make a living themselves. They didn't have time to set up a class for folks like me who were just plain green. But I learned so much from cooks who were not famous, never were on a cooking show, never featured in a magazine. Folks like Tokio, Black Betty, Cowboy Fred, Philip from Philly, Irish Danny McHugh. And in the midst of that my lifelong love of books bore new fruit by teaching me all about the vast world of cooking. My library began with a book by James Beard (*Theory and Practice of Good Cooking*). Then came others like the Time-Life *Good Cook* series helmed by the amazing Richard Olney. Soon came books by the Michelin three-star chefs of France, and then Paula Wolfert, Jacques Pépin, Al "A.J." McClane, Paul Prudhomme, Elizabeth Lambert Ortiz—and on and on until they no longer fit on my desk and began to fill the walls and bookshelves. Thirty years' worth! But now has come the time to *merge* these essential rivers found in both hands-on experience and the books into a cooking school.

Along with partner Candace Walsh we are operating a school named In the Kitchen with Norman Van Aken in the Wynwood area of Miami. Candace and I believe that today, in this country (and increasingly in others), there is a disparity between food knowledge and food preparation skills. Americans eat out in increasing numbers at fine dining establishments. We have celebrity chefs. Food programming on TV is at an all-time high, and the media inundates us with all things food. Every major American city hosts a food festival that brings together consumers with the chefs they idolize and the foods they crave. There are many various food movements with artisanal purveyors.

Good food has never been more part of the American consciousness than it is now. However, at the same time, home economics has dropped from most education curriculums. The family dynamic has changed. We have more single-parent- and two-parent-income households, which means there is less time for parents to teach their children how to cook. We have high-quality prepared foods readily available to take home for the family dinner, and we eat out.

The media and restaurants have set the bar high for what you might wish you could be preparing in *your* kitchen. However, consumers have not been given the tools to do so. We want to cook flavorful, beautiful, and nutritious food at home for our family and friends. We know what that is supposed to look and taste like, but people often don't know how to achieve this.

Our school's mission is to bridge this gap and fulfill the role that home economics courses and family cooking traditions now very rarely provide. We provide hands-on, small-group courses focusing on all things food. Our programs span the globe and cover the gamut of cooking techniques. Our ultimate goal is to create schools across the country and become a new benchmark in cooking education for nonprofessionals.

I realize I have been blessed to find a "job" that is actually a life's passion! The gracious thing to do is to share it and leave a legacy of knowledge that others can build on. Though I love the restaurant business still and I'm very proud of our restaurants, to do them alone I determined was not my way of giving back the teachings of the countless people who instructed me or inspired me. At ITK we have a wide-open curriculum with no degree to attain other than the degree of self-actualization each student aspires to. And our students range from seven to ninety-seven years of age (so far!).

So . . . on we go, with family all around
 . . . still holding the knives
 . . . still stirring the spoons
 . . . but with a forum to teach others
   and enjoy the ongoing *feast*
    . . . and a legacy of sharing food
     . . . and knowledge.

Coconut Milk Rice Pudding
WITH BUCKWHEAT HONEY, MANGO, AND TOASTED COCONUT

The simplicity of this dish is deceptive in terms of the amount of love that pours out of it. It helps if your mother made rice pudding for you when you were a child. If not, your opportunity to start that tradition with your family can begin right here! Our mother taught my sisters, Jane and Bet, to make this without the providence of the mangos, since it was back in our childhood days in Illinois. But the coconut was manageable. Now it all is.

Serves 4 to 6

½ cup arborio rice

½ cinnamon stick

½ teaspoon grated lime zest

½ teaspoon kosher salt

¼ teaspoon coriander seeds

2 cups whole milk

1 (13½-ounce) can unsweetened coconut milk

2 egg yolks

⅓ cup sugar

1 teaspoon vanilla extract

Buckwheat honey

Mango slices

1 cup toasted unsweetened shredded coconut

Put the rice, cinnamon stick, lime zest, salt, coriander, whole milk, and coconut milk in a heavy saucepan and simmer, covered, for 20 minutes, stirring occasionally. Uncover and cook for 10 more minutes, stirring more frequently as it thickens.

Once the rice seems close to being done, whisk the egg yolks, sugar, and vanilla together in a bowl. Measure the volume of the rice mixture. When the rice mixture has reduced to 3½ cups, temper in the yolk mixture by adding about ½ cup of the hot rice at a time to the yolks, stirring, until the yolks are nicely warmed up. Then combine both in the saucepan and cook, continuing to stir, until the mixture coats the back of a spoon. Remove to a bowl to cool and thicken the rest of the way.

Serve warm or chilled, with a drizzle of buckwheat honey, some mango, and toasted coconut.

Note: We buy our buckwheat honey at the famed farmstand curiously (but fittingly once you hear the story) named Robert Is Here. I also love this honey on multigrain toast with Cowgirl Creamery Mt. Tam cheese that has been properly tempered (brought to room temperature). For that matter, try cheeses of many locales.

Devil's Food Cake
WITH CHOCOLATE GANACHE, PEANUT BUTTER FROSTING, AND A FLORIDA KEYS HONEYED PEANUT BRITTLE

Moans may be heard.
That is all.

Makes 1 (8-inch) layer cake

For the honeyed peanut brittle:

2 cups sugar

¼ cup water

4 ounces unsalted butter, plus more for greasing

⅓ cup corn syrup

⅓ cup Florida Keys or Tupelo honey

½ teaspoon baking soda

1½ tablespoons salt

1½ cups unsalted peanuts, chopped well with a knife

For the devil's food cake:

4 ounces unsalted butter, plus more for the pans

2 cups dark brown sugar

1 cup sour cream

1 teaspoon vanilla extract

4 large eggs

1 cup hot brewed coffee

4 ounces bittersweet chocolate (65%), finely chopped

9 ounces cake flour, plus more for the pans

1½ tablespoons unsweetened cocoa powder

2 teaspoons baking soda

½ teaspoon kosher salt

Make the honeyed peanut brittle: Line a baking sheet with a silicone mat or a piece of parchment paper sprayed with baking spray. In a medium-size pot, combine the sugar, water, butter, corn syrup, and honey. Cook the mixture until the sugar dissolves and the syrup is a medium amber color. When it reaches that color, immediately add the baking soda and salt, whisking constantly. Add the peanuts, and pour the mixture out onto the prepared baking sheet. Let cool completely in the refrigerator to prevent stickiness.

Make the devil's food cake: Preheat a convection oven to 325 degrees or a regular oven to 350 degrees. Butter three 8-inch round cake pans, line the bottoms with parchment, then butter the parchment. Put a little flour in each pan, roll around to coat, and dump out the excess.

Begin creaming the butter and brown sugar in a stand mixer fitted with a paddle attachment on medium. When creamy, add the sour cream and vanilla and beat until smooth. Add the eggs one at a time, beating continuously. Set aside.

Pour the hot coffee over the chopped chocolate. Set aside for 2 minutes, then whisk until smooth.

Sift the flour, cocoa powder, baking soda, and salt in a bowl or on top of a sheet of parchment paper so it's easier to pour into the mixer.

Resume mixing on low, then alternately add the dry and wet mixtures, scraping down the sides of the bowl as needed to incorporate all the ingredients.

Pour about 1¾ cups (or 486 grams) of the batter into each of the prepared cake pans. Bake for about 24 minutes, rotating the pans halfway through. The cakes should pull away from the sides a bit, and an inserted toothpick should come out clean. Let cool for 20 minutes, then flip out of the pans and remove the parchment to finish cooling on wire racks.

continued ➜

For the chocolate ganache:

1 cup heavy cream

4 tablespoons sugar

1½ teaspoons vanilla extract

10 ounces bittersweet chocolate (65%), finely chopped

¼ teaspoon kosher salt

2 ounces unsalted butter, softened

For the peanut butter frosting:

8 ounces butter, softened

1 pound creamy peanut butter

¾ teaspoon kosher salt

4 cups confectioners' sugar

¼ cup whole milk

½ teaspoon vanilla extract

Make the chocolate ganache: Bring the cream and sugar to a scald in a heavy saucepan, add the vanilla, then pour the mixture over the chopped chocolate in a heatproof bowl. Let stand for 2 minutes, then whisk until smooth. Whisk in the salt and butter. Cover the surface with plastic wrap and set aside until cool.

Make the peanut butter frosting: Beat the butter, peanut butter, and salt in the clean bowl of a stand mixer. Stop the mixer, add the confectioners' sugar, then start the mixer on low to incorporate. Once the sugar is mostly incorporated, turn up the mixer and beat to make a smooth, thick paste. Stop the mixer and add the milk and vanilla extract. Start the mixer on low again to incorporate, then remove the bowl, scrape down, and finish mixing by hand. Chill for about 30 minutes to firm up a bit.

Assemble the cake: Place one of the cake rounds on a presentation plate. Take one-third of the ganache, mound it in the center of the round, and spread to within ½ inch of the edge. Put another cake round on top, press into place, repeat with the remaining ganache, and then press the last round on top.

Put the peanut butter frosting on the top of the cake and, using a long metal spatula, spread to the edges and carefully down the sides to cover completely. Remember that frosting moves out and down, but not back up the cake. Make swirls and peaks in the frosting as you like. Place in the fridge to firm up the frosting again for 15 minutes.

Meanwhile, chop the brittle into nickel-sized pieces. Put these pieces in a bowl and, using your hands, gently press the brittle against the sides of the cake until the sides are well covered. Chill until ready to serve.

Turrón-Studded Chilled Chocolate Brownies

Turrón, which is much like nougat, hails from Spain. In the Spanish shops you will find a number of different renditions of it; you will want to try a few types for the cultural immersion into chocolate, nuts, honey, and such. Why deny oneself, I say! And broken up into brownies? It is dreamy. Like a Cervantes dream . . .

Makes 12 brownies

½ cup (1 stick) unsalted butter

8 ounces bittersweet chocolate (65%), finely chopped

1½ cups all-purpose flour

¼ cup unsweetened cocoa powder

½ teaspoon kosher salt

1½ cups sugar

¼ cup virgin coconut oil

3 eggs

1 tablespoon vanilla extract

8 ounces white *turrón*, coarsely chopped

Preheat a convection oven to 325 degrees or a regular oven to 350 degrees. Have a (9-inch) square baking dish ready.

Melt the butter in a saucepan, then remove from the heat and drop in the chopped chocolate. Let stand for 2 minutes, then stir until smooth.

Sift the flour with the cocoa powder into a bowl. Whisk in the salt and set aside.

Stir the sugar into the melted chocolate mixture; then stir in the coconut oil, eggs, and vanilla.

Finally, stir in the flour mixture. Pour the batter into the baking pan, then sprinkle the *turrón* all over the surface, pushing it into the batter slightly. Bake for 40 minutes, rotating the dish halfway through. Let cool to room temperature. Loosen from the pan. Cut the brownie into 12 squares and then chill them, wrapped tightly in plastic.

There is nothing more perfect than these with a cold glass of milk. Simple.

Babas au Coctel

In 1987 or so I asked Susan Porter, our very gifted pastry chef at Louie's Backyard in Key West, to make us a version of the classic *babas au rhum*. She did, and her *Babas au Louie's* recipe still is made in many places. Our son spent some formative years playing at Louie's, so I asked if he'd like to contribute his take on *babas* for this book. The family ties of *babas* have special resonance when you learn that they are descended from the Polish pastries called *babkas* and that *baba* means either "old woman" or "grandmother." The family that bakes together gets to eat these *Babas au Coctel* together too! Thanks to Justin *and* to Susan.

Makes approximately 22 *babas*

For the *babas*:

1 (¼-ounce) envelope (2¼ teaspoons) active dry yeast

¼ cup warm water (110 degrees)

3 cups all-purpose flour

¼ cup sugar

½ teaspoon kosher salt

4 large eggs, beaten

2 teaspoons grated orange zest

1 cup (2 sticks) unsalted butter, cut into pieces and softened

For the rum syrup:

½ cup sugar

½ cup dark rum

For serving:

½ cup apple or apricot jelly, heated

> *Serving suggestion:* **Serve with whipped cream and the freshest fruits of the season that you love.**

Make the *babas*: Bloom the yeast in the warm water for 10 minutes.

In a separate bowl, whisk the flour, sugar, and salt together.

Using an electric mixer fitted with a paddle attachment, combine ½ cup room-temperature water, the eggs, orange zest, and bloomed yeast with any residual water. Add the flour mixture and mix on low to make a very loose dough with no "dry spots," about 2 minutes. Add the butter in pieces, still mixing on low, and beat for about 15 seconds more.

Fill greased popover pans halfway with the batter, cover with plastic wrap, and set aside to proof until risen to fill the pans, about 2 hours.

Preheat the oven to 375 degrees.

Bake the *babas* for 10 minutes. Rotate the pan and bake for 10 more minutes, or until golden. Let cool slightly, then remove from the pans to wire racks.

Make the rum syrup: In a small saucepan, combine the sugar and 1¼ cups water and simmer until dissolved. Remove from the heat and stir in the rum. Dip the cooled *babas* in the rum syrup for no longer than 5 seconds, then return them to the rack.

Brush the *babas* with the jelly to give them an attractive shine. Serve.

Gloriann Rivera and Norman Van Aken in the kitchen at 1921

10

COCKTAILING
Drinks

The Bearded Arm Wrestler

By now I would think most everyone in the world knows about the Hemingway Days that happen each July in Key West. Ernest Hemingway machismo is celebrated as part of the festival with an arm-wrestling contest. (It is a bit less famous than the Hemingway Look-Alike Contest, but it has its fans.) In one of the inaugural years I participated and was glad to make it past the first round before losing to a shrimper from over on the Gulf Coast who couldn't understand how a "cook could even give him a contest." (Papa Hemingway was more of a boxer than an arm wrestler, but I think a boxing tournament might have been more difficult to organize, so this prevailed as the contest of brawn.) This drink displays its own strength—as you will be able to attest after you make and taste yours. And if you make it to Key West for Hemingway Days, stop in the Island Bookstore for a fine collection of books by the man who once lived in old Cayo Hueso.

Makes 1 cocktail

2 ounces agricole rhum

¾ ounce fresh-squeezed lime juice

½ ounce fresh-squeezed grapefruit juice

½ ounce maraschino liqueur

½ ounce simple syrup (see box)

Maraschino cherries for garnish

Combine the rhum, juices, liqueur, and simple syrup in an ice-filled shaker; shake. Strain over crushed ice into a cocktail glass and garnish with cherries.

SIMPLE SYRUP

½ cup sugar

In a small pot over medium heat, combine the sugar with ½ cup water and simmer, stirring, until the sugar dissolves. Let cool.

The Mustachioed Swimmer

1 ounce Appleton Estate V/X rum

1 ounce apple brandy

1 ounce fresh-squeezed lime juice

¾ ounce simple syrup (page 201)

Lime wedge for garnish

If you read my memoir, *No Experience Necessary* (and I hope you do), you will learn that I once not only made a drink for the legendary Tennessee Williams, but he kissed me too. Williams was a common sight in the old days in Key West. He was not bothered by the locals one bit as he sauntered down to the same beach we frequented to take his routine and obviously restorative swim many afternoons. He would dry his face and then sink down on a beach towel to sun a bit before heading back to his Duncan Street home—and probably a cocktail of his own.

Makes 1 cocktail

Combine the rum, brandy, lime juice, and simple syrup in a shaker and fill with ice. Shake and strain into a coupe glass and garnish with a lime wedge.

Dance Card Darlin'

5 fresh mint leaves, plus 1 sprig for garnish

1 bar spoon of sugar

3 (⅜-inch-thick) slices peeled cucumber

1 orange wedge

½ ounce fresh-squeezed lime juice

½ ounce Old Sour (page 216)

3 ounces Pimm's No. 1

2 ounces Fever Tree ginger beer

The Key West–based novel *92 Degrees in the Shade*, by Tom McGuane, features a kind of crazy-brilliant fisherman named Nichol Dance. The great Warren Oates played him in the movie version, which was one of the zanier movie sets that ever hit Florida. This is a play on this name and also about taking chances, which wild Nichol Dance did plenty of in the memorable McGuane novel. Care to dance?

Makes 1 cocktail

Chill a collins glass in the freezer. Once chilled, muddle the mint leaves with the sugar lightly in the glass. Then add the cucumber and orange, crush them, and top with ice.

In a mixing tin, shake the lime juice, Old Sour, and Pimm's vigorously with ice, then strain into the glass. Top with the ginger beer and stir gently.

Garnish by smacking the mint sprig gently in your palm and placing it in the drink, along the side of the glass. Serve with a straw.

Mojito Coast

Novelist Paul Theroux wrote the book *Mosquito Coast*, which was subsequently made into a movie starring Harrison Ford. While filming a part in Belize, Harrison took a break and came to Key West. I was pretty dumbstruck when I saw him sitting solo in our dining room at Louie's Backyard at the time. He had an aura about him. I'm not sure if Theroux ever made it there or not. But if he makes it to where I'm cooking, I'll buy him one of these.

Makes 1 cocktail

1 tablespoon Escabeche Spice Rub (page 220)

Extra-virgin olive oil to fry the garlic slices

3 thin slices of garlic

6 fresh mint leaves, plus 1 sprig for garnish

3 bar spoons demerara sugar

2 bar spoons cumin seeds, toasted

1 lime wedge

1 ounce fresh-squeezed sour orange juice

1¾ ounces Havana Club Añejo Reserva rum

2 ounces Fever Tree soda water

3 dashes Regan's orange bitters

Dampen the rim of a collins glass and dip half of it in the Escabeche Spice Rub, then place in the freezer.

In a small pan, heat a little oil over medium-low heat, then add the garlic. Control the heat so that the slices just become fragrant and turn a golden color, rather than golden-brown, then remove to a plate lined with a paper towel. Set aside.

In a mixing glass, combine the mint leaves, demerara sugar, cumin seeds, and lime wedge; muddle the mixture. Add the sour orange juice, fill the glass with ice cubes, then add the rum. Top the glass with the shaker tin and shake vigorously.

Strain (using a julep strainer if possible) the drink into the prepared collins glass. Top with the soda and stir gently. Garnish with the bitters, then gently smack the mint sprig in your palm and place it in the glass. Finally, add the fried garlic slices and serve with a straw.

My Little Half-Tropical Maid

I played in a band for a while in the '70s. My great friend Warren was our frontman (and a much more talented musician than me). One of our mutual favorite bands of that era was the Amazing Rhythm Aces, who came out with an album titled *Stacked Deck* in 1975 that we could not get enough of. One song really spoke to us and our natural male . . . shall we say . . . "longings"; it was titled "Emma Jean," and Russell Smith sings about how he wants to be invited to the house she shares with her girlfriend for some "gin and lemonade." He also refers to her with yearning as his "little half-tropical maid." Great songs lead to great drinks, say we. And Warren can still sing the hell out of that tune.

Makes 1 cocktail

2 ounces London Dry gin

¾ ounce Old Sour (page 216)

¾ ounce fresh-squeezed lemon juice

1½ ounces Fever Tree ginger beer

1 sprig fresh tarragon

1 lemon wheel

In a collins glass, combine the gin, Old Sour, and lemon juice. Fill the glass with ice and stir until the glass feels cold and looks frosty. Slowly pour in the ginger beer, then stir gently to combine.

Give the tarragon a gentle smack in the palm of your hand to release its aroma, and place it in the drink, along the side of the glass; garnish with the lemon wheel.

Rum Running Margarita

Janet has raised the eyebrows of *many* a bartender when she orders essentially a margarita . . . but with spiced rum steading for the tequila. Here, we "spice" our own with our son Justin's recipe for allspice dram, also known as pimento dram. Cocktails are a wonderful way to unite generations, we say. Janet doesn't go for a salt rim, but if you do, by all means . . .

Makes 1 cocktail

1 ounce fresh-squeezed Key lime juice

½ ounce simple syrup (page 201)

½ ounce allspice dram, homemade (recipe on facing page) or store bought (available online)

1½ ounces añejo rum

¾ ounce Grand Marnier

2 dashes Peychaud's bitters

Combine the Key lime juice, simple syrup, and allspice dram in a mixing glass. Fill with ice, then add the rum, Grand Marnier, and bitters. Top with the shaker tin and shake until well chilled. Strain into a rocks glass with fresh ice.

Florida State Trooper

An Orange Whip is a sweet cocktail, made with rum and vodka, containing the base alcohols mixed with cream and orange juice. It is typically blended to a froth like a milkshake and poured over ice in a collins glass. The drink had a resurgence after the release of *The Blues Brothers*. In that movie, John Candy's character, Jake's parole officer, attends the film's pivotal fund-raising concert in order to arrest the performing band, but decides he wants to see them perform first and orders drinks for himself and the uniformed state troopers he is with, saying: "Who wants an orange whip? Orange whip? Orange whip? Three orange whips!"

Note: We use St. Augustine vodka because it is local, made from Florida sugar cane, and is delicious. To make it a little different from the orange whip, I substituted Galliano or Liquor 43, which adds more orange flavor without weakening the drink.

Makes 1 cocktail

1½ ounces St. Augustine vodka

1½ ounces Galliano or Liquor 43

3 ounces fresh-squeezed orange juice (Valencia preferred)

2 ounces heavy cream

Blend all the ingredients briefly with a hand blender. Pour into a glass over ice and stir.

ALLSPICE DRAM

¼ cup allspice berries

1 cup white rum

1 cinnamon stick

12 ounces water

1 cup dark brown sugar

Using a mortar and pestle (or spice grinder), crush (or chop) the allspice coarsely. Put in a mason jar and cover with the rum. Secure the lid and shake well once a day for 4 days, leaving in a cool dark place. On the fifth day, break the cinnamon stick in half and steep for 1 week more.

After the 12 total days, bring 1½ cups water and the brown sugar to a boil in a saucepan, stirring to dissolve. Let cool.

Meanwhile, double-strain the rum mixture using a fine-mesh strainer, then a coffee filter, into the bottle you plan to store the dram in. Add the cooled syrup to the bottle. Shake and set aside for 2 days before using.

Your Scotch Grandma

My mom was a Scotch drinker and also part Scottish on her daddy's side. Each winter after our son was born, she came and stayed with us in our home. She loved Florida. When the cocktail hour rolled around she enjoyed a glass of Scotch—"on the rocks" was fine by her. When asked about what cocktail we would honor her with in this book, I said to our son, her grandson, "Let's be sure to create one your Scotch-loving grandma would approve of." Her cigarette lighter was as much a part of her daily outfit as her funky collection of hats. We use her lighter to "toast" the citrus peel for this drink. And then we raise our glasses high to the woman who began this whole dance.

Makes 1 cocktail

2 ounces Scotch (Grandma drank Old Smuggler . . . you can join her on that or take your own route)

1 ounce sweet vermouth (preferably a good one, such as Dolin, Carpano Antica, or Ransom)

2 dashes Angostura bitters

1 thin slice lemon peel

Put the Scotch, vermouth, and bitters in a mixing glass with ice. Stir until chilled, then strain into a chilled coupe or martini glass.

Garnish by flaming the lemon peel over the drink and discarding it after.

Seminole Peacemaker

Our research says that this Black Drink was many times more caffeinated than a cup of coffee, which is why I keep the cold brew uncut at full strength. The Fernet and vanilla give the drink a nice herbal spice, which I imagine the original Black Drink may have had, and then gives you the caffeine kick.

Makes 1 cocktail

2 ounces Fernet Branca

1½ ounces Cold Brew Coffee (see box)

½ ounce Vanilla Simple Syrup (see box)

Shake all the ingredients in a shaker with ice and strain into a coupe glass.

COLD BREW COFFEE   ¾ cup coffee beans

Very coarsely grind the coffee beans. Put in a large container. Add 4 cups cold water. Stir gently to be sure all grounds are moistened. Cover the container with cheesecloth (do not cover with a lid, as the coffee needs to release gasses as it brews). Let stand at room temperature for 12 to 15 hours.

Remove the cheesecloth and use it to line a fine-mesh sieve set over a large pitcher. Pour the coffee through the sieve into the pitcher (do not stir); rinse the jar and set aside. Discard the cheesecloth with the grounds.

Line the same sieve with a large coffee filter and set it over the jar. Strain the coffee through the sieve into the jar. (It may take up to 45 minutes for all of the coffee to drip through; do not stir or the coffee may become cloudy.) Cover and chill. Coffee concentrate can be kept in the refrigerator for 2 weeks.

For the cocktail above, do *not* dilute. If used for regular drinking, fill a glass with ice and add 1 part coffee concentrate to 1 part milk or water.

VANILLA SIMPLE SYRUP   1 cup sugar / 1 vanilla bean, split

Combine the sugar and ½ cup water in a saucepan. Scrape the seeds from the vanilla bean and put the seeds and scraped pod in the pan. Bring to a boil, then remove from the heat and let cool. Remove the vanilla bean pod.

Mount Dora Muleskinner

This drink's name refers to a scene in the great movie *Little Big Man*, directed by Arthur Penn and starring Dustin Hoffman and Faye Dunaway. In one scene an amazingly pompous General George Custer declares that he can discern Hoffman's character's occupation just by the way he stands. Custer: "Lieutenant, it's amazing how I can guess the profession of a man just by looking at him! Notice the bandy legs, the powerful arms. This man has spent years with mules. Isn't that right?" Hoffman's befuddled Jack Crabb character falls in line meekly at that point. Custer bellows out at him smugly, "You, sir . . . are a *muleskinner*!" When someone pompous comes along, my son, Justin, and I use that line as a bit of code to amuse ourselves. The nice thing about the small towns of Florida is that the pompous are so laughably out of place.

Makes 1 cocktail

Note: Florida Farm Distillers is a microdistillery located on a small cattle farm near Umatilla, Florida (very close to our restaurant in Mount Dora). Owners Marti and Dick Waters believe that their personal and detailed attention makes Palm Ridge Reserve stand out from mass-produced liquors. The boutique operation produces a 90-proof young Florida bourbon-style whiskey. This limited-quantity, select whiskey (only five hundred cases per year) is non-chill filtered, mellowed with toasted orange and oak woods, and left to finish in small charred oak barrels.

2 ounces Palm Ridge Reserve (preferred) whiskey

1 ounce fresh-squeezed lime juice

1 ounce Ginger-Sage Simple Syrup (see box)

Soda water

Candied or fresh sage leaves for garnish

In a shaker, combine the whiskey, lime juice, simple syrup, and ice. Shake well and strain into a copper mule cup or collins glass filled with ice. Top with soda water and garnish with sage.

GINGER-SAGE SIMPLE SYRUP

1½ cups sugar

½ cup diced fresh ginger

½ cup chopped fresh sage

Combine the sugar, ginger, and 1 cup water in a saucepan and bring to a boil. Remove from the heat and immediately add the sage. Allow to steep and cool for 30 minutes, then strain.

11

OUR ROOT CELLAR AND MISS LAZY SUSAN STUFF

Relishes, Salsas, Sauces, and More

Piccalilli Relish

The term *piccalilli* originated in the fascinating fusing of food cultures from Britain and India. In the American South, *chow chow* refers to a very similar tart mélange of vegetables and spice. I like both terms. With more folks rediscovering the magic of pickles, this is one not to forget.

Makes 5 cups

1½ pounds green tomatoes, cored and finely chopped

1 sweet onion, finely chopped

2 stalks celery, chopped

1 yellow bell pepper, chopped

1 red bell pepper, chopped

¼ cup kosher salt

1 cup sugar

⅔ cup apple cider vinegar

1 tablespoon dry mustard powder

1 tablespoon yellow mustard seeds

2 teaspoons celery seeds

1 tablespoon crushed red pepper

½ teaspoon ground coriander

Toss the tomatoes, onion, celery, and bell peppers in a large bowl with the salt. Cover with plastic wrap and let sit at room temperature for 4 hours or overnight.

Transfer the vegetables to a strainer and press gently to extract excess juice; discard those now salty juices.

Transfer the vegetables to a 6-quart saucepan and add all the remaining ingredients. Cover, bring to a boil, then reduce the heat to medium-low and simmer, stirring occasionally, until vegetables are very soft, about 30 minutes.

Transfer relish to a bowl and let cool.

Once it has cooled to room temperature, cover, and refrigerate for up to 2 weeks.

Mango-Lime Coulis

We have an abundance of beautiful mangos where we live—in fact, a veritable plethora during some months of the year. This recipe is for those who want to enjoy the fruit but in a more savory way. When I was a little boy my family ate canned peaches in heavy syrup. This is like a badass version of that, I suppose. Try it with barbeque or grilled foods.

Makes 2½ cups

5 tablespoons fresh-squeezed lime juice

2 teaspoons grated lime zest

2 teaspoons liquid Sugar in the Raw

2½ cups peeled and cubed mango

Put the lime juice and zest and the liquid sugar in a heavy saucepan over medium heat. Stir and bring to just below a simmer. Let cool to room temperature. Add the mango and serve.

Use: **We use this on our Rhum and Pepper Painted Pork Belly (page 131), but if you are fans of tartness, this would be wonderful with the richness of a cheesecake. If, on the other hand, you like less tart, simply add some more of the Sugar in the Raw or other sweetener.**

Corn Relish

This relish is yet another way to offer vegetables, always a good thing. We get amazing sweet corn here, but even in places that are not so fueled with sunlight one can find plenty of "sweet" in this simple relish.

Makes a little over 1 cup

¼ cup sherry vinegar

2 tablespoons sugar

¾ teaspoon kosher salt

¼ teaspoon turmeric

1½ cups cooked sweet corn kernels (from about 2 ears)

½ serrano chile, seeded and minced

1 jarred piquillo pepper, drained and minced

1 teaspoon cracked black pepper

Combine the vinegar, sugar, salt, and turmeric in a saucepan and bring to a boil, stirring to dissolve the sugar. Add the corn and boil for 1 minute more. Remove from the heat and stir in the serrano, piquillo, and black pepper. Mix well and let cool to room temperature. Cover and refrigerate until ready to serve.

Use: Black Grouper with Split-Roasted Tomatoes, Sweet Onion "Cream," and Corn Relish (page 102).

Sweet-Hot Pepper Jelly

Sweet, hot, and a mate for many a sandwich or snack. I learned this originally from my mother, who was expert at canning. It was one of those childhood activities that probably and almost undoubtedly made me find a life inside a happy kitchen.

Makes about 5 cups

2 cups pureed seeded red bell peppers

2 tablespoons crushed red pepper

6½ cups sugar

1½ cups apple cider vinegar

2 tablespoons powdered pectin

In a heavy saucepan, bring the pureed bell peppers to a boil with the crushed red pepper, sugar, and vinegar. Simmer for about 7 minutes. Skim off the foam as necessary.

Remove from the heat and let stand, stirring occasionally, for 20 minutes. Return to the heat and boil hard for 2 minutes. Remove from the heat and stir in the pectin. Skim as necessary. Strain through a fine-mesh sieve over a bowl, discarding the solids. Pour into heatproof jars, let cool, cover, and put in the refrigerator until set.

Use: Golden Corn "Hoe Cakes" with Sweet-Hot Pepper Jelly and Chicharrón Crumbles (page 87).

Pickled Roasted Gingered Beets "with a Guest"

The "guest" here is the *umami*-bedecked traveler known as "fish sauce." It adds that "sixth taste" not normally found in a pickling agent. The earthiness of the roasted beets really allows for its intriguing powers. The pickle works without it, but you might want to give it a try.

Makes about 3 cups

1½ pounds beets, cleaned, 1 inch of the stem left on, not peeled

1 cup distilled white vinegar (tarragon or other white vinegars work well too)

⅓ cup sugar

1 tablespoon kosher salt

3 tablespoons julienned fresh ginger

2 kaffir lime leaves, torn; or 1 large bay leaf, broken

1 tablespoon fish sauce

Preheat the oven to 350 degrees.

Enclose the beets in separate "pouches" of aluminum foil. Roast the beets on a rimmed baking sheet to protect against any leaks. Roast for about 1 hour, until the beets are easily pierced with a knife.

Open the foil packages and let the beets cool enough to handle them. Peel (discarding the peel, stems, and root) and cut into shapes or sizes as desired. The smaller the pieces, the more intense the pickling will be. Set aside.

In a saucepan, combine the vinegar, sugar, salt, ginger, and kaffir lime leaves. Bring to a boil, then remove from the heat and let steep for about 15 minutes. Add the fish sauce and stir. Pour over the beets and let stand until cool. (Strain if you wish, but I like the visual of the ginger and lime leaves left in.)

The beets will improve in flavor for a few days and last about 10 days in the refrigerator.

Old Sour

This recipe was part of the old Key West cooking repertoire long before I rolled into the Island Town. It is used as a "spritz" on all kinds of foods that need a bit of acidity. We utilize the locally grown Key limes; Persian limes can be used as a substitute if you need one.

Makes about 2 cups

2 cups fresh-squeezed Key lime juice

1 tablespoon kosher salt

A few drops of hot sauce

Combine all the ingredients and let sit for a day or so. Strain the liquid through a cheesecloth into a bowl, passing it through three or four times to remove all undissolved salt and fibers. Pour into a clean mason jar or bottle with a stopper on top.

Place in the refrigerator for 2 weeks to "cure" before using. It can be stored in the refrigerator for up to 2 months.

Pineapple-Lychee Chutney

When we were invited to a project creating both the Tropical Exotic Fruit posters and *The Great Exotic Fruit Book*, we had the wonderful opportunity to delve into the breadth of south Florida's bio-diversity. We were guided by many Florida farmers and took some master classes at the Kampong in Coconut Grove from the wise and gentle Larry Schokman. Larry led us past the common mangos and pineapples and into the world of mangosteens, rambutans, and lychees. We feature lychees here even though we know they are not widely available. (They can be enjoyed after freezing, by the way.) Feel free to substitute something luscious that's in season. The recipe will still work out fine!

Makes 4 cups

1 small red onion, diced (about 1½ cups)

1 mango, peeled and diced

½ pineapple, diced (about 3 cups)

½ cup sugar, or more to taste

1 tablespoon 5 Spice Powder (see box)

Kosher salt and cracked black pepper

1 cup apple cider vinegar, or more to taste

1 tablespoon peeled and chopped fresh ginger

1 star anise

10 lychees, peeled, seeded, and chopped

In a large bowl, combine the onion, mango, pineapple, sugar, 5 Spice Powder, and salt and pepper to taste.

Put the vinegar, ginger, and star anise in a saucepan and simmer until reduced to ¾ cup; strain into a bowl and discard the solids.

Pour the vinegar mixture over the mango mixture and transfer to a large heavy saucepan. Cook over medium heat for about 20 minutes, then let cool to room temperature. Drain off the excess juices into another pan.

Cook the juices until reduced to an almost syrupy consistency, then pour it back into the fruit mixture. Add the lychees and taste for acidity; add more vinegar or sugar if needed.

Cover and refrigerate for up to 3 weeks.

OUR 5 SPICE POWDER

1 teaspoon ground cinnamon

1 teaspoon toasted fennel seeds, ground

1 teaspoon ground star anise

1 teaspoon ground cardamon

1 teaspoon ground cayenne

Mix all the ingredients together and keep in an airtight container in a cool, dark spot for up to 6 months.

Haitian Pikliz Slaw

This is a traditional condiment I first had in a Little Haiti fried chicken place, and then again not long afterward at a culinary school where an enterprising young student from inner-city Miami was creating her own artisanal line of it. I shared that story with the award-winning author Edwidge Danticat, who wrote the amazing novel *Breath, Eyes, Memory*. Edwidge beamed upon hearing of her, and also at me for caring about something so dear to the Haitian kitchen history. Upon tasting it I was a convert, and I think you will be too.

Makes about 1 quart

3 cups finely shredded cabbage (I do this *carefully* on a Japanese-style mandoline cutter)

2 cups finely shredded carrots

1 to 2 Scotch bonnet chiles, seeded and minced

½ sweet onion, diced

6 scallions, chopped

2 shallots, finely chopped

3 cloves garlic, minced

2 tablespoons fresh thyme leaves, roughly chopped

¼ teaspoon ground allspice

Kosher salt and cracked black pepper

¼ cup fresh-squeezed lime juice

1 cup apple cider vinegar or white wine vinegar

½ cup liquid Sugar in the Raw or regular granulated sugar

Combine the cabbage, carrots, chiles, onion, scallions, shallots, garlic, thyme, allspice, and salt and pepper to taste in a bowl. Stir well. Pour in the lime juice and vinegar and stir again. Add the liquid sugar.

Cover and refrigerate for 1 to 3 days before using. Taste and season again if needed. This will keep up to 3 months in the refrigerator.

Note: Many Haitians will add more chiles than we have called for. They grew up with heat levels that would kick most of us in the ass. Follow your own path on that ingredient! Note also that most recipes don't call for any kind of sugar. Acidity, too, is a bit more prized in some cultures than others. You can try it without sugar and then go in the direction that best suits your taste buds.

Use: I like this with any kind of fried or fatty foods when spice is appreciated by the guests. We serve it with oxtails (page 123), and we also love it on fried chicken.

Fried Pickle Spears

Fried fish sandwiches are very, very popular in Florida. But if you want a purer taste of fish and also a more pronounced crunch, we suggest you try these on a grilled or oven-cooked fillet of fish before placing it all between the buns. They make a good snack as is, dipped in a sour cream–based sauce. You see fried pickles often down here. Spear style is our preference.

Makes 10 spears

8 pickle spears (pick the style you like), well drained

¼ cup all-purpose flour

1 egg, beaten together with 1 tablespoon water

½ cup panko breadcrumbs, briefly pulsed in a food processor

Cracked black pepper

Canola, vegetable, or peanut oil for deep-frying

Hot sauce (optional)

Blot the pickles *quite* dry and lay them on paper towels for about 2 minutes.

Dredge the spears in flour. Dip them in the egg wash and dredge them in the breadcrumbs. Season with black pepper. Allow to sit for a few minutes.

Heat enough oil to submerge the pickles in a deep-fryer or heavy pot to 375 degrees.

Cook the pickle spears in the oil for about 1 minute, until golden brown. Remove to paper towels and serve hot, with hot sauce if you'd like.

Serving suggestion: Sour cream is nice on these. Fat and acid are lifelong pals.

Use: **We make these for our Steadman's Boatyard Grilled Citrus and Soy Fish Tacos (page 79).**

Preserved Lemons

Preserved lemons are a great pantry tool and can be used for many things. We first discovered this wonder when studying the works of the one and only Paula Wolfert years ago.

Makes 6 preserved lemons (the usable part is the rind)

6 lemons, scrubbed and patted dry

1 cup kosher salt

½ teaspoon crushed red pepper

2 bay leaves, broken

1½ cups fresh-squeezed lemon juice

3 tablespoons extra-virgin olive oil

Cut the blossom and stem ends off the lemons and then cut them into wedges.

Toss the lemons, salt, crushed red pepper, and bay leaves together in a large bowl. Transfer to a mason jar. Pour the lemon juice over the cut lemons and seasonings and add the oil. Cover tightly.

Let the jar stand for at least 1 week, shaking it once every day.

When the time is up, remove the lid. If any scum came to the surface, skim off and discard it. Put the lemons in a clean container and refrigerate. They will improve in flavor over time.

Rinse away the salt before using them. It is only the *rinds* that we use—scrape away and discard the flesh.

Rhum and Pepper Paint

We have done many dishes with this particular "paint." I began making versions of it in 1984 and settled on a "final" recipe about ten years later. Though the recipe has become fixed, the uses for it change frequently, sometimes because the folks I cook with come up with new ways to use it.

Makes 2 cups

½ cup plus 2 tablespoons whole black peppercorns

¾ tablespoon whole cloves

2 cups sugar

2½ cups soy sauce

3 cups light or spiced rhum

½ cup grated lemon zest (no white pith)

½ cup fresh-squeezed lemon juice

Notes: **It is better to remove the "paint" from the heat a bit early if you are unsure of its thickness while reducing. It needs to be as thick as warm molasses but actually *not* any thicker. If it results in the 2-cup yield here it is likely to be ideal.**

Toast the black peppercorns and the cloves together in a dry skillet over medium-high heat until you see puffs of smoke.

Grind them together in a spice grinder and transfer to a heavy, deep saucepan. Add the remaining ingredients and bring to a boil. The mixture will begin to foam as it reduces. It will also flame from all of the rum in it. Be ready with a pan or lid to place on top of the flame after it burns the alcohol off for a few seconds. When the mixture is reduced by half, strain it through a chinois or very-fine-mesh sieve and into a bowl. Let cool to room temperature.

This "paint" will keep a long time in the refrigerator. When you use it, only take out what you need and pour it into a bowl; don't dip meat into the larger amount, which will spoil it.

Uses: **Rhum and Pepper Painted Pork Belly (page 131).**

Escabeche Spice Rub

This is an indispensable spice mixture you will find yourself using on countless things. *Escabeche* comes to us via the Spaniards. The word means "pickled, spiced fish," and it surely derives from the Spanish *pesca*, or "fish." We use it on chicken and pork with a free hand!

Makes 1 scant cup

¼ cup cumin seeds

¼ cup whole black peppercorns

5 tablespoons sugar

2 tablespoons kosher salt

Put the cumin seeds and peppercorns in a dry skillet and toast over medium heat until fragrant, 30 to 60 seconds. Let cool, then transfer to a spice grinder and grind until fine. Pour into a bowl, add the sugar and salt, and stir well. Store in an airtight container until ready to use.

Use: **Use it on just about anything!**

Korean Spice Mix

This is a nicely balanced spice mix with an unusual (to an American palate, at least) yet highly welcome range of flavors. Try it as a stand-alone spice rub for a roasted chicken sometime.

Makes ⅓ cup

1 tablespoon canola oil

2 teaspoons dark toasted sesame oil

2 cloves garlic, minced

5 teaspoons Korean chile powder (aka *gochugaru*) or another mild chile powder

3 teaspoons sugar

1 teaspoon Sichuan peppercorns, ground

1 teaspoon ground black pepper

Combine all of the ingredients and mix well. Store in a small resealable plastic bag or a glass jar with a lid in a cool, dark spot for up to 6 months.

Use: "Koreatown" Fried Chicken (page 147).

Coffee Spice Rub

My fellow chef and pal (and occasional bandmate) Robert Del Grande of Texas was the first person I saw using coffee as a spice rub component. The complex notes of coffee add lively harmony to the staples of salt, pepper, sugar, and other spices found in many a rub.

Makes ½ cup

2 tablespoons finely ground coffee (decaf is fine too)

1½ tablespoons kosher salt

1 tablespoon granulated (white or raw) sugar

1 tablespoon brown sugar

1½ tablespoons granulated garlic

1 heaping teaspoon cracked black pepper

¼ teaspoon ground cayenne

¼ teaspoon ground cumin

¼ teaspoon smoked pimentón

Mix all the ingredients together. Store in a tightly covered container in a dark, cool spot until ready to use.

Uses: Coffee-Rubbed T-Bone Steaks (page 120).

"Galbi" Marinade

This marinade of Korean origin, sometimes spelled *kalbi*, comes from the word for "ribs" and is the traditional kind of marinade you find on Korean short ribs. I found this marinade works so well on a slew of things to grill that I didn't want to confine it to one (albeit wonderful) dish, so cut loose and try it on whatever suits your fancy. See the dish in this book using shrimp, for instance (page 88); it was listed as one of the "World's 50 Most Delicious Foods" in a poll compiled by CNN a few years back!

Makes 2¾ cups

6 tablespoons sugar

6 tablespoons soy sauce

2 tablespoons crushed red pepper

¾ cup apple, peach, or Asian pear juice

½ cup dark toasted sesame oil

8 cloves garlic, minced

¼ cup finely minced fresh ginger

Kosher salt and cracked black pepper

Combine the sugar, soy sauce, crushed red pepper, apple juice, sesame oil, garlic, ginger, and 1 teaspoon salt and 1 teaspoon pepper, or more to taste, in a mixing bowl. This makes enough to marinate 3 to 4 pounds meat; it is best to marinate in the refrigerator overnight if possible.

Note: We have reduced this marinade by half or so and used it as a brush-on BBQ sauce to great effect.

Classic Sour Orange *Mojo*

There are plenty of bottled *mojos* being produced. Avoid them! Manufacturers have yet to capture the perfection of what you can make at home. We use *mojo* as a marinade for chicken, pork, and steak (especially flank and skirt steak). It will keep in the refrigerator up to a month.

Makes 1½ cups

6 cloves garlic, chopped

1 Scotch bonnet chile, seeded and minced

½ teaspoon kosher salt

2 teaspoons toasted cumin seeds

1 cup extra-virgin olive oil

⅓ cup fresh-squeezed sour orange juice

2 teaspoons sherry vinegar

Cracked black pepper

Mash the garlic, chile, salt, and cumin together in a mortar with the pestle until fairly smooth. Scrape into a bowl and set aside.

Heat the oil in a pan until fairly hot (about 300 degrees) and *carefully* pour it, whisking, over the garlic mixture. Let stand for 5 minutes. Whisk in the sour orange juice and the vinegar.

Season with the black pepper to taste and set aside in the refrigerator until ready to use, up to 1 month.

Note: Sour oranges, *naranja agria* in Spanish, are much more sour than regular oranges. If you don't have sour oranges, you can use a combination of lemon and lime juice if need be. It is not quite the same, but workable.

Tomatillo Salsa

Tomatillos are a hallmark of Latin-Caribbean cooking and hopefully will become more so in yours via this salsa. The presence of masa is not typical in salsas, but it is traditional.

Makes about 2 cups

3 large tomatillos, husks and stems removed, rinsed, and cut in half

¾ cup chopped sweet onion

1 large jalapeño chile, stemmed, seeded, and cut into quarters

3 cloves garlic, peeled

1 teaspoon freshly ground cumin seeds

A pinch of ground cloves

Leaves from 1 sprig fresh thyme

Leaves from 1 sprig fresh oregano, plus 2 tablespoons leaves

3 tablespoons sherry vinegar

3 cups Chicken Stock (page 237)

3 tablespoons masa harina mixed to a smooth paste with 4 tablespoons water

½ cup fresh Italian parsley, chopped

½ cup fresh cilantro leaves, chopped

Put the tomatillos, onion, jalapeño, garlic, cumin, cloves, thyme, the leaves of 1 sprig oregano, the vinegar, and ½ cup of the stock in a heavy-duty blender. Process on high until smooth, about 2 minutes.

Put the remaining 2½ cups stock in a large saucepan. Bring to a boil and adjust the heat to maintain a gentle simmer. Add the pureed mixture to the hot stock, bring to a simmer, and cook for 3 minutes.

Whisk the thinned masa into the sauce and bring back to a simmer, whisking often.

Cook uncovered over low heat, whisking occasionally, until reduced to 2 cups, about 10 minutes.

Put the sauce, parsley, cilantro, and the remaining 2 tablespoons oregano in the blender. Process until smooth. Serve or refrigerate in an airtight container for up to 1 week.

Use: **Route 27 Turkey Neck Tamales (page 65).**

Caramelized Pineapple Salsa

The famous natural sweetness of pineapple is ramped up via caramelization for this simple, fresh, and versatile salsa. You can bake the pineapple, but even more fun is to caramelize it until very dark with a blowtorch. As Julia Child supposedly once said, "Every girl should have a blowtorch." Janet is that girl here!

Makes 1½ cups

1 cup diced pineapple

1 tablespoon sugar

¼ cup finely diced sweet onion

1 cup diced peeled and seeded ripe tomato

½ Scotch bonnet or other chile, seeded and minced

2 tablespoons chopped fresh cilantro or mint leaves

1 tablespoon sherry vinegar

1 teaspoon fresh-squeezed lime juice

2 tablespoons extra-virgin olive oil

¼ teaspoon kosher salt

¼ teaspoon cracked black pepper

Preheat the oven to 475 degrees.

Toss the pineapple with the sugar in a bowl. Put the pineapple in a nonstick baking pan or ovenproof skillet. Place in the oven for 6 to 7 minutes and check for caramelization. It could take another few minutes. The sugar content in the pineapple will vary, hence the variable cooking time. When there is a nice color, remove and let cool a bit. Set aside.

In a bowl, combine the caramelized pineapple, onion, tomato, chile, cilantro, vinegar, lime juice, oil, salt, and black pepper. Cover and chill if not using right away. (The salsa is best if used within a day or so.)

Note: Some tomatoes are thin skinned enough to not need peeling. Seeding them is a matter of personal preference too.

Our House Vinaigrette

Clearly when you name something "our house," you use and enjoy it often. Here's to sharing ours.

Makes 1¾ cups

A pinch of kosher salt

2 tablespoons minced shallot

½ tablespoon Dijon mustard

⅓ cup red wine vinegar

1 tablespoon balsamic vinegar

1 tablespoon honey

½ cup canola oil

¾ cup extra-virgin olive oil

2 tablespoons sesame oil

2 tablespoons chopped fresh Italian parsley

Cracked black pepper

Whisk the salt, shallot, mustard, and vinegars together in a medium bowl or shake them in a lidded mason jar.

Add the honey, all the oils, the parsley, and pepper to taste. Whisk or cover and shake well. Season to taste.

Set aside in the refrigerator until needed, up to 3 weeks.

Buttermilk–Creole Mustard Dressing

We love the punchy and zesty flavors of this creamy dressing. The buttermilk supplies a vibrant tang that adds another kind of lift. You can use this on the "Florida Pinks" Shrimp salad (page 49), but it is a fine partner to raw vegetables too.

Makes about 5 cups

¾ cup apple cider vinegar

6 tablespoons honey

4 cloves garlic, minced

6 tablespoons Creole or "country Dijon" mustard

1 cup plus 2 tablespoons sour cream

1½ cups buttermilk

¾ cup heavy cream

½ cup mayonnaise

½ to 1 teaspoon salt

1 teaspoon cracked black pepper

In a medium-size nonreactive bowl, combine the vinegar, honey, garlic, and mustard. Whisk in the remaining ingredients one by one. Season to taste with salt and pepper.

Cover and refrigerate until needed, up to 2 weeks.

Fermented Black Bean Butter

What's old is new again, and that is the case with fermentation, now trending as a food preparation. This butter sauce goes with our Grilled Swordfish (page 110), but you can serve it with a wide range of seafoods and even grilled or baked chicken.

Makes 1 cup

½ cup dry white wine

2 tablespoons mirin (sweet rice wine)

¼ cup rice vinegar

½ shallot, minced

1½ tablespoons minced fresh ginger

1 tablespoon minced garlic

1 jalapeño chile, seeded and finely minced

¼ cup Chicken Stock (page 237)

½ cup heavy cream

¼ cup fermented black beans, soaked for about 10 minutes in a little cool water, rinsed, and drained

½ cup (1 stick) cold butter, cut into small pieces

3 tablespoons chopped fresh cilantro leaves

In a small saucepan, combine the white wine, mirin, vinegar, shallot, ginger, garlic, and jalapeño. Cook over high heat until reduced by half, about 3 minutes.

Add the stock and cook to reduce the mixture until fairly thick. Add the cream and bring to a simmer for about 10 seconds. Add the fermented black beans and whisk in the butter bit by bit. (Do not strain this butter sauce.) Add the cilantro. Keep warm until ready to use.

Red Chimichurri

¼ cup plus 2 tablespoons olive oil

½ cup red wine vinegar

1½ tablespoons Spanish pimentón

2 teaspoons ground cayenne

4 cloves garlic, minced

1 teaspoon toasted and ground black peppercorns

1 teaspoon toasted and ground cumin seeds

1 bay leaf, broken in half

½ teaspoon kosher salt

Chimichurri originated in Argentina and Uruguay and is a popular sauce for grilled meat in many Latin American countries. Apparently the word *chimichurri* comes from Jimmy McCurry, an Irishman who fought alongside Argentine soldiers in the fight for Argentine independence in the nineteenth century. The sauce became popular and the recipe was passed on. However, "Jimmy McCurry" was difficult for native Spanish speakers to say. Some sources claim that the sauce's name is a corrupted version of its creator's, while others say the sauce's name was changed in his honor.

There is a green version and a red one. I would not be surprised to learn of more. This baby is *not* shy, by the way. Use sparingly until you have experienced it.

Makes 1 cup

Combine all of the ingredients and mix well. Store in the refrigerator in a glass jar with a tight-fitting lid.

Strawberry-Ancho-Guava Jam

This is a unique BBQ-type sauce. I call it a "jam" to differentiate it (and because I *like* the word *jam*). I created this sauce for the Florida Strawberry Growers Association. It may be a bit surprising to use strawberries in this way, but their sweetness is not entirely different from that of tomatoes when the luscious red berries are in season. The guava adds an exotic touch we love.

Makes 5 cups

3 dried ancho chiles, stems and seeds removed

12 cloves garlic, peeled

1¼ cups bottled Asian plum sauce

3 tablespoons sherry vinegar

½ teaspoon kosher salt

½ tablespoon cracked black pepper

1 pound fresh Florida strawberries, washed, hulled, patted dry, and thinly sliced

¾ cup guava jam (store bought)

Toast the chiles in a dry skillet until fragrant. When they are cool enough to handle, chop them or cut them with scissors into pieces.

Put the garlic cloves and chiles in a heavy saucepan with 4 cups water and bring to a boil. Lower the heat to a high simmer and cook until the water is *almost* gone, about 30 minutes. Keep a close eye on it as it reaches the end of evaporating.

Put the mixture in a food processor and pulse until smooth. Add the plum sauce, vinegar, salt, and black pepper and process until smooth.

Gently fold in the sliced strawberries. Return the mixture to a saucepan and heat through. Stir in the guava jam.

Set aside, covered in the refrigerator, until needed, up to 3 weeks.

Use: We use this on our Cornbread-Stuffed Quail with Strawberry-Ancho-Guava Jam and Sweet and Sour Parsnips (page 154), but you can use it about anywhere you would a BBQ sauce.

Chipotle BBQ Sauce

The number of ingredients here may surprise you (many fine barbeque sauces will have a lot of ingredients), but it is super simple to mix up and packs a nice punch from both chiles and the acids in the recipe. Good on any kind of thing you love to cook on a grill when in "BBQ mode."

Makes 4 cups

2 tablespoons olive oil or canola oil

½ large red onion, peeled and chopped

3 cloves garlic, minced

¼ cup fresh-squeezed orange juice

½ cup plus 1 tablespoon white wine vinegar

1 (14-ounce) can whole plum tomatoes

1 cup diced pineapple

¼ cup molasses

1 tablespoon dark brown sugar

1 tablespoon granulated sugar

1 tablespoon cracked black pepper

½ tablespoon Hungarian hot paprika

½ tablespoon toasted and ground cumin seeds

1 teaspoon chili powder

¼ cup chipotles in adobo

¼ cup Creole or Dijon mustard

2 tablespoons soy sauce or tamari

1 tablespoon Worcestershire sauce

¼ cup chopped fresh basil

Heat a large heavy saucepan over medium heat and add the oil and onion. Stir. Cook until the onion is darkened a little on the edges, 10 to 15 minutes.

Add the garlic and stir for about 1 minute. Add all the remaining ingredients and bring to a simmer.

Puree in a blender or food processor. Let cool and serve, or cover and refrigerate.

Basic and Beautiful Tomato Sauce

The name says it all. Try it and see if you agree.

Makes 3 cups

2 tablespoons extra-virgin olive oil

2 cloves garlic, thinly sliced

½ cup diced sweet onion

1 teaspoon crushed red pepper

2 cups canned whole tomatoes, pureed (I like San Marzano–type tomatoes)

2 tablespoons red wine or, for a slightly sweeter version, balsamic vinegar

2 or 3 fresh basil leaves or 1 sprig fresh thyme

Kosher salt and cracked black pepper

Heat the oil over medium heat in a heavy-bottomed straight-sided saucepan. Add the garlic, onion, and crushed red pepper. Cook for 5 minutes, stirring.

Add the tomatoes, wine, and basil and season with salt and pepper to taste. Cook for about 30 minutes more, until the sauce is thick, stirring often. You want a steady heat. Season to taste.

Set aside, covered to keep warm, or refrigerate and reheat when ready to serve.

Rosa's "Two Way" Tomato Sauce

This somewhat piquant and spicy sauce is often called a "gastrique" in fancy kitchens. The power of a well-made one is the one-two punch of sweet meets acid. The fruits more often used are clearly sweeter than tomatoes. But those tasting our sauce who have that culinary background might compare it to a gastrique all the same. Does this make it better? No. What makes it useful, though, is the range of flavors it imparts. I learned it from a Cuban Italian woman named Rosa.

Makes 3 cups

¼ cup finely diced fatty bacon

1 tablespoon olive oil

4 cloves garlic, thinly sliced

1 shallot, sliced

¼ cup sugar

½ tablespoon crushed red pepper

⅓ cup red wine vinegar

1½ cups Chicken Stock (page 237)

1 (28-ounce) can whole tomatoes, crushed up by hand

Kosher salt and cracked black pepper

¼ cup fresh basil leaves, chopped

Heat a large heavy saucepan over medium heat.

Add the bacon and oil. Cook until the bacon is beginning to crisp and has given off some of its fat.

Add the garlic and shallot, and sauté, stirring occasionally, until *lightly* browned, 5 to 6 minutes.

Add the sugar, stirring well and mashing it in with a heavy wooden spoon to break up. Cook for about 2 minutes, taking care not to allow this to burn. (Sugar accelerates the possibilities of burning.)

Add the crushed red pepper. Stir briefly. Add the vinegar and stir well, as the sugar needs to be well dispersed. Add the stock. Increase the heat and bring to a high simmer; cook until reduced by half or a bit more, 10 to 12 minutes.

Add the tomatoes and their juice. Season with a bit of salt and black pepper and bring just to a boil, then lower the heat and cook, stirring, for about 10 minutes. Remove from the heat. Add the basil and stir. Season with more salt and black pepper if needed. Serve warm, or let cool, cover, and refrigerate.

Note: You can blend the sauce if you want a smoother consistency, but do so before adding the basil so you keep those pretty flecks within the sauce.

Charred Scallion–Toasted Almond Romesco

Romescos date back to nearly ancient Spain and so figure into many dishes that continue to descend from that amazing land.

Makes 1 cup

20 scallions, including some of the green part, trimmed of the roots but otherwise left whole

Peanut oil

Kosher salt and cracked black pepper

1 ripe tomato, cored and halved

¼ sweet onion, halved

½ poblano chile, stemmed, halved, and seeded

1 dried ancho chile, stemmed, seeded, toasted, then soaked in warm water until soft and drained

1 pimiento (about ½ cup), drained

2 teaspoons fresh-squeezed lemon juice

1½ tablespoons dark toasted sesame oil

1 cup sliced almonds, toasted

Preheat the oven to 350 degrees.

Rinse the trimmed scallions, shake them dry, and then towel-dry them too.

Heat a large nonstick skillet over medium heat. Add oil to just coat the bottom and then add the scallions in a single layer. Cook, turning only occasionally, until they are charred. (If you stir them too much they will not develop the char.) This will take about 15 minutes total. Season with salt and pepper and set aside on a plate; blot off any excess oil.

Put the tomato, onion, and poblano in a lightly oiled baking pan. Oil the vegetables a bit too. Roast them in the oven. Take the tomato out after 10 minutes and set it on a plate. Remove the skin. Roast the onion and poblano for a total of about 30 minutes. Remove and set aside to cool. Peel the poblano. If the onion has any "papery" skin, discard that too.

In a food processor or blender, put the charred scallions, tomato, onion, poblano, dried chile, pimiento, lemon juice, sesame oil, and salt and pepper as needed. Pulse until smooth. Strain through a medium-mesh strainer set over a bowl and push as much of the puree through into the bowl; discard the solids in the strainer. (This step pulls out the strands of the scallions, which are not a good texture.)

Clean out the food processor or blender. Return the sauce to the processor, along with the almonds, and pulse again. Check for seasoning and set aside, covered and refrigerated, until ready to serve.

Use: **This is a sauce that we use on our Smoked Fish Dip on Corn Cakes (page 99), but it goes with many dishes.**

Sriracha Hollandaise

The pleasures of a great hollandaise don't go in and out of season, much like Mozart or Cole Porter music. It also is quite capable of taking on a new traveling partner. Sriracha, in this case.

Makes 1½ cups

1 cup (2 sticks) unsalted butter

3 egg yolks

1½ teaspoons fresh-squeezed lemon juice (if needed)

Kosher salt and cracked black pepper

Tabasco sauce or ground cayenne

Sriracha

Cut the butter into several pieces and melt it. Set aside.

Put the egg yolks and a few drops of water in a stainless-steel bowl and whisk very well.

Heat a saucepan of water that will hold the bowl without letting the bowl come into contact with the water, like a double boiler. Keep over medium heat.

Put the bowl of egg yolks over the simmering water and whisk (not just stir!) the eggs. Allow them to thicken gently and evenly. When you can draw a line with the whisk across the bottom of the bowl and see the bottom for a quick count to three, they are thick enough.

Remove the bowl from the heat and, very gradually at first, whisk in the melted butter. If the sauce gets too thick, whisk in the lemon juice (if you need it, add a few drops of warm water as well). When all of the butter is incorporated, whisk in salt and pepper to taste.

Whisk in the Tabasco and sriracha a little at a time, tasting to see if the strength level is for you. If not, bump a few more drops in there. Keep warm until ready to serve.

Note: I do not clarify butter for sauce béarnaise or hollandaise. That is a restaurant trick to help "hold" the sauce over the longer periods of service a restaurant might require, but we do not need to do it for quality home cooking. It has an additional downside in that sauces made with clarified butter don't have quite as luxurious a mouthfeel as those made with whole butter.

Piccalilli Tartar Sauce

6 raw egg yolks

1 cup extra-virgin olive oil

1 cup canola oil

2 tablespoons Champagne vinegar

2 teaspoons apple cider vinegar

6 tablespoons Piccalilli Relish (or other favorite pickle relish) (page 214)

¼ cup finely diced red onion

2 tablespoons fresh-squeezed lemon juice

4 teaspoons Dijon mustard

2 to 3 teaspoons Tabasco sauce

2 hard-cooked eggs (yolks sieved, whites minced)

Kosher salt and cracked black pepper

Once you make the Piccalilli Relish, it will be an easy jump to fit it into a tartar sauce. To hasten the process, you can skip the homemade mayo for a store-bought version.

Makes 4 cups

Put the raw egg yolks in a mixer and beat until pale. This takes a few minutes, so be patient.

Add the olive and canola oils very slowly until it is all incorporated, alternately adding the vinegars a few drops at a time to help balance the emulsification.

When all of the oils and vinegars are well incorporated, remove the bowl from the mixer. Pour the mixture into a bowl and add the Piccalilli Relish and onion. Stir in the lemon juice, mustard, and Tabasco. Stir in the hard-cooked eggs. Season with salt and pepper to taste.

Cover and refrigerate until ready to serve.

Use: Spiny Lobster Hash Cakes (page 22).

Sorghum and Horseradish Sour Cream

½ cup sour cream

2 tablespoons sorghum syrup

1 tablespoon prepared horseradish sauce (not the creamy kind)

The balance of sweet-meeting-heat in a soft embrace of fat is the triple kisser to many successful sauces that go with crispy things like empanadas, fritters, and their cousins. There is no cheese in this sauce, so the finger-waggers on serving fish with cheese can take a break too.

Makes ⅔ cup

Combine all the ingredients in a bowl. Refrigerate, covered, until ready to serve.

Colonial Drive Dipping Sauce

The "drive" in this recipe title comes from a part of Orlando that is a wide-open celebration of Asian flavors. If you can't visit the actual spot, you can taste the DNA here.

Makes 2⅔ cups

⅔ cup thinly sliced shallots (3 to 4 shallots)

½ bulb fennel, minced

1 cup fresh cilantro leaves, minced

3 scallions, white and light green parts, thinly sliced into rings (about ½ cup)

6 tablespoons packed light brown sugar

¼ cup packed minced garlic (5 to 6 cloves)

5 tablespoons soy sauce or tamari

4 tablespoons peanut or canola oil

1 tablespoon dark toasted sesame oil

Juice and minced zest of 4 limes

3-inch piece fresh ginger, peeled and grated (1½ tablespoons)

2 tablespoons fish sauce

2 Scotch bonnet chiles, seeded and minced

1 teaspoon ground cumin

Kosher salt and cracked black pepper to taste

Combine all of the ingredients together and set aside, tightly covered in the refrigerator, until needed, up to 1 month.

Comeback Sauce

Comeback Sauce came out of Mississippi and, like mayo, spread. The southern-hospitality charm in the name might have a bit to do with it, but the beguiling combination of fat, acid, and spice truly makes it a versatile tablemate. We lace ours with Pickapeppa sauce, which was invented in 1921 in Jamaica. Combining Mississippi and Jamaican powers makes perfect sense to me.

Makes 1⅔ cups

¼ cup extra-virgin olive oil

¼ cup Heinz chili sauce

¼ cup ketchup

½ tablespoon Pickapeppa sauce

½ tablespoon Worcestershire sauce

1 teaspoon stone-ground mustard

1 cup mayonnaise

Kosher salt and cracked black pepper to taste

½ tablespoon fresh-squeezed lemon juice

1 teaspoon minced garlic

Put all of the ingredients in a blender and blend well. Taste and adjust the seasonings as needed. Store in the refrigerator and allow the flavors to marry for at least a few hours.

Use: We use this for the normal "mayo" part of our Fully Loaded Cracked Conch Po' Boy (page 76), but the uses are legion.

House Pork Sausage

Making your own pork sausage is not only fun but also economical. And you can control the outcome in ways store bought don't allow.

Makes 3 pounds

2 pounds boneless pork butt or shoulder, cut into 1-inch pieces

1 pound pork fat, cut into 1-inch pieces

5½ tablespoons pureed chipotles in adobo

½ teaspoon ground cayenne

½ teaspoon crushed red pepper

1 teaspoon ground cumin

2 teaspoons kosher salt

1 teaspoon coarsely cracked black pepper

¼ cup sherry vinegar

1½ teaspoons minced fresh thyme leaves

Canola oil or rendered bacon fat for cooking

Put the meat, fat, and also a meat grinder's grinding blade and plate in the freezer for 30 minutes before doing the grind. (It makes the meat cut more cleanly instead of getting squished as it goes through, which results in a texturally *much* better sausage.)

Grind the pork meat and pork fat in the meat grinder with a plate with ¼-inch holes. Put the mixture back in the freezer for 15 more minutes. Grind again with the same plate.

Mix the chipotles, cayenne, crushed red pepper, cumin, salt, black pepper, vinegar, and thyme together very well and add to the meat, quickly mixing it in well. Cover and refrigerate for at least 1 hour.

Form the mixture into patties of the size you like, cover, and refrigerate until ready to cook.

Cook the patties in oil or bacon fat until nicely browned on both sides and cooked through.

Use: Marjorie's Corn Cakes (page 61).

Candied Bacon Bits

These might need to be offered with a warning label. They are that good!

Makes about ½ cup

4 slices bacon, cut into ½-inch pieces

1 tablespoon dark brown sugar

2 teaspoons apple cider vinegar

Kosher salt and cracked black pepper

Note: **This can be served in many ways. We are now testing it with a pumpkin chiffon pie at our cooking school, for example.**

Cook the bacon in a large nonstick skillet over medium heat until crisp and well rendered, 6 to 8 minutes.

Using a slotted spoon, remove the bacon from the skillet and save the fat for another use.

Return the bacon to the skillet and add the brown sugar and vinegar. Cook over low heat, stirring constantly, until the bacon is evenly coated.

Transfer to a plate in a single layer and season to taste with salt and pepper. Let cool completely. Store in a covered container in the refrigerator or freezer.

Lardons

This is a classic recipe, the kind I have learned to make by studying the cookbooks of that mentor of many—Jacques Pépin.

Makes about 1½ cups

8 ounces slab-style bacon

Cut the bacon into baton shapes about ¾ inch long by ½ inch wide by ½ inch thick.

Put them in a small heavy saucepan with 3 tablespoons water. Place over medium to medium-low heat and cook for about 15 minutes. Use a transparent lid if you have one, as it helps you monitor the water level. You want to be sure to add a bit more water if it evaporates too quickly as you cook. Stir or shake the pan from time to time.

You can't judge by the same color as when cooking bacon normally (without water). So carefully pull out a piece and taste it. The texture of lardons is less crunchy and more meaty.

Use: "Florida Pinks" Shrimp with Buttermilk–Creole Mustard Dressing (page 49). Excellent for salads.

Drain the lardons in a strainer, reserving the rendered fat for other uses. Transfer to paper towels until ready to use. Lardons may be prepared in advance and rewarmed.

Smoked Fish Dip

It kind of catches me when people say we don't have the "four seasons" in Florida. I find myself not saying anything. Why argue? But when you live here in Florida the majority of your life, you come to perceive seasonality very subtly. Let's just put it this way: We eat ceviche in hot weather and smoked fish dip in cool weather!

Makes 1 cup plus 2 tablespoons

2 cups smoked fish (mullet and wahoo are big in Florida; feel free to smoke your own like we do, but very good store-bought versions exist and can be overnighted to your door)

5 tablespoons sour cream

3 tablespoons cream cheese

½ teaspoon Dijon or "yellow" mustard

½ teaspoon Tabasco sauce

1 teaspoon Pickapeppa sauce (A.1. is a reasonable alternative)

1 teaspoon your favorite spice blend or Escabeche Spice Rub (page 220)

3 tablespoons spicy pickle relish (we like "Wickles" brand out of neighboring Alabama)

Lightly crumble the fish.

Combine the sour cream, cream cheese, mustard, Tabasco, Pickapeppa, and spice blend in a mixer until smooth. Fold in the fish and pickle relish. Chill, covered, until ready to serve.

Serving suggestion: Offer with crackers or "Those Toasts" (page 242) to keep it simple.

Braised Turkey Necks

Braising turkey necks—like braising almost anything—seems like a nearly lost art. But braising unlocks the deepest of flavors and is not difficult. In fact, Janet began braising turkey necks when she was still a little girl cooking by her mother's side. The meat went (and still goes!) into turkey stuffing. And it is good to know we are using more of the turkey than the legs, thighs, and breasts as we seek to cook "nose to tail."

Makes 3½ cups meat and 4 cups broth

4 pounds turkey necks, rinsed and patted dry

Kosher salt and cracked black pepper

¼ cup olive oil

4 tablespoons unsalted butter

6 cloves garlic, sliced

1 sweet onion, diced

3 stalks celery, diced

2 large carrots, peeled and diced

1 fennel bulb, tops removed, diced

1 cup dry white wine

4 cups Chicken Stock (page 237)

3 sprigs fresh thyme

1 bay leaf, broken in half

Season the turkey necks with salt and pepper. Heat the oil in a large soup pot or Dutch oven over medium-high heat. When hot, working in batches, add the turkey necks and brown them on all sides, 10 to 15 minutes total. Transfer them to a platter as they brown.

Add the butter to the pot, then add the garlic, onion, celery, carrots, and fennel and stir to coat. Season with salt and pepper and cook until the vegetables are caramelized, 10 to 15 minutes, being careful not to scorch the bottom of the pot. Transfer the vegetables to a bowl and set aside.

Add the wine to the pot and deglaze it, scraping the bottom with a wooden spoon. Return the turkey necks and vegetables to the pot and pour in the stock and 4 cups cool water. Bring to a simmer, then lower the heat and skim any impurities that have risen to the top. Add the thyme and bay leaf, cover, and simmer for 1½ to 2 hours, until the turkey is quite tender.

Remove the necks to a clean pan and let cool for a few minutes. Strain the broth through a fine-mesh strainer into a clean bowl.

When the turkey is just cool enough to handle (it is an easier task if the meat is still pretty warm), take it off the bones, pulling it apart with your fingers, then cut it into bite-sized pieces. You can cook the broth in a saucepan to reduce it to a gravy-like consistency and add it to the meat to amp up the flavor, or save the broth and use it to fortify other soups and sauces. You can also take all of the neck bones and make a second "wetting" of the bones to glean every last drop of flavor from them, as we do in our kitchens.

Use: Route 27 Turkey Neck Tamales (page 65).

Chicken Stock

Please make your own homemade chicken stock. It is not only more economical it is spiritual and creates a base of flavor that the store-bought stuff has yet to attain.

Makes 2 gallons plus 1 quart

Canola or other light oil

7 pounds skin-on chicken, cut into 8 parts

3 large sweet onions (about 3 pounds), peeled and chopped

1½ pounds peeled and chopped carrots

1 pound celery, chopped

½ bulb fennel (with fronds from the whole bulb), chopped

White wine or water if needed

3 heads of garlic, cut in half crosswise

24 black peppercorns

2 to 3 bay leaves, broken

2 dried ancho chiles, cut in half

1 bunch fresh thyme

1 bunch fresh Italian parsley

Preheat the oven to 400 degrees.

Lightly oil the cut-up chicken and put it in two large roasting pans. Roast until lightly browned, 35 to 45 minutes.

Remove from the oven, turn the chicken over, and add about half of the onions, carrots, celery, and fennel (don't overcrowd the pans).

In the resulting chicken fat, brown the remaining vegetables in another sauté pan over medium to medium-high heat, stirring. Return the chicken and vegetables back to the oven. Roast for another 15 to 20 minutes.

Take the pans out of the oven and transfer everything from the pans to a large stockpot and cover with cold water. If you have bits of meat, skin, and so on stuck to the pans, pour some white wine or water into the pan and using a flat wooden spoon scrape those bits up and add them to the stockpot. Bring to a good high simmer (*not* a boil) and skim off any impurities that come to the top of the pot. This will take a few rounds and a bit of time. But it is what you do to get a good clear final stock. Add the garlic heads, peppercorns, bay leaves, chiles, thyme, and parsley. Let simmer gently over low heat for 4 to 5 hours, skimming as necessary.

Put a large strainer in a large bowl. Scoop the liquid and solids into the strainer. You will probably need two or more of these.

When you are done straining all from the stockpot, strain the liquid a second time to remove finer solids. Use a fine strainer and a bowl set over an ice-water bath. Leave until cool enough to pour into containers with tight-fitting lids.

Refrigerate or freeze until ready to use. Label and date the containers for clarity in your life.

Shrimp Stock

Perhaps your seafood market will sell you fresh shrimp shells, but if not simply save the shells from the meals you make with shrimp that call upon you to peel the shrimp. We freeze them in batches stored in resealable freezer bags until we have enough to make the stock. Crab shells can also be used in all or part of the quantity. The stock is best used within 3 days but can be frozen for up to 4 months.

Makes about 3 quarts

½ cup canola or other light oil

2 pounds shrimp shells (heads can be included if you can get them . . . and it would be nice in that they contain a ton of flavor)

2 large sweet onions, peeled and chopped

1 pound carrots, peeled and chopped

8 ounces celery, chopped

½ bulb fennel (with fronds from the whole bulb), chopped

2 cups white wine

2 heads of garlic, cut in half crosswise

6 sprigs fresh thyme

6 sprigs fresh Italian parsley

12 black peppercorns, lightly crushed

2 bay leaves, broken

Preheat the oven to 375 degrees.

Oil the shrimp shells (and heads if you have them). Put them in a baking pan and roast until somewhat colored, about 30 minutes.

Remove the pan from the oven and add the onions, carrots, celery, and fennel. Stir and return the pan to the oven for 30 minutes. Add the wine.

Transfer everything from the pan to a stockpot and cover with 1 gallon cool water.

Bring to just a boil and skim any impurities that come to the top of the pot, then lower the heat to medium.

Add the garlic heads, thyme, parsley, peppercorns, and bay leaves. Adjust the heat as needed to let the liquid simmer for about 1 hour, skimming as necessary.

Put a large-holed strainer in a bowl large enough to hold all of the liquid. Scoop the liquid and solids into the strainer. Discard the shells and vegetables.

When you are done straining all of it, use a fine-meshed strainer to strain off the remaining solids into a bowl set over an ice-water bath. Leave until cool enough to pour into containers with tight-fitting lids.

Refrigerate or freeze the stock until ready to use.

Bacon-Speckled Hush Puppies

These hush puppies are adaptive to so many fillings you can either put add-ons straight into the batter or "sandwiched" into halved hush puppies. Try grilled or sautéed wild mushrooms, crabmeat, or cooked shrimp. For a straight, nonmeat version, omit the bacon from the recipe. Have your variations as you wish!

Makes about 20 hush puppies

2 cups plus 2 tablespoons stone-ground self-rising yellow cornmeal

½ cup self-rising all-purpose flour

2 tablespoons sugar

½ teaspoon kosher salt

1 teaspoon baking soda

½ teaspoon baking powder

1½ cups buttermilk

1 egg, lightly beaten

1 cup finely diced sweet onion

½ Scotch bonnet chile, seeded and finely minced

2½ tablespoons cooked diced bacon

Vegetable, peanut, or canola oil for deep-frying

1 teaspoon Escabeche Spice Rub (page 220)

Combine the cornmeal, flour, sugar, salt, baking soda, and baking powder in a medium-size bowl.

In a separate bowl, whisk together the buttermilk and egg. Add the wet ingredients to the dry ingredients, whisking until just combined. Add the onion, chile, and bacon. Stir and set aside to rest for about 5 minutes.

In a deep heavy pot, heat 2 to 3 inches of oil to 350 degrees.

Spoon heaping tablespoons of the batter into the hot oil using two spoons—one to help push the other's batter into the oil. (It also prevents oil from splashing up onto your hands.)

Cook for 1½ to 2 minutes, carefully turning the "puppies" over once or twice to cook evenly. When they are golden and cooked through (check one to test it), lift them out with a slotted spoon and drain on paper towels. Sprinkle the warm "puppies" with the Escabeche Spice Rub, place on a cookie rack, and keep warm until ready to serve.

Note: These can be frozen and reheated after the frying step. The batter also can be made a few days in advance and held in the refrigerator.

Smoky Chile Buttermilk Biscuits

Breakfast starts with a *bang* when the smoke rises from the chipotle chile powder we employ in these lusty biscuits. Biscuits are treasured all over the American South, of which Florida is a proud and historic member.

Makes about 12 (3-inch) biscuits

6¾ cups all-purpose flour, plus more for the work surface

3½ tablespoons baking powder

1½ teaspoons salt

¼ cup sugar

2 tablespoons chipotle chile powder

1 cup (2 sticks) cold butter, plus 2 to 3 tablespoons melted butter (or olive oil)

2 cups buttermilk

Maldon salt to sprinkle on top

Into a large bowl, sift together the flour, baking powder, salt, sugar, and chile powder.

Cut the cold butter into pieces. Work them into the flour mixture with a pastry cutter until it resembles coarse meal.

Form a well in the flour mixture and add the buttermilk. Blend with a fork at first and then use your hands until the dough forms a ball. Wrap with plastic wrap and let rest in the refrigerator for about 1 hour.

Preheat the oven to 425 degrees.

Turn the dough out onto a floured work surface. Roll out to 1 inch thick. Cut rounds about 2¾ inches in diameter using a floured drinking glass or biscuit cutter. Do not twist the cutter when cutting, as that move crimps the edges of the biscuit and shortens its rise.

Place on a parchment paper–lined baking sheet and bake for 15 to 20 minutes, until golden.

Remove from the oven and brush lightly with the melted butter or olive oil. Season with the Maldon salt to taste. Gently lift them off the pan and let cool on a wire rack. Serve warm or at room temperature.

Serving suggestion: These make great sandwich-stuffing muffins due to the savory "hit" of them. I also enjoy them split, toasted, and topped with homemade egg salad.

14 Corn Sticks

We make these in heavy old-fashioned cast-iron corn stick pans. Lodge makes a fine version. There are seven indents in them to mimic the shapes of perfect small ears of corn, and the batter makes two batches. I asked Janet, "What we are calling these babies?" She is very practical, not so much like her husband, hence the name.

Makes 14 (cute as hell) corn sticks (about 13 ounces cornbread)

Light oil or rendered bacon fat for the corn stick pan

3 eggs, beaten

1 cup sour cream

¼ cup vegetable oil

1 cup self-rising cornmeal

1 tablespoon sugar

1 teaspoon kosher salt

Preheat the oven to 400 degrees. Grease the corn stick pan and heat in the oven (set it on a baking sheet so it's easier to remove from the oven) while the temperature is reached.

In a large bowl, combine the eggs, sour cream, and the vegetable oil. Add the cornmeal, sugar, and salt and stir until just combined.

Carefully take the hot cornbread pan out of the oven. Spoon the batter into the preheated pan. The batter "sears" when you put it in this hot mold, which actually reduces sticking.

Bake for about 20 minutes, until golden brown. Remove from the oven and let cool slightly. Carefully remove the "sticks" from the mold, taking care not to dig at them with a knife or any item that could gouge the beauty of cast iron.

Serve warm. The mold for the corn sticks we have makes seven sticks, so we repeat the cooking part one more time. If we are lucky, *some* of the first seven are still not devoured by the time the rest are done.

Note: Some folks like to smear some butter on the corn sticks while they are still piping hot. I *like* folks like that.

Use: Apalachicola Oyster Pan Stew with Sherry Cream and Corn Sticks (page 31) and Cornbread-Stuffed Quail with Strawberry-Ancho-Guava Jam and Sweet and Sour Parsnips (page 154).

"Those Toasts"

The Florida Cookbook has been a great resource for me in learning about Florida's historical and regional foods. The coauthors' deep love of Florida has stood the test of time. One of them, Caroline Stuart, became a very good friend of ours. She has a fascinating history. She actually worked on a daily basis with Beard at his famous home in Greenwich Village teaching cooking classes and helping with his books. Another part of why I admire her is due to her gracious generosity. James Beard shared some very valuable cooking tools with her, and Caroline in turn shared them with me, Emeril Lagasse, Jeremiah Tower, Dean Fearing, and Justin Van Aken during a celebration we had upon the tenth anniversary of NORMAN'S at The Ritz-Carlton, Grande Lakes, Orlando when she gave each of us a tool from the hands of Beard himself. I "toast" Caroline with this recipe—an original from The Florida Cookbook with some slight changes by us. I make a point to bring out Beard's knife when I prepare these simple and addictive toasts.

Makes about 50 quarter cuts of the toasts; the thickness of the bread creates some variation in yields

12 ounces thinly sliced firm whole wheat or white sandwich bread

¼ cup butter, melted

¼ cup finely grated Parmesan cheese

Preheat the oven to 250 degrees.

Line a large baking sheet with aluminum foil.

Cut the crusts off the bread, working with four slices stacked, then cut into quarters. Fit them closely together on the pan in a single layer. Brush generously with the melted butter, then sprinkle with Parmesan cheese.

Bake on the middle oven rack until crisp, about 45 minutes.

Let cool to room temperature, then pack in a sealable container. They'll keep for up to 1 week at room temperature.

Serving suggestion: These can be topped with a wide range of ingredients. For Janet's Smoky Tomato Soup (page 14), we like to top it with a fine blue cheese.

Journey Bread
(A.K.A. JOHNNY BREAD AND JOHNNY CAKE)

Given the many varieties of recipes for this unleavened cornmeal bread, I wondered why? Finally, a Caribbean native told me he thought it was because the word *johnny* was probably a corruption of the word *journey*, and naturally, you ate whatever kind of bread was available on open-boat journeys from one island to the next. Whether in the Caribbean or in the swamps and marshes of the Deep South or on the Great Plains of the Midwest among the Amerindians, johnnycakes filled a lot of hungry travelers' bellies.

In long-distance swimmer Diana Nyad's memoir, *Find a Way*, she recounts her experiences in achieving her goal of swimming without a shark cage from Cuba to Key West. She writes, "By 3 a.m., my mind was at its *bleakest* moment. I had been swimming in pitch darkness for six hours. That's when I began singing in my head 'Needle,' from Neil Young's *Harvest* album. It has a *surfy*, steady rhythm that helped me sustain my 52 strokes per minute. I also related to Neil's voice, which had the right level of vulnerability . . . and *pain*." When I read those words of hers, I thought of the sailors, seekers, dreamers also seeking to survive on those waters, clutching their Journey Bread, trying to make it. Ms. Nyad's bread was a *song*.

Makes 1 (9-inch) square pan

¾ cup self-rising cornmeal

1 cup all-purpose flour

1 teaspoon baking powder

1 teaspoon baking soda

½ teaspoon kosher salt

3 tablespoons honey

1 egg, lightly beaten

3 tablespoons butter, melted, plus more for the pan

1¼ cups buttermilk

1 Scotch bonnet chile, seeded and minced

Preheat the oven to 400 degrees. Generously butter a 9-inch square baking pan.

In a large mixing bowl, combine the cornmeal, flour, baking powder, baking soda, and salt. In a separate bowl, beat together the honey, egg, melted butter, buttermilk, and chile until lightly frothy.

Add the flour mixture to the buttermilk mixture and beat until just blended, about 30 seconds. Pour the batter into the prepared baking pan and bake on the middle rack of the oven for 25 to 30 minutes, until an inserted toothpick comes out clean. Remove from the oven and let cool for 10 minutes. Turn out onto a wire rack and cut into portions as desired.

Janet's Multigrain Croutons

We urge you to make your own croutons. Leftover bread is almost always on hand, so it makes sense to put it to such a tasty use.

Makes 2 cups

3 cups cubed multigrain bread (½-inch cubes)

¾ cup olive oil (or flavored oil of your choice, such as herb, garlic, pepper, and so on)

Kosher salt and cracked black pepper

Preheat the oven to 350 degrees.

Toss the bread cubes in a mixing bowl with the oil to coat. Season with salt and pepper to taste. Put the bread cubes on a nonstick baking sheet or one lined with parchment paper. Toast in the oven for 10 minutes. Remove the baking sheet, stir the cubes around some, and return to the oven for about 10 more minutes, until golden brown and crunchy.

Let cool completely on a wire rack. Store in a resealable plastic bag with a paper towel inside, or in an airtight container with a paper towel laid over the top of the croutons.

Use: **"Florida Pinks" Shrimp with Buttermilk–Creole Mustard Dressing (page 49), or any time you want croutons.**

Plantain Chips

Florida fosters the joys and pleasures of bringing Latin and Caribbean cooking into our lives. One way is as easy as making plantain chips, a nice alternative to that all-American snack the potato chip.

Makes 10 to 12 chips

Peanut oil for deep-frying

1 green plantain, peeled and sliced lengthwise as thinly as possible

Kosher salt and cracked black pepper

In a deep heavy skillet, heat the oil to 350 degrees. Drop the plantain slices into the oil one at a time (so they don't stick together) and fry for about 2 minutes, or until crisp and golden.

Remove from the skillet with a slotted spoon and transfer to a bowl lined with paper towels. Season with salt and pepper to taste and serve.

Use: **We feature these with our Raw Diced Tuna (page 41), but I also like to sprinkle or scatter chips of many kinds across a sandwich. A humble sloppy Joe would be "the bomb," as we say in the current vernacular, with these chips on top of the meat.**

ACKNOWLEDGMENTS

To every book that came into my hands and taught me new things.

To everyone who cooked and taught me something I didn't know the moment before that moment.

To the people of my adopted state of Florida.

To the people of Illinois who always welcome us back home . . . for walks along Diamond Lake and pizzas at Bill's with family and friends.

The teams at 1921 by Norman Van Aken in Mount Dora, In the Kitchen with Norman Van Aken Cooking School, Three, and No. 3 Social in Miami and *NORMAN'S* at The Ritz-Carlton, Grande Lakes, Orlando.

Lisa Ekus, my great friend and gifted book agent.

To my publisher University Press of Florida. And with a big shout-out to Sian Hunter and Marthe Walters.

RockawayPR with special thanks to Alexis and Heather.

Dennis Hayes, my "coconut brother" and sage friend.

Veronica "Fuzzy" Randall, who guided the very beginnings of this book and now guides from Heaven.

Debi Harbin, this book's primary and ultra-positive photographer.

Justin Van Aken for jump-starting the chapters on cocktails and desserts and *always* being our loving son. And to Lourdes, his beautiful wife who has the gift of loving and teaching children.

Candace and Graham Walsh for their support in helping me achieve a long-time dream of building a cooking school . . . and then went . . . 3 times further . . . Candace is a role model for aspiring young women. She really knocks me out with her humor, her vision, and her grit.

Ken Mazik, Donna Brown, and Larry Baker for welcoming us with open arms to Mount Dora and then building us an astonishingly beautiful restaurant that is breathing new winds in both cuisine *and* museum artistry.

And to my Janet . . . who never quits, who always wants to help, who asks for nothing, who gives *everything*.

Staff of 1921 by Norman Van Aken in Mount Dora

1921 by Norman Van Aken General Manager Scott Geisler and Chef Camilo Velasco

INDEX

Following page: Chef's Tasting Menu Room at 1921 by Norman Van Aken

Award-winning chef and restaurateur Norman Van Aken invites you to discover the richness of Florida's culinary landscape. This long-awaited cookbook embraces the history, the character, and the flavors of the state that has inspired Van Aken's famous fusion style for over forty years.

Drawing from Florida's vibrant array of immigrant cultures, and incorporating local ingredients, the dishes in this book display the exciting diversity of Van Aken's "New World Cuisine." Recipes include Key lime beignets; cornbread-stuffed quail with strawberry-ancho-guava jam and sweet and sour parsnips; "Spanglish" tortillas with hash browns, creamed spinach, and serrano ham; pork stew with raisins, tamarind, plantains, and chiles; and fully loaded cracked conch po' boys.

While preparing these dishes, readers will enjoy advice and stories straight from the kitchen of a master chef. Van Aken infuses his recipes with tips, techniques, and personality. He reveals the key to a good gumbo, praises the acidity of a pickled peppadew, connects food innovation to jazz and blues music, describes hitchhiking adventures across the state with his wife, Janet, and tells the tale behind the Mustachioed Swimmer, a cocktail named for Tennessee Williams.

Norman Van Aken's Florida Kitchen is a delicious read—the definitive guide to the historic past and multicultural future of Florida's abundant foodways. With its forward-thinking blend of old and new, thoughtful step-by-step instructions for wonderful meals, and plenty of friendly conversation, this book is a rare immersion in a culinary artist's world.